T0207172

Communications
in Computer and Information Science 1411

More information about this series at http://www.springer.com/series/7899

Cédric Grueau · Robert Laurini ·
Lemonia Ragia (Eds.)

Geographical Information Systems Theory, Applications and Management

6th International Conference, GISTAM 2020
Prague, Czech Republic, May 7–9, 2020
Revised Selected Papers

 Springer

Editors
Cédric Grueau
Polytechnic Institute of Setúbal
Setúbal, Portugal

Robert Laurini
Knowledge Systems Institute
Skokie, IL, USA

Lemonia Ragia
Technical University of Crete
Chania, Greece

ISSN 1865-0929 ISSN 1865-0937 (electronic)
Communications in Computer and Information Science
ISBN 978-3-030-76373-2 ISBN 978-3-030-76374-9 (eBook)
https://doi.org/10.1007/978-3-030-76374-9

This Springer imprint is published by the registered company Springer Nature Switzerland AG
The registered company address is: Gewerbestrasse 11, 6330 Cham, Switzerland

Preface

This book includes extended and revised versions of a set of selected papers from the 6th International Conference on Geographical Information Systems Theory, Applications and Management (GISTAM 2020), exceptionally held as a web-based event, due to the COVID-19 pandemic, during May 7–9, 2020.

GISTAM 2020 received 62 paper submissions from 38 countries, of which 15% were included in this book. The papers were selected by the event chairs and their selection was based on a number of criteria that included classifications and comments provided by Program Committee members, session chairs' assessments, and also the program chairs' global view of all the papers included in the technical program. The authors of selected papers were then invited to submit revised and extended versions of their papers having at least 30% innovative material.

The International Conference on Geographical Information Systems Theory, Applications and Management aims at creating a meeting point of researchers and practitioners that addresses new challenges in geo-spatial data sensing, observation, representation, processing, visualization, sharing, and managing, in all aspects concerning information communication and technologies (ICT) as well as management information systems and knowledge-based systems. The conference welcomes original papers of either practical or theoretical nature, presenting research or applications, of specialized or interdisciplinary nature, addressing any aspect of geographic information systems and technologies.

We are confident that the papers included in this book will strongly contribute to the understanding of some current research trends in geographical information systems theory, applications, and management, specifically with relation to geographic information retrieval, big data, real-time sensors, spatial information and society, spatial modeling and reasoning, spatio-temporal data acquisition, earth observation and satellite data, and ecological and environmental management.

We would like to thank all the authors for their contributions and the reviewers for their hard work which has helped ensure the quality of this publication.

May 2020

Cédric Grueau
Robert Laurini
Lemonia Ragia

Organization

Conference Chair

Lemonia Ragia   ATHENA Research & Innovation Information Technologies, Greece

Program Chairs

Cédric Grueau   Polytechnic Institute of Setúbal, Portugal
Robert Laurini (Honorary)   Knowledge Systems Institute, France

Program Committee

Andrea Ajmar   Politecnico di Torino, Italy
Rute Almeida   University of Porto, Portugal
Costas Armenakis   York University, Canada
Thierry Badard   Laval University, Canada
Jan Blachowski   Wroclaw University of Science and Technology, Poland
María Camacho Olmedo   Universidad de Granada, Spain
Manuel Campagnolo   Instituto Superior de Agronomia, Portugal
Cristina Catita   Universidade de Lisboa, Portugal
Filiberto Chiabrando   Politecnico di Torino, Italy
Eliseo Clementini   University of L'Aquila, Italy
Antonio Corral   University of Almeria, Spain
Joep Crompvoets   Catholic University of Leuven, Belgium
Paolo Dabove   Politecnico di Torino, Italy
Anastasios Doulamis   National Technical University of Athens, Greece
Nikolaos Doulamis   National Technical University of Athens, Greece
Suzana Dragicevic   Simon Fraser University, Canada
João Fernandes   Universidade de Lisboa, Portugal
Ana Fonseca   Laboratório Nacional de Engenharia Civil, Portugal
Cidália Fonte   University of Coimbra, Portugal
Cheng Fu   University of Zurich, Switzerland
Sébastien Gadal   Aix-Marseille University, France/CNRS UMR 7300 ESPACE, France/North-Eastern Federal University, Russia
Auroop Ganguly   Northeastern University, USA
Jinzhu Gao   University of the Pacific, USA
Lianru Gao   Chinese Academy of Sciences, China
Gilles Gesquière   LIRIS, France
Fabio Giulio Tonolo   Politecnico di Torino, Italy

Michael Vassilakopoulos	University of Thessaly, Greece
Benoit Vozel	University of Rennes I, France
Lei Wang	Louisiana State University, USA
Christiane Weber	CNRS UMR TETIS, France
Stephan Winter	The University of Melbourne, Australia
Laszlo Zentai	Eötvös Loránd University, Hungary

Invited Speakers

Alexander Zipf	Heidelberg University, Germany
Paraskevi Nomikou	National and Kapodistrian University of Athens, Greece
Andrew U. Frank	Vienna University of Technology, Austria

Contents

Spatial Information Technology: Past, Present, Future

Andrew U. Frank[✉]

Geoinformation, Technical University Vienna,
Gusshausstrasse 27-29, 1040 Wien, Austria
`frank@geoinfo.tuwien.ac.at`

Abstract. I have participated for about 40 years in the most astonishing technical development of Geographic Information Systems and seen the inclusion of spatial information technology in nearly all forms of it: spatial database technology, GPS, the web, mobile smart phones. Ubiquitous computing and connectivity became possible. The article will firstly reviews the history of GIS use and divides the development of the enabling technology for GIS use approximately in decades. The development can be broken in roughly decades characterized by the technology which enabled the then dominant GIS use.

The article will then includes some tentative ideas for developments which could occur in the next decade. I will try to draw some conclusions from the review: why did some technologies become successful in the marketplace and while some other did not? What makes a technology to become a smashing commercial success? Google maps might be the most spectacular, but by far not the only example.

My experience leads me to believe that commercial success is the result of the combination of three conditions:

- a fundamental human need is at the core - e.g. people need to navigate in the world and must avoid to get lost,
- a cost-effective technical means to satisfy this need is available - e.g. widely available smartphones, and,
- a business-opportunity is identified - e.g. selling advertisement.

1 Introduction

Telling history involves always a personal slant: what is considered important enough to be told, what is left out? My involvement started the day before Christmas 1977 when Prof. Rudolf Conzett at ETH Zurich asked me to investigate the application of database management system software to cadaster data. *Multipurpose cadaster* was then an emerging concept to combine the different kinds of spatial data collected in city administration in maps which could be superimposed on light tables. Multipurpose cadaster was one of the technologies which eventually became *GIS*.

Nearly 40 years later – at the time when I retired from the chair for Geoinformation at the Technical University Vienna, Geoinformation is an established,

© Springer Nature Switzerland AG 2021
C. Grueau et al. (Eds.): GISTAM 2020, CCIS 1411, pp. 1–17, 2021.
https://doi.org/10.1007/978-3-030-76374-9_1

widely used technology: Think of Google Maps and car navigation! My professional career has evolved around GIScience research at ETH Zurich, at University of Maine as part of the NCGIA and eventually at TU Wien. During these years, I had the pleasure to meet and work with most of the pioneers of GIS in person.

The *first part* of this article will review the GIS history from my observations during these years. I will divide the development into five periods of (roughly) a decade, referring to what I considered dominant practice. Eventually, I add some predictions for the 2020 decade.

The development of GIS is driven by enabling technologies; therefore, for each decade, I will first characterize the new, generally used information and surveying technologies and then describe the geographic information practice and the geographic information research enabled by the technology; I will then highlight changes in the available data and software. The reduction of prices for information technology was and still is the most important driver of development in recent years. The reduction in IT prices follows Moore's law[1]; the development of IT has drastically reduced the costs of determining a location on the earth's surface by using GPS (from an estimated \$1,000 to \$.01 per point[2]).

The *second smaller part* of the article is an attempt to draw some conclusions from observing the history of GIS business. What were the success stories? Why did some technology advances lead to business successes—and other not? What combinations of technology advances were necessary to start a successful business venture?

For example, computer mapping was available since early 1990, but became successful only when the technical solution combining GPS with smart phones were widely available and "payment" by clients accepting advertisement a form of compensation.

2 Decade Around 1970

Likely the first conference which can be counted as GIS precursor conference was the AutoCarto conference in 1974 in Reston VA.[3] One of the first theory-oriented GIS conferences attended by those who would become influential in GIS development in the decades to come. The first academic GIS conference was

---

[1] Gordon Moore, co-founder of Fairchild Semiconductors and Intel, empirically observed that computer performance doubles every 18 months or every 10 years the performance increases by a factor of about 100 ($2^{(120/18)} = 101.6$), or the costs decrease by the same factor. For example, the price of a GPS receiver decreased from \$30,000 to \$3 between 1990 and 2010. Processors improved by a factor of 10^{10} between 1970 and 2020 as a combination of price reduction from \$10 million to \$100 (i.e. 10^4), an increase in speed by 10^5 and with 10 more processor cores - together roughly 10^{10} .

[2] Since the Euro has not been used over the entire period under review, I am giving prices in "units" that correspond approximately to one Euro or one US\$.

[3] https://cartogis.org/docs/proceedings/archive/auto-carto-1/index.html.

organized a few years later by the "Harvard Laboratory for Computer Graphics and Spatial Analysis" [20].[4]

I attended at the beginning of my doctoral studies at the ETH Zurich probably the first European non-English language conference on "Land Information Systems" in Darmstadt [23], together with my advisor R. Conzett and W. Messmer (from city surveying Basel which operated one of the first city "GIS" at the time).

Before starting my Ph.D. at ETH Zurich[5] I had experienced IT technology in a major Swiss bank with punched cards and suffered batch processing during my undergrad studies, where Niklaus Wirth taught me Pascal. I was allowed to do my Ph.D. research at the new "Center for *Interactive* Computing" at ETH (ZIR), where I experienced a user friendly version of a time sharing, interactive operating system (TOPS-10 on a DEC-10 computer from Digital Equipment Corp.) derived from Multics.[6]

2.1 Technology

The typical IT technology in this decade was processing tasks in batches, without user interaction with big mainframe computers in data centers; tasks were entered as stacks of punched cards. They produced stacks of printed paper, often with hundreds of pages which where then distributed to users.

Maps were drawn slowly on very expensive mechanical drafting tables. Graphic displays were either static (Tektronix Storage Tube) or extremely expensive dynamic vector displays.[7]

Surveying offices used the first electronic pocket calculators (e.g. HP 35) and less often desktop calculators for geodetic coordinate calculations; larger computational tasks were handed over to data centers.

2.2 Geographic Information Practice

Archives of paper maps, blueprint copying machines and light tables for overlaying plans dominated technical offices. Few departments of large organizations used small computers to keep cadastral and utilities mapping up to date.[8]

---

[4] https://en.wikipedia.org/wiki/Harvard_Laboratory_for_Computer_Graphics_and_Spatial_Analysis.

[5] My topic was to study the suitability of database management systems for (multipurpose) cadaster; the supervisors were R. Conzett (surveying) and C.A. Zehnder (IT) from ETH Zurich [27].

[6] Most modern OS derive in some form from MULTICS; most notably Multics is the precursor for Unix, which is the precursor for Linux ... see https://en.wikipedia.org/wiki/Multics.

[7] The ETH "Center for Interactive Computing" (ZIR) had one dynamic vector display, an Evans & Sutherland Picture System 2, which could draw wire frame representations of a very small village; the price tag was above one million dollar.

[8] Surveying offices in e.g. the towns of Vienna, Basel, Hamburg, or the Dutch Rijkwaterstaat.

In Canada, Roger Tomlinson – known as the "inventor" of the term GIS – developed the "Canadian Geographic Information System" since 1962.[9]

2.3   Research

There were experiments with cartographic production in England [4] or at the Harvard Graphics Lab [20] for applications in local planning, forestry etc. Steiner in Zurich used minicomputer for a "geographical data processing system" [55].[10]

2.4   Software

Software was supplied by the manufacturers and only worked on their systems; in contrast to the 1960s, software in the 1970s had now has a price and is no longer a free add-on to the pricey expensive hardware.

3   Decade Around 1980

At the FIG conference in Montreux I was involved in the definition of the term *Land Information System*:

> A land information system is a tool for legal, administrative and economic decision-making and an aid for planning and development which consists, on the one hand, of a data base containing spatially referenced land-related data for a defined area, and, on the other hand, of procedures and techniques for the systematic collection, updating, processing and distribution of this data.
>
> The base of a LIS is a uniform, spatial reference system for the data in the system which also facilitates the linking of the data within the system with other land-related data [25].[11]

Soon afterwards the distinction between Land Information System (LIS) and Geographic Information System (GIS) was abandoned in favor of the now common GIS terminology [28].

After completing my dissertation at ETH [27], I became professor of Geographic Information Systems at the University of Maine. A few years later, my research group joined a team formed with the geography departments of the University of California, Santa Barbara and New York State University in Buffalo to win an NSF funded competition [1] and started the NCGIA (National Center for Geographic Information and Analysis) in 1987 [44].

---

[9] https://en.wikipedia.org/wiki/Canada_Geographic_Information_System.

[10] Other reviews, slightly english-language centered are by [14,15]. Notable is an early publication in 1988 with contributions from Dangermond, Coppock, Chrisman, Rhind, Tomlinson and Goodchild.

[11] The definition was produced in parallel in German, French and English in a small hotel room in Montreux in a long night discussion; it survived the change in terminology from LIS to GIS.

3.1   Technology

Mini computers for less than one million dollar and graphic workstations with raster displays were affordable even for smaller organizations. The necessary software for GIS was purchased from various companies, often together with the necessary hardware. Graphics [24] and database management programs became standardized [12]. Microcomputers, such as the IBM PC introduced 1981, were still very limited and had no graphics capabilities.

3.2   Geographic Information Practice

Reports of successful and cost-effective utility mapping operations are published by US companies, often referred to as AM/FM (for automated mapping/facilities management) [57]. These systems operated by large utility companies produced documentation of existing installations for maintenance. Various manufacturers (for example Intergraph[12] and Synercom) offered software and hardware for graphical systems with few very expensive workstations (approximately half a million dollar per seat). For urban planning and environmental projects, software from ESRI[13] brought together data from different sources. All these systems were proprietary and the exchange of data between the systems was challenging.

3.3   Research

The use of database management systems for spatial data requires more elaborate data storage structures than is customary for administrative applications [27]; metadata (i.e. data about the data) must describe the data quality [9,10]. The Global Positioning System (originally Navstar later became known as "GPS"[14]) was developed at the Johns Hopkins University Applied Physics Laboratory on behalf of the United States Department of Defense. Tests for geodetic use began after sufficient satellites were operational and the system was approved for civilian use [36].[15]

Cartographic representations were the primary product from GIS at the time. The data structures (i.e. unconnected lines and anchor points for area descriptions - referred to as "spaghetti & meat balls") were sufficient to obtain cartographic output, but not for the management of public utilities planning and management.

The US government had collected data describing the street network to organize the decennial population census; the data structure recorded topology in a format which is often referred to as Dual Independent Map Encoding (DIME) [16]. Instructions for wayfinding could be produced if additional rules of road traffic (especially turning restrictions) where added [61]. First trials showed the

---

[12] https://en.wikipedia.org/wiki/Intergraph.

[13] https://en.wikipedia.org/wiki/Esri.

[14] https://en.wikipedia.org/wiki/Global_Positioning_System.

[15] https://en.wikipedia.org/wiki/Global_Positioning_System#Predecessors.

importance of presentation of instructions to the user [39,42]. Experimental car navigation systems with dead-reckoning to determine location were not commercially successful; it took another 20 years of technological development [13,31].

The need to transfer the large amount of geographical data recorded in on paper maps into a digital system became recognized. Laserscan built an automatic digitizing device for the Dutch Rijkswaterstaat where lines were optically tracked.[16]

At the same time the Ohio State University equipped vehicles with position sensors and video cameras to record street data digitally [48], these were the forerunners of the technology Google Maps used twenty years later to collect street data.

3.4 Data

Extensive digitization projects were started in many places (e.g. city of Vienna for multi-purpose digital map, the French national mapping agency started a project to digitize the topographic map series) and projects were already completed in smaller regions (e.g. city of Basel). The data set including all streets in the United States was prepared by the US Bureau of the Census; it is topologically encoded [17,60].

3.5 Software

GIS software was produced by specialized companies - often tied to hardware of specific manufacturers. Software production creates a natural monopoly, few companies dominate the market.[17] Changing the software manufacturer is almost impossible because the data collected was recorded in the manufacturers proprietary format and translation to the format of another vendor was very difficult.

4 Decade Around 1990

I taught at the University of Maine in the United States for about 10 years and did research at NCGIA until I was appointed to the Vienna University of Technology in 1992.

4.1 Technology

Local networks connect large and very expensive mainframes with terminals, workstations on the raster screens of which graphic representations are finally possible. Around 1995 the restrictions on the Internet (Arpanet, NSFNET) on

---

[16] http://www.laser-scan.com/demo/laser-scan-history/.

[17] The production of software is a large investment to produce initially but to produce more copies is inexpensive; this creates a "natural monopoly". A company having a product can undercut any competing offer and no other vendor will reasonably attempt to make the large investment when the primary vendor will always be able to reduce his price and make it impossible for him to recoup his investment.

research institutions were lifted and access was made available to everyone. The NSCA Mosaic Browser, available since 1993, allowed the Internet not only for email but also for access to linked documents - the World Wide Web became a reality [2].

GPS is increasingly used to obtain point coordinates. Calculations were carried out on PC or workstations and the map layout coded there; maps were later plotted on expensive large pen plotters.

4.2   Geographic Information Practice

Urban and regional GIS emerged, connected map with data from the administrative departments. Employees connected with terminals at their workplace could obtain spatial analysis on demand. The centrally managed data could be updated by decentralized employees. The vision of a GIS with central data storage avoiding multiple copies of data to maintain, as it was imagined as a goal in FIG documents and in the work of researchers at the University of Wisconsin [11,46] twenty years before, became slowly reality.

Applications outside of public administration, for example for the real estate market or fleet management, appeared and were cost effective for private companies. MapQuest used the US government road data from the US census to display route descriptions in the web browser; the user then prints ed the description and used it as a reference while driving.[18] This application was probably the first geographic service to be accepted by a wide audience. At the end of the decade, the first train schedule information systems for the railroad were created (in Europe SBB 1988, DB 1990) and accessible by the public using a web browser as well.[19]

4.3   Research

An NCGIA initiative led to an analysis of the economic impact of geographic data and in particular the use of location data for commercial exploitation [7,8].

Mobile phones used GPS to determine the location GPS-based devices were patented in 1995; in the USA it becomes mandatory that all mobile phones from 1998 onward transmit at least the position as radio cell identifier in an emergency E-911 call [52]. Leading GIS researchers recognized ethical and social issues involved [18,19].

The standardization of query languages became urgent with the emerging internet; the research addressed methods of qualitative spatial reasoning necessary for query languages qualitative spatial reasoning [21,22,30,51]. Transfer of data between systems was impeded by the differences in encoding semantics; standards for interoperability were urgently required [6], but the necessary theory was lacking [59]. GIS, which could also record, document and display changes in time, were designed and theoretically justified but not widely used for lack of software [29,33,43].

---

[18] https://en.wikipedia.org/wiki/MapQuest.

[19] https://de.wikipedia.org/wiki/Elektronische_Fahrplanauskunft.

4.4 Data

Federal government data in the United States is free of copyright, accessible and usable by everyone even commercially. MapQuest and similar companies used the road data from the Bureau of the Census to develop commercially viable applications. In Europe, the national surveying offices defended the copyright on their geographic data and only allowed commercial use within restricted and expensive agreements; many national mapping agencies made even experiments and research difficult. Therefore there are hardly any commercial GIS applications in Europe (with few exception like e.g. WiGeoGIS[20] in Vienna) even if this would make economic sense [40]. National Geoinformation policies to create and maintain a spatial data infrastructure were proposed [41] but had limited influence; Rhind and Onsrud debate the role of copyright on GIS commercialization [49,54].

4.5 Software

GIS programs were increasingly being built for the "PC" and the Windows operating system from Microsoft. The GRASS GIS program system[21] built up by the US Corps of Engineers gains wider usage.

The exchange of data structured for use with proprietary software was complicated and costly. Various US government agencies, universities and industry founded under the leadership of David Schell 1994 the Open Geospatial Consortium[22] to advance software standards. The contribution of OGC was to create a channel for the exchange of information between public authorities and potential providers which leads to realistic standards. The very strict US public procurement law restricts contacts between providers and potential buyers and among the providers in enforcing anti-trust regulations. The OGC standards severed the close connection between proprietary software and GIS data and allowed smaller, specialized companies to deliver individual components in an open GIS program. The EU promoted the European software industry, consisting of small companies, with the GIPSIE project.[23]

5   Decade Around 2000

5.1 Technology

PCs were available at practically every employee's desk and connected to the World Wide Web - data is available regardless of the location of storage. The

---

[20] https://www.wigeogis.com/en/home.

[21] More information about the current state of the open source GIS program is found at https://de.wikipedia.org/wiki/GRASS_GIS and https://grass.osgeo.org/. A text book is Neteler and Mitasova [45].

[22] http://www.opengeospatial.org/ogc/histor   and   https://de.wikipedia.org/wiki/Open_Geospatial_Consortium.

[23] https://cordis.europa.eu/event/id/11209-gipsie-information-day/de.

reduction of prices of GPS receivers and microcomputers allowed applications that were previously not economically feasible. Mobile phones that finally fit in trousers and handbags and whose position within a radio cell are known are spreading rapidly, as are battery-powered laptop computers that can connect to the Internet via the mobile phone network. Users have, in principle, *access to all the data in the world everywhere and always.*

5.2 Geographic Information Practice

Car navigation devices with

- GPS positioning,
- locally stored road network, and
- usable graphical screen

were sold at a price that is acceptable for private users and are spreading rapidly.

Al Gore[24] envisioned a virtual earth where a user can zoom in on his home town and then on his street; it was realized around 2005 by Google Earth and Google Maps in a comprehensive and widely used application, which later included directions for road transportation, time-tables of public transport, etc.

Ruggedized laptop computers became small enough to allow direct recording of spatial data in the field and proved cost effective in forestry, agriculture and similar industries.

5.3 Research

Using available spatial and population statistics data achieved better targeting for advertisement of services and goods. Targeting advertisement based on the location of a person allows more situation and location aware adverts. In 2004 a specialized conference on location-based services started at the Vienna University of Technology.[25] The determination of positions of customers within buildings remains an open but important question with numerous applications [34].

The integration of data from different sources with different goals when collecting was studied not only as a question of data structuring but also identifying the differences in the meaning of the data (a.k.a semantics). Interoperability of semantics was increasingly understood and connected to quality of the data.

5.4 Data

It was observed that only a few data sets are important for most applications and it would be economically advantageous to make them generally available for all uses:

- transport network,

---

[24] US Vice President 1993–2001 serving President Bill Clinton.
[25] https://lbsconference.org/former-lbs-conferences/.

- political boundaries,
- digital terrain model,
- hydrography,
- land use and land cover.

Data quality requirements for spatial resolution are usually low and errors in the data are tolerable in many cases [26,35].

The desired reduction of apparently duplicate data collections is sometimes not possible because different legal definitions underlie the administrative application, e.g. different definitions of "forest" produce requirements for different data sets which use the definition appropriate for the agencies; observing two agencies collecting data with the same label are not always indicating wasteful duplications!

5.5   Software

The open source movement in computer science was gaining traction and was used by large companies for the creation of complex systems (IBM with Eclipse or Google with Android); the open QGIS[26] was created using GRASS and various other free software packages.

6   Decade Around 2010: The Present Situation

6.1   Technology

Better resolution for small screens, better batteries, higher transmission rates in the mobile network and tiny, powerful computer chips allow graphic access to the WWW on the new smart phones. The higher resolution of the screen is attractive for map drawings. The new device can be used to place a phone call, but users learn rapidly to appreciate all the other functions found on the WWW. Social media, platforms for the exchange of information in more or less closed groups become extremely popular. The smart phone uses the GPS location to track the users location and add location data to all data collected. Producing enormous amounts of spatial data.

Vehicles with many sensors collect street images for different collectors (Google and others); laser scanners allow precise mapping of a site by surveyors.

Google collected practically all text document on the web and scanned a substantial share of all books found in university libraries.[27] The collected immense amount of data is used to train natural language components which later are used in commercial applications, but is – due to copyright restrictions – not widely available.

---

[26] https://en.wikipedia.org/wiki/QGIS.
[27] https://en.wikipedia.org/wiki/HathiTrust.

6.2   Geographic Information Practice

Geographic information is used everywhere and at all times by everyone – everyone and every company uses location data in applications to find people and find addresses, customers search for services, and companies offer services nearby, etc. Applications are designed for the web right from the start. The use of geographic information is practically only limited by the number and the usability of programs on the smart phone. Mobile devices serve as sensors: traffic volumes and traffic jams can be detected from observing the movement of users and lead to better route guidance. Applications for accessing popular services are often duplicated by resellers and it becomes difficult for the user to identify the genuine informative one, e.g. the authoritative time-table of a public transport company, the cinema program, without confusion by unwanted and unhelpful offers.

Organizations and administration begin to use smart phone applications to update data their employees collect, but allow citizens to send messages (with location and photo) to record problems needing an intervention. Dispatchers collect data from employees and forward jobs to them - all as applications on the smart phone.

6.3   Research

The connection of data with other databases became possible with the concepts of the Semantic Web [5]. The data are structured in binary relations with RDF [38] and found with the query language SPARQL [50]. Typically are these operations buried in lower layers of application programs and combined with attractive graphics.

Assembling GIS applications with data from different sources and connecting them with the dialog with the user, reveals the lack of systematic understanding of meaning. The adequate solution of tasks in space depends on the context; for example, the decision as to what is "close" and what is "far" includes many aspects of the situation of the person making the decision, e.g. tourism or commercial travel, the mode of transportation. ... [32].

6.4   Opening Up of Government Data

Based on a decision by the UK government in 2011[28] geodata is released from copyright in the UK; other local authorities were quickly following the trend (e.g. City of Vienna). Commercially significant is not so much the access to the basic geographic data (which is already largely available through Google Maps), but the detailed descriptive data which providers use in different business models. Data is often provided free of charge to the user who are then constrained to accept some advertising. Commercial applications can often charge a fee for access. There are often restrictions put in place to channel web traffic to governmental agencies and avoid commercial enterprises benefiting from public data.

---

[28] https://en.wikipedia.org/wiki/Open_Data_in_the_United_Kingdom.

For example, it took a long time long till Google Maps could include the schedules of e.g. the Vienna city public transport schedule system.

Free geographic data collected by volunteers in the Open Street Map Project is of sufficient quality and is accessible across the board.[29] It is used as an alternative to the proprietary Google Maps data.

7 What May Come: The Next Decade

7.1 Technology

Computer downsizing and performance increases likely continue. Novel ideas are "wearable" computers, which are incorporated into clothing and are with you at all times; unsolved is the communication between user and computer. Invisible sensors that collect data about the behavior of their users or people around them will increase. Using cars as sensors is no longer a technical issue, but mostly a legal and social question. Semantics, cognition and context (as three key words) are captured primarily using statistical methods.

The penetration of IT into all activities and the current low level of data protection and security promote crime: Nobody places leaves a cars unlocked on a city streets, but putting their computers - even if only an integrated computer in a washing machine or in a refrigerator - unprotected on the Internet is common practice.

7.2 Geographic Information Practice

Surveying will specialize in high precision and surveillance tasks. Surveyors are familiar with observing movement of objects and spatial-temporal planning. The importance of time-related data will increase in most applications and often time-related data will replace static data.

The quality of the data can be displayed and the demands on the quality of data for various applications can be assessed. Applications must include warnings for users, if the data necessary for a decision is not available or is not available in sufficient quantity.

Games that connect virtual worlds with real space – Pokémon Go was one of the first[30] – are successful and complementary to classic sports. Just as today the timetable information – once a domain of specialized railway officials – is automated, simple legal cases (and other activities of human "experts") can be automated [56]. The same should also apply to routine decisions in building law.

Sensors automatically detect certain situations (e.g. crowds in public transport, traffic jams) and make this information available to others for their decisions in the form of programmed components that can be integrated into applications. This extends the field of work of the "quantity surveyor" and the property valuation specialist.

---

[29] https://en.wikipedia.org/wiki/OpenStreetMap.
[30] https://en.wikipedia.org/wiki/Pokémon_Go.

7.3   Research

The statistical procedures for the acquisition of semantics should be supplemented with rule-based, ontological procedures. Since space and time are the fundamental indices in almost all areas of life and have likely fundamentally influenced the development of human cognition, spatial thinking and the "digital version" of it will be a prerequisite for the intelligent integration of data from different sources: sensor data must be combined with verbal data to make meaningful messages.

Research on human-computer interaction, especially user interfaces, in connection with natural language technologies are recognized as the most important topics for overcoming practical obstacles in the use of IT. The protection of spatio-temporal information to ensure the level of "privacy" necessary for a human society becomes an important topic for the development of technology, law and practice. How can information be obtained for the planning of business or public decisions without conclusions being drawn about the behavior of individuals [58]?

The context of information communicated must be considered. Understanding the pragmatics of natural language are difficult to integrate with programmed applications. The contrast between the "closed world" logic of most administrative activities and the "open world" logic [53] must be used for spatial reasoning in most cases calls for "intelligent" systems that choose between the two logics depending on the situation [3]. Computer security and defense against crime when dealing with spatial data is an issue: how to prevent the misuse or falsification of sensor data?

7.4   Data and Software

Data and software are increasingly becoming a "free good" that can be used by everyone. Business models must move their focus away from the copyright of data [37] and concentrate on value produced for the user. The spatial professional in practice becomes an expert in situation-appropriate applications of processes that run on public data with public software. Remember the famous joke from the early years of automobiles, where a repair bill read: "Material used: 1 screw 10 cents, Known where to apply it $19.90, Total $20"!

8   Conclusion

8.1   Enabling Technologies

The development of IT, especially of ever smaller computers that provide more performance with less power consumption, but also the development of batteries, cellular networks and finally GPS, have allowed new applications. Applications become economically viable, as a combination of price and usability, including the form factor. I conclude that the development of technology, driven by research, is the primary engine of change and that the social changes, which are becoming apparent in politics are the consequences of the development of technology, including new institutions (in the sense of Douglas North [47]).

8.2   Innovative Companies

Many of the pioneers have disappeared over time. Rarely have small companies, which were first on the market, survived in the long term against being pushed out or bought up by monopolists (e.g. Microsoft has successfully forced the first browser by Netscape out through marketing practices later considered illegal). The increasing complexity of IT through intensely networked systems forced the transition to open source models of software production and increases the chances for new ideas in startups - which are then taken over by monopolists.

8.3   It Takes Fifteen to Twenty Years from Research to Practice

The examples shown here, such as GPS, topological relations, data acquisition from moving vehicles, demonstrate a time lag of 15 to 20 years between the "invention" is discussed in research groups till it is put into practice. Novel ideas are often documented at an early stage in a research publication, but only years later the announcement of a product follows, and only much later, after the idea has been incorporated into education and has proven to be economically worthwhile, it will be sold and money earned with it. This is hardly documented and is - in retrospect - difficult to observe.

9   Coda

The real and the virtual world seem to merge on the web, but in the end, real physical space is essential for humans; we can order food from a take out and ask a delivery service to bring it to our home—but the food is better physically real and nourishing! The same applies for many other substantial aspects of human life.

Maintaining the synchronization between the real physical world and the virtual image is a demanding task; for example, the state of the road network, public transport etc. must be up-to-date. The user must become more conscious of the difference between reality and its representation; if there is a discrepancy between the physical reality and the information in a database then we should believe the real world situation; knowledge can be wrong, the state of reality cannot.

My experience leads me to believe that commercial success is possible as a combination of three conditions:

– a fundamental human need is at the core - e.g. people need to navigate in the world and must avoid to get lost;
– a cost-effective technical mean to satisfy this need is available and,
– a business-opportunity is identified.

A long term successful business is only possible if the services rendered or the product sold is solid and substantially satisfies the user needs, as expressed by Abraham Lincoln:

You can fool all the people some of the time, and some of the people all the time, but you cannot fool all the people all the time.

References

1. Abler, R.: The National Science Foundation - National Center for Geographic Information and Analysis. Int. J. Geograph. Inf. Syst. **1**(4), 303–326 (1987)
2. Andreessen, M.: NCSA Mosaic Technical Summary 605 (1993)
3. Arenas, M., Gottlob, G., Pieris, A.: Expressive languages for querying the semantic web. In: Proceedings of the 33rd ACM SIGMOD-SIGACT-SIGART Symposium on Principles of Database Systems, pp. 14–26. ACM (2014)
4. Bell, S., Bickmore, D.: Interactive cartography at the ECU: regional geography à la mode. In: Unit, E.C., Merriam, D.F.(ed.) Recent Advances in Geomathematics, an International Symposium, pp. 117–134. Pergamon Press (1978)
5. Berners-Lee, T., Hendler, J., Lassila, O.: The semantic web. A new form of web content that is meaningful to computers will unleash a revolution of new possibilities. Sci. Am. **284**(5), 28–37 (2001)
6. Buehler, K., McKee, L. (eds.): OpenGIS Guide: An Introduction to Interoperable Geoprocessing, Part 1 of the Open Geodata Interoperability Specification (OGIS). The Open GIS Consortium, Inc. (OGC)
7. Calkins, H.W., Obermeyer, N.J.: Taxonomy for surveying the use and value of geographical information! Int. J. Geograph. Inf. Syst. **5**(3), 341–351 (1991)
8. Calkins, H.W., Onsrud, H., Obermeyer, N.: Use and value of geographic information: initiative 4 specialist meeting summary report and proceedings, 89-7
9. Chrisman, N.: An interim proposed standard for digital cartographic data quality: supporting documentation. In: Moellering, H. (ed.) Digital Cartographic Data Standards: An Interim Proposed Standard, vol. 6. National Committee for Digital Cartographic Data Standards (1985)
10. Chrisman, N.R.: Digital cartographic data quality 15(1)
11. Clapp, J.L., Moyer, D.D., Niemann, B.J.: The Wisconsin land records committee: its background, status, impact, and future. In: GIS/LIS'88, Third Annual International Conference, vol. 2, pp. 766–773. ACSM, ASPRS, AAG, URISA (1988)
12. CODASYL: Report of the data base task group (1971)
13. Cooke, D.F.: Vehicle navigation appliances. In: Seventh International Symposium on Computer-Assisted Cartography, pp. 108–115. ASP and ACSM (1985)
14. Coppock, J.T., Rhind, D.W.: The history of GIS. In: Maguire, D.J., Goodchild, M.F., Rhind, D.W. (eds.) Geographical Information Systems: Principles and Applications, vol. 1, pp. 21–43. Longman Scientific & Technical (1991)
15. Coppock, T.: Retrospect and prospect: a personal view. In: Masser, I., Blakemore, M. (eds.) Handling Geographical Information, vol. 1, pp. 285–304. Longman Scientific, Harlow & Technical (1991)
16. Corbett, J.: Topological principles in cartography. In: 2nd International Symposium on Computer-Assisted Cartography, pp. 61–65 (1975)
17. Corbett, J.P.: Topological principles in cartography. Tech. Report: U.S. Dept. of Commerce, Bureau of the Census (1979)
18. Dobson, J.E., Fisher, P.F.: Geoslavery **22**(1), 47–52(2003)
19. Dobson, J.: The "g" in GIS - what are the ethical limits of GIS? **13**, 24–25(2000)
20. Dutton, G.H. (ed.): Harvard Papers on Geographic Information Systems: Laboratory for Computer Graphics and Spatial Analysis. Graduate School of Design, Harvard University, Cambridge, MA, Proceedings of the First International Advanced Study Symposium on Topological Data Structures for Geographic Information Systems held at Endicott House, Dedham, MA, from 16–21 October 1977

21. Egenhofer, M.J., Frank, A.U., Jackson, J.P.: A topological data model for spatial databases. In: Buchmann, A.P., Günther, O., Smith, T.R., Wang, Y.-F. (eds.) SSD 1989. LNCS, vol. 409, pp. 271–286. Springer, Heidelberg (1990). https://doi.org/10.1007/3-540-52208-5_32

22. Egenhofer, M.J.: A formal definition of binary topological relationships. In: Litwin, W., Schek, H.-J. (eds.) FODO 1989. LNCS, vol. 367, pp. 457–472. Springer, Heidelberg (1989). https://doi.org/10.1007/3-540-51295-0_148

23. Eichhorn, G. (ed.): Landinformationssysteme. TH Darmstadt, Berlin

24. Encarnacao, J., et al.: The workstation concept of GKS and the resulting conceptual differences to the GSPC core system. In: ACM SIGGRAPH Computer Graphics. vol. 14, pp. 226–230. ACM (1980)

25. FIG Féderation International des Géomètres (ed.): XVIe Congrès International des Géomètres

26. Frank, A.U.: Analysis of dependence of decision quality on data quality. J. Geograph. Syst. **10**(1), 71–88 (2008)

27. Frank, A.U.: Data structures for land information systems - semantical, topological and spatial relations in data of geo-sciences - in German (1983)

28. Frank, A.U.: Landinformationssysteme - ein Versuch zu einer Abgrenzung I/81, 23–30 (1979)

29. Frank, A.U., Medak, D.: Formal models of a spatiotemporal database. In: Richta, K. (ed.) DATASEM'99 - 19th Annual Conference on the Current Trends in Databases and Information Systems, pp. 117–130. Dept. of Computer Science, Czech Technical University (1999)

30. Freksa, C.: Qualitative spatial reasoning. In: Mark, D.M., Frank, A.U. (eds.) Cognitive and Linguistic Aspects of Geographic Space, pp. 361–372. NATO ASI Series D: Behavioural and Social Sciences, Kluwer Academic Press (2014). https://doi.org/10.1007/978-3-319-05732-3_3

31. French, R.: Automobile navigation in the past, present and future. In: Chrisman, N.R. (ed.) Auto-Carto, vol. 8. pp. 542–551. ASPRS & ACSM (1987)

32. Hahn, J.: Context Algebra applied to spatial concepts. PhD thesis. Geoinformation, Technical University Vienna (2016)

33. Homsby, K., Egenhofer, M.J.: Qualitative representation of change. In: Hirtle, S.C., Frank, A.U. (eds.) COSIT 1997. LNCS, vol. 1329, pp. 15–33. Springer, Heidelberg (1997). https://doi.org/10.1007/3-540-63623-4_40

34. Huang, H., Gartner, G.: A survey of mobile indoor navigation systems. In: Gartner, G., Ortag, F. (eds.) Cartography in Central and Eastern Europe, pp. 305–319. Springer, Heidelberg (2009). https://doi.org/10.1007/978-3-642-03294-3_20

35. Krek, A.: An agent-based model for quantifying the economic value of geographic information. PhD thesis. Technical University Vienna (2002)

36. Leick, A.: Macrometer satellite surveying. J. Surv. Eng. **110**(2), 146–158 (1984)

37. Lessig, L.: Remix Making Art and Commerce Thrive in the Hybrid Economy, Penguin Press, New York (2008)

38. Manola, F., et al.: RDF primer. W3C Recommend. **10**(1–107), 6 (2004)

39. Mark, D.: On giving and receiving directions: cartographic and cognitive issues, pp. 562–571. Auto-Carto 8, ASPRS & ACSM

40. Martinez-Asenjo, B., Frank, A.U.: An economic overview of European NAMs transformation from government departments into public corporations. Geoinformatics, Jan/Feb 2002

41. Masser, I.: All shapes and sizes: the first generation of national spatial data infrastructures. J. Geograph. Inf. Sci. **13**(1), 67–84 (1994)

42. McGranaghan, M.: Human interface requirements for vehicle navigation aids, pp. 396–402. Auto-Carto 8, ASPRS & ACSM (1987)
43. Medak, D.: Lifestyles - a paradigm for the description of spatiotemporal databases. PhD thesis. Wien: Technical University Vienna (1999). isbn: 978-3-901716-39-3
44. NCGIA: The U.S. National Center for Geographic Information and Analysis: an overview of the agenda for research and education 2(3), 117–136 (1989)
45. Neteler, M., Mitasova, H.: Open Source GIS: a GRASS GIS Approach, vol. 689. Springer, Heidelberg (2008). https://doi.org/10.1007/978-0-387-68574-8
46. Niemann, B.J.J., Sullivan, J.G.: Results of the Dane county land records project: implications for conservation planning. In: Chrisman, N.R. (ed.) Auto-Carto 8, pp. 445–455. ASPRS & ACSM (1987)
47. North, D.C.: Institutions, Institutional Change and Economic Performance, Cambridge University Press, Cambridge (1997)
48. Novak, K.: Mobile mapping systems: new tools for the fast collection of GIS information. In: Optical Engineering and Photonics in Aerospace Sensing, pp. 188–198. International Society for Optics and Photonics (1993)
49. Onsrud, H.J.: The role of law in impeding and facilitating the sharing of geographic information, In: Sharing Geographic Information, pp. 292–306 (1995)
50. Prud'Hommeaux, E., et al.: SPARQL query language for RDF. In: W3C recommendation 15 (2008)
51. Randell, D.A., Cui, Z., Cohn, A.: A spatial logic based on regions and connection. In: Brachmann, R., Levesque, H., Reiter, R. (eds.) Third International Conference on the Principles of Knowledge Representation and Reasoning, pp. 165–176. Morgan-Kaufmann, Los Altos (1992)
52. Reed, J.H., Krizman, K.J., Woerner, B.D., Rappaport, T.S.: An overview of the challenges and progress in meeting the e-911 requirement for location service. IEEE Commun. Mag. 36(4), 30–37(1998)
53. Reiter, R.: Towards a logical reconstruction of relational database theory. In: Brodie, M.L., Mylopoulos, J., Schmidt, J.W. (eds.) On Conceptual Modelling, Perspectives from Artificial Intelligence, Database and Programming Languages, pp. 191–238. Springer, Heidelberg (1984). https://doi.org/10.1007/978-1-4612-5196-5_8
54. Rhind, D.: Data access, charging and copyright and their implications for GIS. In: Proceedings of EGIS 1991, vol. 2, pp. 929–945. EGIS Foundation (1991)
55. Steiner, D.: A minicomputer-based geographical data processing system. In: Map Data Processing, pp. 1–25. Elsevier (1980)
56. Susskind, R., Susskind, D.: The Future of the Professions: How Technology Will Transform the Work of Human Experts. Oxford University Press, Oxford (2015)
57. Tripp, R.E.I.: Tracking AM/FM benefits at Carolina Power & Light Company. In: Proceedings of AM/FM Conference XIV, vol. 1, pp. 793–802. AM/FM International (1991)
58. Tyagi, A.K., Sreenath, N.: A comparative study on privacy preserving techniques for location based services. Br. J. Math. Comput. Sci. 10(4), 1–25 (2015)
59. Vckovski, A.: Interoperability and spatial information theory. In: International Conference and Workshop on Interoperating Geographic Systems (1997)
60. White, M.S.: A survey of the mathematics of maps. In: Auto Carto IV, vol. 1, pp. 82–96 (1979)
61. White, M.: Digital map requirements of vehicle navigation. In: Chrisman, N.R. (ed.) Auto-Carto 8, pp. 552–561. ASPRS & ACSM (1987)

Location Extraction from Twitter Messages Using a Bidirectional Long Short-Term Memory Neural Network with Conditional Random Field Model

Zi Chen$^{(\boxtimes)}$ (iD), Badal Pokharel (iD), Bingnan Li (iD), and Samsung Lim (iD)

School of Civil and Environmental Engineering, University of New South Wales,
Sydney, Australia
zi.chen1@student.unsw.edu.au, {b.pokharel,bingnan.li,
s.lim}@unsw.edu.au

Abstract. In the context of disaster management, location information is crucial in disaster scenarios to infer the incident location and facilitate disaster relief. In recent years the advent of social media has brought not only great opportunity to enhance disaster management in a crowdsourced perspective, but also a major challenge to interpret the noisy information. A conventional approach to location extraction from texts is Named Entity Recognition (NER), however it shows unsatisfactory performance on informal and colloquial texts such as social media messages, especially for the uncommon place names. To address this issue, we proposed a Bidirectional Long Short-Term Memory (LSTM) Neural Network with Conditional Random Field (CRF) layer to identify geo-entities especially the rarely known local places in social media messages, and the use of orthographic, semantic and syntactic features was explored to achieve best performance. The proposed model was tested on a dataset collected from Twitter, showing promising performance in detecting location information when compared with off-the-shelf NER tools.

Keywords: Named entity recognition · Location extraction · Social media · Deep learning model

1 Introduction

Social media can be beneficial in disaster risk reduction, response and recovery process [1], and Twitter stands out as an effective social media platform because of its global extension and the speed in which information gets disseminated [2]. While location information can be crucial in disaster management, Twitter offers three types of information for extracting the location where the incident happens: (i) geo-tagged texts or geo-coordinates (ii) users' locations in their profiles (iii) location mentions in the tweets. The previous studies show that the explicit and accurate information about the place where an event has happened can be gained with the tweets having geo-coordinates

© Springer Nature Switzerland AG 2021
C. Grueau et al. (Eds.): GISTAM 2020, CCIS 1411, pp. 18–30, 2021.
https://doi.org/10.1007/978-3-030-76374-9_2

[3]. However, the tweets containing geo-coordinates are rare among the whole Twitter stream. The location information from the user's profile can be an alternative to detection of the place of event, but its accuracy is not guaranteed. Therefore, the location mentions in the tweet text accounts the most for the location recognition, which requires further text processing.

The text mining technique that is commonly used to extract place names from texts is Named Entity Recognition (NER). This method analyzes the text based on Part-of-Speech (POS) tagging and labels a certain group of words as an entity category including person, organization or location. The technique performs well for well-structured sentences and well-known places, but not so good for the extraction of local geo-entities from social media messages. It is because the texts are usually written in informal or random format due to geographic or non-geographic ambiguities.

In order to improve the extraction of unknown place names from the social media, we proposed a model based on Bidirectional Long Short-Term Memory (LSTM) Neural Network with Conditional Random Field (CRF) layer to recognize the local geo-entities mentioned in social media messages. Stanford Named Entity Recognizer was used to label the training data. The experimentation was carried out to incorporate both syntactic and semantic features in the model. In addition to word embedding, POS tags, letter cases and prepositions are considered as well to augment the model.

2   Related Work

The extraction of location mentions from texts is a long-studied problem since texts are one of the most common forms to encode geographic information, but in this process the geo-referents of the location mentions become ambiguous and even the boundaries of the location mentions in text are difficult to recognize without enough background information, especially when the place name is abbreviated for brevity. Naturally the place name extraction falls into sub-problems: entity delimitation and toponym disambiguation. The former delimitates the boundaries of a place name, which is the focus of our study, and the latter decides the most possible geo-referent to the place name.

While entity delimitation can be solved by matching with gazetteer [4] or hard-coded rules [5], the current NER tools or systems are generally more powerful in extracting location mentions from formal texts in terms of recall. One of the most renowned NER systems is Stanford NER [6] where a Conditional Random Field (CRF) model incorporates long distance features to identify named entities including location. Some researchers have also attempted further augmentation to the NER capability of extracting locations by constructing a gazetteer from word clusters [7]. Web NER aims at separating complex place names from web pages by utilizing capitalization cues and lexical statistics [8].

However, the NER systems have shown unsatisfactory performances on social media messages [9] mainly owing to the informal and irregular expressions as well as the short texts. An outstanding performance has been achieved by Stanford NER when it is retrained by annotated tweets [10], but the annotation of social media messages is time-consuming and elusive on large scale text processing. Meanwhile LSTM is becoming a popular choice of NER owing to its suitability for sequence classification.

Bi-LSTM-CRF networks using contextualized embeddings were employed for chemical NER [11]. An exploratory study on Indonesian Twitter Posts [12] used LSTM for NER and experimented on a small dataset, on which it achieved a F1-score of 0.81 for location recognition.

Recent years have witnessed a lot of efforts attempting to address the problem of extracting location mentions from social media streams. A model to predict the occurrence of location mentions in a tweet was introduced and was found that this preliminary process can enhance the accuracy of entity delimitation [13]. A statistical language model was built in [14] based on augmented and filtered region-specific gazetteers from online resources such as OpenStreetMap (OSM) to extract place names from tweets, a F1-score of 0.85 was achieved while no training data is required.

Unlike the studies above, we mainly focus on the location mentions referring to geo-entities of small scale, which rarely appear in most gazetteers. And a deep learning model is constructed and trained on Stanford NER annotated tweets, without manual annotation.

3   Methodology

3.1   Model

We used a Bidirectional LSTM-CRF (Bi-LSTM-CRF) model, which belongs to the category of Recurrent Neural Networks (RNNs), to label whether a word is an element of a location mention or not. RNN is an appropriate approach for sequence classification due to its capability of passing the output of one node to its successor, which can be interpreted as the influence of a word to the successive word. LSTM is a specialized RNN which performs better on long sequences while the impact of previous layers decay along with vanishing gradient in RNN. LSTM employs a mechanism called forget gates to control the information flow in the neural network.

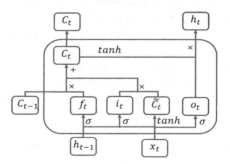

Fig. 1. LSTM cell.

Figure 1 shows the mechanism of an LSTM cell that handles information from previous sequences and current input with forget gate, input gate and output gate. An LSTM cell takes three inputs: previous hidden state h_{t-1}, previous cell state C_{t-1} and current input x_t. The forget gate generates f_t to decide whether to keep previous cell state C_{t-1}:

$$f_t = \sigma(W_f x_t + U_f h_{t-1}) \tag{1}$$

where σ is sigmoid activation function, W_f and U_f are weight matrices for linear transformation and combination of x_t and h_{t-1}, respectively.

Input gate is to decide whether to update current cell state C_t with new candidate value $\widetilde{C}_t$ by i_t:

$$i_t = \sigma(W_i x_t + U_i h_{t-1}) \tag{2}$$

$$\widetilde{C}_t = tanh(W_C x_t + U_C h_{t-1}) \tag{3}$$

where $tanh$ stands for a hyperbolic tangent activation function. The current cell state C_t is updated by:

$$C_t = f_t * C_{t-1} + i_t * \widetilde{C}_t \tag{4}$$

Output gate controls the update of current hidden state h_t:

$$o_t = \sigma(W_o x_t + U_o h_{t-1}) \tag{5}$$

$$h_t = o_t * tanh(C_t) \tag{6}$$

The outputs of an LSTM cell are current cell state C_t and current hidden state h_t where C_t and h_t are passed to the next time step $t+1$. The label y_t of input x_t is determined by h_t:

$$y_t = softmax(W_y h_t + b_y) \tag{7}$$

On the basis of LSTM, Bi-LSTM model is trained on two directions of the input sequence, forward and backward, providing comprehensive context information of the target word. Bi-LSTM model has been implemented on NER tasks and shown competitive performances on benchmark datasets [15].

Conditional Random Field (CRF) is a graph-based sequence labelling algorithm to predict a label for each element in a sequence. A set of feature functions $f(X, i, y_i, y_{i-1})$ is defined to model the interdependency of input sequence X, position i, current state y_i and previous state y_{i-1}. The selection feature functions are task-specific. For instance, in POS tagging task if a word ends with '-ness' and y_i is NN (noun, singular or mass) the feature function $f_j(X, i, y_i, y_{i-1})$ is set to be 1, or otherwise 0. This shows that the feature functions quantify semantic or syntactic rules and evaluate the factors determining the label of a token. The interdependency can be modelled between not only neighboring states but also states at a distance in a sequence. It is assumed in CRF that the conditional probability $P(Y|X) \propto exp\{\sum_{i=1}^{n} w^T \cdot f(X, i, y_i, y_{i-1})\}$ where the weight w represents the significance of different feature factors in determining the final class label. It is optimized by minimizing $-log(P(Y|X))$. CRF maximises the conditional probability of the whole sequence while removes the constraint of limited dependency among states Y in Hidden Markov Model (HMM).

In the combination of LSTM and CRF, CRF takes the output of LSTM layer as the feature functions and automatically learns characteristics and regulations of a valid output sequence, which not only avoids manual work to select feature functions but also captures the interaction between LSTM output sequences.

As seen in Fig. 2, features of the input sequence are passed to the forward and backward LSTM layers respectively in our model, the two outputs are subsequently concatenated and passed to a fully connected layer. Finally, a CRF layer verifies the validity of LSTM output sequence and predicts the probability distribution over all the class labels in the sequence.

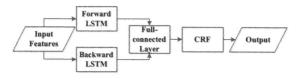

Fig. 2. Bi-LSTM-CRF model architecture.

Additionally, a regularization method called label smoothing is employed to rectify the noisy labels generated by Stanford NER. For a one-hot label vector y, label smoothing constructs a softened label vector $y' = (1 - \alpha) * y + \alpha * u$ where u is a uniform distribution over K classes and α is a hyperparameter. Label smoothing is commonly used to avoid overfitting in deep learning models. However, it also contributes to correcting the noisy labels in this case.

3.2 Features

Apart from the Bi-LSTM-CRF model, we tested the impacts of five categories of features on the classification results: word embedding, character embedding, POS tags, capitalization and prepositions. Word embedding is a word representation method that maps words to continuous vectors in higher dimensions. It is grounded on Distributional Hypothesis that words with similar contexts are inclined to have similar semantic meanings [16], and word embedding encodes the context information in the vector. Therefore, the similarity of two words can be evaluated by the cosine value of their word vectors.

One of the most popular approaches of word embedding is the Skip-Gram model. It is a fully connected neural network that takes the one hot encoding vector of the target word w_i as input and produces the conditional probability that an arbitrary word w_j from the vocabulary occurs in the context window of w_i. Parameters θ of the model are optimized by maximizing the log-likelihood sum of $P(w_j|w_i; \theta)$. Another widely used word embedding model is GloVe [17], short for Global Vectors. Unlike Skip-Gram model which is trained by maximum likelihood estimation of the conditional probability of neighboring words, GloVe is trained on global statistics of a word-word co-occurrence matrix obtained from training corpus. In the co-occurrence matrix X, X_{ij} represents the co-occurrences of word i and word j and $P_{ij} = X_{ij}/X_i$. In order to measure the semantic similarity between words, a ratio $F(i, j, k) = P_{ik}/P_{jk}$ is defined on a third entry word k. If the ratio approximates to 1, word k is either highly or barely relevant to both word i and word j. Otherwise word k is relevant to word i or word j, according to offset of ratio. Specifically, F is an exponential function to fulfil the symmetry of word relations:

$$F\left((\boldsymbol{u}_i - \boldsymbol{u}_j)^T \cdot \boldsymbol{u}_k\right) = \frac{P_{ik}}{P_{jk}} = \frac{F\left(\boldsymbol{u}_i^T \cdot \boldsymbol{u}_k\right)}{F\left(\boldsymbol{u}_j^T \cdot \boldsymbol{u}_k\right)} \tag{8}$$

where $\boldsymbol{u}_i, \boldsymbol{u}_j$ and $\boldsymbol{u}_k$ are the corresponding word embeddings of word i, j and k. Therefore we have:

$$\boldsymbol{u}_i^T \boldsymbol{u}_k = log(X_{ik}) - log(X_i) \tag{9}$$

The right term $log(X_i)$ is invariant of word k, it is split into two bias terms to comply with the symmetry of relation between word i and k:

$$\boldsymbol{u}_i^T \boldsymbol{u}_k + b_i + b_k = log(X_{ik}) \tag{10}$$

The cost function over vocabulary V is defined as:

$$J = \sum_{i,j=1}^{V} f\left(X_{ij}\right)(\boldsymbol{u}_i^T \boldsymbol{u}_j + b_i + b_j - log\left(X_{ij}\right))^2 \tag{11}$$

$$f\left(X_{ij}\right) = \begin{cases} \left(\frac{X_{ij}}{X_{max}}\right)^{\alpha} & if \ X_{ij} < X_{max} \\ 1 & otherwise \end{cases} \tag{12}$$

where f is a weighting function to adjust the cost for word pairs of different co-occurrence frequencies and α is empirically set at 0.75.

GloVe provides pre-trained word embeddings which are used in this paper. The GloVe word embeddings are trained on an enormous Twitter dataset of 2 billion tweets covering a vocabulary of 1.2 million words.

An outstanding challenge in the processing of social media texts lies in the out-of-vocabulary words. The evolving lexicon of cyberspeak far surpasses the limited dictionary of numbered training materials, not to mention misspellings and emoticons. The out-of-vocabulary words are often marked as unknown words and share the identical embedding, neglecting their semantic and syntactic diversities. However, the constituents that form all words possibly occurring among social media texts in English are restricted to 26 l, 10 digits and some other special characters, which inspires the introduction of character embedding as an alternative to word embedding. Training of character embedding is similar to word embedding where a substantially smaller character dictionary is pre-defined, and the character sequence is projected to a matrix made up of character embeddings. The character matrix is processed by a one dimensional convolutional or recurrent layer to extract the features of word segments or subwords, which are commonly recognized as prefixes, suffixes or roots.

The other three features, POS tags, capitalization and prepositions are regarded as categorical data and encoded into integers. POS tags are the labels that denote the part of speech of a word such as noun, verb or adjective. Since the location mentions are mostly comprised of nouns, POS tags can signify the possible occurrence of location mentions.

Another factor that could influence the identification of location mentions is the capitalization or case of a word. We consider the capitalization in four categories: upper case, lower case, title case and other.

Prepositions that can describe places or directions such as 'at' or 'in' are also important indicators of location mentions. We collect all the prepositions regarding locations in a list and encode the occurrence of prepositions in tweets as the list index. The three indexed categorical features are mapped and trained into corresponding embeddings in the Bidirectional LSTM-CRF model. Another factor to consider in the model is the errors in features resulted from the informality of social media data. The errors caused by upstream tasks or writing mistakes may severely impact the downstream task of geo-entity recognition. For example, POS tag is a major indicator to identify proper nouns, but the performance of POS taggers on informal and noisy social media data is constantly in doubt. Therefore, a fully connected layer is designed in the proposed model to correct the errors in input features in order to minimize their influence on model performance. Meanwhile the errors are infrequent compared with the majority of unpolluted data, which requires merely a minor correction on the original embedding layer. To this end, a fully connected layer with an L2 regularizer is added after the POS tag embedding layer and case embedding layer to correct the noise in features such as POS tagging errors or case misuse. The corrected embedding layers are concatenated with the pre-trained word embedding and preposition embedding for each token or word as can be seen in Fig. 3.

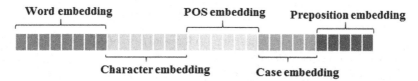

Fig. 3. Concatenated feature embeddings.

As the features employed to describe the data are heuristic, we also explore the contribution of each feature to the correct location mention labelling by adjust the dimension of the feature in the following experiments.

4 Experiments

4.1 Dataset

The dataset we used in the experiments was collected from Twitter via its official application programming interfaces (APIs). From to 21st to 30th of August 2017 two consecutive typhoons *Hato* and *Pakhar* affected Southern China area while two populated coastal cities Hong Kong and Macau were severely impacted. We collected and reduplicated tweets from the two areas during the typhoon-impacted period and extracted typhoon-related tweets by an augmented Convolutional Neural Network (CNN), resulting in 10,996 tweets ready for location extraction.

4.2 Pre-processing

The named entities including location mentions in the tweets were annotated via Stanford NER tools, and POS tagging was implemented likewise using Stanford POS tagger. Among 10,996 tweets location mentions were found in 4,215 tweets. Considering that Stanford NER tools can ignore the unknown places only familiar to locals, we only used the 4,215 positive tweets as training data.

In order to test the proposed model on its capability of detecting local place names, we manually selected and labelled 100 tweets in which Stanford NER misclassified the place names. The word embeddings with dimension of 200 were pre-trained by the Skip-Gram model on the Twitter stream we collected. The embeddings of POS tags, capitalization and prepositions were trained along with the model.

4.3 Model Training

In the training process we leave out one tenth of the training data, which is 422 tweets, for validation, and 3,793 for training. If the validation loss is not improved in 5 epochs the training process will be terminated.

Figure 3 shows the variation of accuracy and loss for training set and validation set when all the four features are employed. The validation accuracy is improved to 96% in comparison to 92% when only word embedding is used, which proves that the utilization of syntactic features such as POS tags can boost the model performance. In the following subsection we will examine how the features influence the model on the test set (Fig. 4).

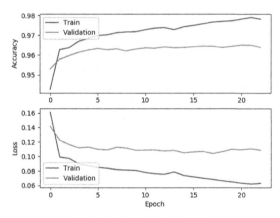

Fig. 4. Model training [18].

4.4 Feature Evaluation

4.4.1 Individual Application of Feature

We first verify every feature separately on the test set. In the training process all the tweets are padded to the same length for alignment, the padded element is labelled 0 as its location mention category. A word that is part of a location mention is labelled 1, and other words are 2. The positive label 1 accounts for an extreme small proportion in the true labels of test set at 1.18%.

In Table 1 we present the precision, recall and F1-score of each label when only word embedding is applied. The proposed model performs well on label 0 and 2 that constitute majority of labels but shows poor performance in predicting location mentions particularly in terms of recall. The precision has not reached 0.5 and F1-score is merely 0.11.

Table 1. Classification results on word embedding.

Label	Precision	Recall	F1-score
0	0.98	0.99	0.99
1	0.42	0.06	0.11
2	0.91	0.94	0.93

We further investigate the classification performance of individual application of character embedding, POS tags, capitalization and Prepositions on label 1, as shown in Table 2. The noise correction layer for POS embedding and case embedding is tested separately as well to verify its effectiveness. Best performance is achieved by POS tags on precision and F1-score, and case embedding with noise correction layer reaches highest recall. The singular employment of prepositions produces inferior outcomes compared to POS tags and capitalization, but still outperforms the results of word embedding. The unsatisfactory outcomes produced by prepositions are reasonable for that preposition is an indicator of neighboring words for geo-entity recognition. For POS embedding and case embedding, the use of noise correction layer lowers precision and increases recall, this tradeoff has no significant contribution for POS embedding but enhances F1-score of case embedding considerably. This indicates that capitalization in social media texts is comparably noisy than POS tags produced by Stanford POS Tagger and less informative than formal texts.

Table 2. Classification results on other features.

Feature	Precision	Recall	F1-score
Character embedding	0.57	0.55	0.56
POS tags	**0.66**	0.65	**0.66**
POS tags w/correction	0.62	0.71	**0.66**
Capitalization	0.60	0.54	0.57
Capitalization w/correction	0.55	**0.72**	0.62
Prepositions	0.58	0.09	0.15

In general, individual application of feature produces unsatisfactory results, which is mostly caused by the imbalanced nature of data where location mentions are exceedingly infrequent.

4.4.2 Combination of Features

After the performance of individual features is tested, the concatenated embedding that encompasses all the features are verified in experiments as well as the noise correction layers. In Table 3, the concatenated embedding has yielded favourable outcomes in comparison with individual features. The introduction of noise correction layer has considerably improved recall as well as F1-score, which means that in social media data the errors of POS tagging and case misuse have notably affected the sequence labelling task. The noise correction layer has corrected most of these errors, whereas it also imports minor noise resulting in slight decrease of precision.

Table 3. Classification results on other features.

Model	Precision	Recall	F1-score
Bi-LSTM-CRF without noise correction layer	0.82	0.60	0.69
Bi-LSTM-CRF with POS correction layer	0.81	0.62	0.70
Bi-LSTM-CRF with case correction layer	0.78	0.68	0.72
Bi-LSTM-CRF with both noise correction layers	0.77	0.71	0.74

We compare the proposed model to Stanford NER and two off-the-shelf NER tools TwitterNLP [19] and TwitterNER [20] that are specialized for Twitter data. TwitterNLP reconstructed an NLP pipeline including POS tagging, shallow parsing, capitalization informativity classifier and NER tagger. Capitalization informativity classifier was designed to determine if a tweet informatively capitalized since the capitalization in social media messages are generally less reliable. Each component of the NLP pipeline was adapted and re-trained on Twitter data. The NER tagger in TwitterNLP consisted of two parts: named entity segmentation and classification. In named entity segmentation orthographic, contextual and dictionary features were employed on a Conditional Random Fields model to label IOB (Inside-Outside-Beginning) tags for text sequences, and LabeledLDA [21] was applied in named entity classification to model the label distribution over the text segments linked to an entity.

TwitterNER provides a semi-supervised approach for named entity recognition in tweets. It utilized diversified features including orthographic features extracted by regular expressions, gazetteer features, unsupervised features such as word embedding and word clusters, and applied random feature dropout to generate more samples for augmentation of the small training dataset. A linear chain CRF was leveraged for named entity classification.

The experiments were conducted on the same test set. In Table 4 it can be seen that precision, recall and F1-score have been largely increased, which proves the capability of the proposed model on identifying unknown location mentions from social media messages, either with or without the label smoothing. Label smoothing has moderately improved precision of the model while maintaining the same level of recall, thus promotes the overall metric F1-score. It proves that label smoothing is capable of reducing the noise in training labels. Moreover, Bi-LSTM-CRF with label smoothing enhances recall and F1-score significantly with small sacrifice of precision by rectifying the errors in labels.

Table 4. Comparison with baselines.

Model	Precision	Recall	F1-score
Bi-LSTM-CRF without label smoothing	0.77	0.71	0.74
Bi-LSTM-CRF with label smoothing	0.80	0.71	0.75
TwitterNLP	0.30	0.14	0.19
TwitterNER	0.96	0.56	0.71
Stanford NER	0.89	0.58	0.70

The Bi-LSTM-CRF model is proven to have better capability to learn the interdependences between input sequences in both forward and backward directions as well as the output sequences. Without utilization of gazetteers, it achieves promising results on identification of unknown place names from social media texts in the curated test dataset that is difficult to learn.

5   Conclusions

In this paper, a deep learning model based on Bi-LSTM-CRF Neural Network was proposed in order to identify the rarely known local geo-entities mentioned in social media messages. We tested five features of word embedding, character embedding, POS tags, capitalization and prepositions to evaluate their capabilities to differentiate between positive and negative labels. It was found that POS tags contribute the most to classification. The proposed model has achieved competitive results even with noisy training data. The introduction of noise correction layer for features further boosts the performance. However, there still exist areas for further enhancements especially on precision of the Bi-LSTM-CRF model. In order to address the issue of imbalanced datasets, we can further under-sample the majority negative labels, or ensemble the proposed model with other methods suitable for imbalanced datasets such as decision tree models. Moreover, the multiple instance learning framework can be exploited in the model as the training data labelled by Stanford NER possibly contains many false negative labels.

Acknowledgements. This research is sponsored by China Scholarship Council (CSC).

References

1. Ahmed, A.: Use of social media in disaster management. In: International Conference on Information Systems, ICIS 2011. pp. 4149–4159 (2011)
2. Chatfield, A.T., Brajawidagda, U.: Twitter early tsunami warning system: a case study in Indonesia's natural disaster management. In: Proceedings of the Annual Hawaii International Conference on System Science, pp. 2050–2060 (2013)
3. Nakaji, Y., Yanai, K.: Visualization of real-world events with geotagged tweet photos. In: Proceedings of the 2012 IEEE International Conference on Multimedia and Expo Workshops, ICMEW, pp. 272–277. ICMEW (2012)
4. Sultanik, E.A., Fink, C.: Rapid geotagging and disambiguation of social media text via an indexed gazetteer. In: ISCRAM 2012 Conference Proceedings - 9th International Conference on Information Systems for Crisis Response and Management (2012)
5. Cunningham, H., Maynard, D., Bontcheva, K., Tablan, V.: GATE: an architecture for development of robust HLT applications. In: Proceedings of the 40th Annual Meeting of the Association for Computational Linguistics, ACL 2002, p. 1688 (2001). https://doi.org/10.3115/1073083.1073112
6. Finkel, J.R., Grenager, T., Manning, C.: Incorporating non-local information into information extraction systems by Gibbs sampling. In: ACL-05 - 43rd Annual Meeting of the Association for Computational Linguistics, Proceedings of the Conference. pp. 363–370 (2005)
7. Kazama, J., Torisawa, K.: Inducing gazetteers for named entity recognition by large-scale clustering of dependency relations. In: Proceedings of the Conference of 46th Annual Meeting of the Association for Computational Linguistics: Human Language Technologies, HLT, ACL 2008. pp. 407–415 (2008)
8. Downey, D., Broadhead, M., Etzioni, O.: Locating complex named entities in web text. In: IJCAI International Joint Conference on Artificial Intelligence. pp. 2733–2739 (2007)
9. Bontcheva, K., Derczynski, L., Funk, A., Greenwood, M. A., Maynard, D., Aswani, N.: Twitie: An open-source information extraction pipeline for microblog text. In: Proceedings of the International Conference Recent Advances in Natural Language Processing RANLP 2013, 83–90 (2013)
10. Lingad, J., Karimi, S., Yin, J.: Location extraction from disaster-related microblogs. In: Proceedings of the 22nd International Conference on World Wide Web, WWW 2013 Companion. pp. 1017–1020. ACM Press, New York (2013)
11. Awan, Z., Kahlke, T., Ralph, P.J., Kennedy, P.J.: Chemical named entity recognition with deep contextualized neural embeddings. In: IC3K 2019 - Proceedings of the 11th International Joint Conference on Knowledge Discovery, Knowledge Engineering and Knowledge Management. pp. 135–144 (2019)
12. Rachman, V., Savitri, S., Augustianti, F., Mahendra, R.: Named entity recognition on Indonesian Twitter posts using long short-term memory networks. In: 2017 International Conference on Advanced Computer Science and Information Systems, ICACSIS 2017. pp. 228–232 (2018)
13. Hoang, T.B.N., Mothe, J.: Location extraction from tweets. Inf. Process. Manage. **54**, 129–144 (2018). https://doi.org/10.1016/j.ipm.2017.11.001
14. Al-Olimat, H.S., Thirunarayan, K., Shalin, V., Sheth, A.: Location name extraction from targeted text streams using gazetteer-based statistical language models. arXiv preprint arXiv: 1708.03105 (2017)
15. Chiu, J.P.C., Nichols, E.: Named entity recognition with bidirectional LSTM-CNNs. Trans. Assoc. Comput. Linguist. **4**, 357–370 (2016). https://doi.org/10.1162/tacl_a_00104
16. Harris, Z.S.: Distributional structure. Distrib. Struct. Word. **10**, 146–162 (1954). https://doi.org/10.1080/00437956.1954.11659520

17. Pennington, J., Socher, R., Manning, C.D.: GloVe: global vectors for word representation. In: 2014 Conference on Empirical Methods in Natural Language Processing, Proceedings of the Conference, EMNLP 2014. pp. 1532–1543 (2014)
18. Chen, Z., Pokharel, B., Li, B., Lim, S.: Location extraction from twitter messages using bidirectional long short-term memory model. In: Proceedings of the 6th International Conference on Geographical Information Systems Theory, Applications and Management. SCITEPRESS - Science and Technology Publications. pp. 45–50 (2020)
19. Ritter, A., Sam, C., Mausam, E.O.: Named entity recognition in tweets: an experimental study. In: Proceedings of the Conference on Empirical Methods in Natural Language Processing, EMNLP 2011, pp. 1524–1534. Association for Computational Linguistics (2011)
20. Mishra, S., Diesner, J.: Semi-supervised named entity recognition in noisy-text. In: Proceedings of the 2nd Workshop on Noisy User-generated Text (WNUT). The COLING 2016 Organizing Committee. pp. 203–212 (2016)
21. Ramage, D., Hall, D., Nallapati, R., Manning, C.D.: Labeled LDA: a supervised topic model for credit attribution in multi-labeled corpora. In: EMNLP 2009 - Proceedings of the 2009 Conference on Empirical Methods in Natural Language Processing: A Meeting of SIGDAT, a Special Interest Group of ACL, Held in Conjunction with ACL-IJCNLP 2009. pp. 248–256 (2009)

Automatic Processing of Sentinel-2 Data for Monitoring Biodiversity in a User-Defined Area: An Example from Mount Kilimanjaro National Park

Fortunata Msoffe[1,2(✉)] and Dirk Zeuss[1]

[1] Department of Environmental Informatics, Philipps Universität-Marburg,
Deutschhausstrasse, 12, 35032 Marburg, Germany
`dirk.zeuss@uni-marburg.de`
[2] Tanzania National Parks, P.O. Box 3134, Arusha, Tanzania

Abstract. Climate and land-use change continue to pose major threats to global rapid declines in biodiversity and ecosystem functions impacting natural system's resilience and capacity for the provision of ecosystems services. Kilimanjaro Mountain National Park, a cloud tropical montane forest was specifically designated to protect the only free-standing highest mountain in the world. In ensuring long-term protection of this high biodiverse tropical montane forest park, consistent ecological monitoring, including field measurements, is of paramount importance. This study provides a state-of-the-art remote sensing method contribution in the conservation efforts carried out by park staff for protecting this unique national park in the tropics. Our method demonstrates the automatic calculation of derived vegetation indices from Sentinel-2 data of the European Satellite Agency, using the normalized difference vegetation index (NDVI) as an example. The Sentinel-2 satellite mission provides data for consistent and long-term biodiversity monitoring to complement the in-situ observations by focusing on specific areas of interests in and outside the park ecosystems. Our study uses an area in the western edge of the park as an example, which became part of the Kilimanjaro Mountain National Park in 2008 (the "Half-mile strip"). We demonstrate how to automatically download and preprocess Sentinel-2 data for a particular study area and time period, as well as how to calculate various vegetation indices while taking into account the specific cloud coverage in the satellite images for the area in focus. We developed and provide processing routines in the programming environment R, which can easily be adopted to any study area for automatically generating similar outcomes.

Keywords: Biodiversity monitoring · Climate-land-use change · Cloud Coverage · Mount Kilimanjaro National Park · Remote sensing · Sentinel-2 data · Vegetation indices

1 Introduction

It is well known that protected areas particularly those in the tropics face key challenges linked to loss of wildlife habitats, mainly due to land use changes in their surrounding

© Springer Nature Switzerland AG 2021
C. Grueau et al. (Eds.): GISTAM 2020, CCIS 1411, pp. 31–45, 2021.
https://doi.org/10.1007/978-3-030-76374-9_3

ecosystems whilst exacerbated by the increasing impacts of global climate change [1, 2]. Mount Kilimanjaro National Park and its associated ecosystems represent such a world-wide unique and diverse habitat, with its altitudinal range of about 5,900 m associated with climate and vegetation zones changing from the tropical savannas at the lowlands to the afro-alpine grasslands at the top [3]. Apart from the natural ecosystems within the national park, several land use types occur in the vicinity, including intensive annual monocultures (maize, beans and other cereals), perennial coffee-plantations and diverse traditional agro-forestry systems such as the so-called "Chagga-home-gardens", which to some extent retain a semi-natural forest structure [4].

This highest free-standing mountain in Africa acts as a water tower by feeding major river systems in the region. The tropical mountainous forest ecosystems play a major role in the regional climate regulation, while providing many other important ecosystem services to the locals and beyond [2]. It's melting "ice-cap", which is vanishing because of decreasing precipitation [5] rather than by an increasing temperature, is an important tourism attraction by mountaineers and tourists visiting the park every year and has become a global symbol for the accelerating trend of global change [3].

Our study capitalizes on the recently concluded "KiLi1-Project" (running from 2010 to 2018), with the main objective of a follow-up monitoring strategy for the Kilimanjaro Mountain National Park, being the custodian in ensuring the continuity of the ecosystem services provided by the park to the local, national and the international community at large [1, 2]. Apart from the direct ecosystem services provided by the park in its natural settings, it is particularly a key tourist destination in the country, contributing to the local and national economy from the foreign currency accrued through the tourism business and its tripling effects to the local communities surrounding the park [2]. The park management authority vested with the responsibility of protecting this unique tropical montane cloud-forest in the long run, at the face of its increasingly isolation from its surroundings, mainly through habitat conversions from natural forest vegetations to croplands because of the adjacent intensifying land uses spearheaded by increasing human population pressure [4].

We explored the use of current remote sensing opportunities by deploying state-of-the-art data from the Sentinel-2 Multi-Spectral Instrument (MSI) satellite of the European Satellite Agency (ESA), and developed a workflow in the programming environment R, which can easily be adopted to other study areas. The implementation of the workflow will enable in-situ repeated observations up-scale, which are hardly feasible in such a large protected area's challenging terrain by park staff on the ground [2]. The currently available data from the Sentinel-2 MSI provides multi-spectral bands with high spatial resolutions and quick revisit time of five days for both Sentinel-2 A and B satellites [6]. The Sentinel-2 MSI is comprised of 13 spectral bands ranging in resolutions from 10 m, (four bands) inclusive of the visible wavelengths (band 2-Blue, band 3-Green, band 4-Red); 20 m (six bands) inclusive of the new "Red-Edge", near-infra red (NIR) and short-wave infra-red (SWIR) wavelengths; important for vegetation monitoring and with high capabilities for use in ecosystem, biodiversity and conservation monitoring [7]. The other three bands are of 60 m resolution including the aerosol, water vapor and cirrus bands.

Spectral signatures and derived indices like the normalized difference vegetation index (NDVI) are used as a standardized way to measure the health of vegetation by quantifying the ratio of the difference between the NIR (strongly reflected by vegetation) and Red bands (strongly absorbed by vegetation) [8]. NDVI values ranges from −1 to + 1, with a distinct threshold for each land cover type. Negatives likely represent water, while positives close to one indicate dense green leaves. However, values close to zero represent no leaves or degraded forest [2].

In this paper, Sentinel-2 MSI spectral bands and derived products, including vegetation indices like the NDVI, were processed with the following objectives:

- Automatically download Sentinel-2 data for a particular study area.
- Automatically pre-process the downloaded Sentinel-2 data to calculate various vegetation indices for the selected study area and time period.
- Calculate and take into account the specific cloud coverage within the study area for multiple Sentinel-2 data scenes.
- Provide graphical results for assessing the quality of the input data and changes in vegetation indices over time.

2   Materials and Methods

2.1   Study Area

The Kilimanjaro Mountain National Park and its ecosystems are located in the northeast of Tanzania (Fig. 1) and span an elevation gradient from the colline savanna plains (~700 m a.s.l.) to the glaciated areas encircling Kibo summit (5895 m a.s.l.). Its equatorial day time climate is shaped by the passing of the intertropical convergence zone, with more than half of the annual rainfall occurring during the so called long-rainy season (March to May) [9]. While annual precipitation amounts to more than 2500 mm in the southern montane forest belt, the lee ward northern mountain side receives hardly more than 1000 mm [9, 10].

In this study, we focused on an area in the western edge of the Kilimanjaro Mountain National Park (Fig. 1), the so called "Half-mile strip". The border of this study area was digitized in QGIS [17]. The Half-mile strip is an area of interest for the park management due to its proximity to human settlements, its expanding land-use conversions mainly for agricultural activities, and other characteristics such as the presence of access roads for various public services making the park more vulnerable to poaching and other illegal activities [4].

2.2   Sentinel-2 Data

Our study area is covered by the Sentinel-2 tile "T37MBS". We searched for all available L2A scenes of this tile for the period between 2017-01-01 and 2020-09-01 and automatically downloaded them with the R-script provided in the Supplementary Material (Appendix A1), thereby making use of the functions provided by the R package sen2r [11]. A total of 130 L2A scenes were found and downloaded for further processing (Appendix A2).

We clipped and cropped all downloaded scenes with the previously digitized polygon of our study area in order to calculate 17 different vegetation indices as well as the study-area-specific cloud coverage for each scene. It is important to note that the calculation

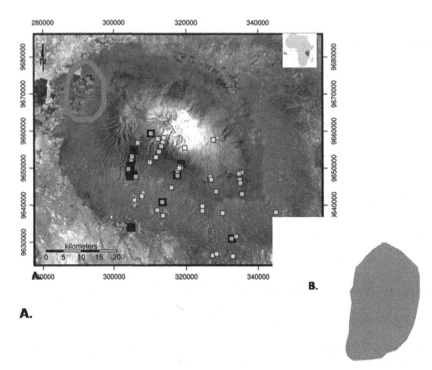

Fig. 1. Study area in the Kilimanjaro Mountain Ecosystem in Tanzania. A) Distribution of the established sampling sites in the KiLi1 project along the elevational and land use gradients [9]. B) Area used in this study (the "Half-mile strip").

of cloud coverage within the study area is much more appropriate compared to selecting scenes based on the overall cloud coverage because low overall cloud coverage could still be related to high cloud coverage in the study area, and vice versa. Only scenes with less than 10% cloud cover in the study area were selected for further analyses. Our R script for batch processing of multiple Sentinel-2 scenes is provided in Appendix A3 and can easily be adjusted for any other study area. The code is also available via our github repository at https://github.com/envima/sentinel-kili and might be extended in the future.

2.3 Vegetation Indices

In this study, indices extraction focused on the western edge of the Kilimanjaro Mountain National Park boundary, an area that was annexed into the park in 2008, formally "the Half-mile strip" zone of the former Kilimanjaro Forest Reserve [2, 3]. We calculated 17 different vegetation indices (Table 1) in this particular study area according to a standardized workflow (Fig. 2, Appendix A3) with a spatial resolution of 10 m and for 130 points in time (scenes). For convenience, we present only exemplary results for the well-known NDVI in the main text. For the complete results see Appendix A2.

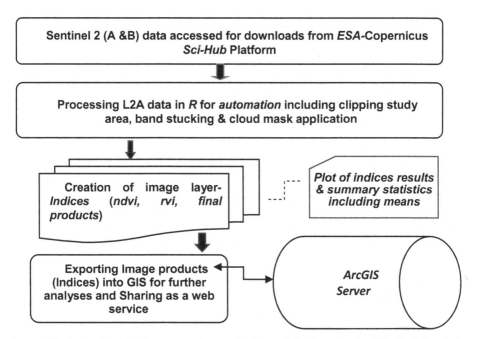

Fig. 2. Workflow for obtaining, processing, analyzing, and sharing outputs of Sentinel-2 satellite data through the TANAPA GIS Server (adopted from Msoffe et al. [2]).

Table 1. Indices processed in this study (adopted from Xu and Su [16]).

Index	Description
CTVI	Corrected transformed vegetation index
DVI	Difference vegetation index
EVI	Environmental vegetation index
EVI2	2-band Enhanced vegetation index
GEMI	Global environmental monitoring index
GNDVI	Green normalized difference vegetation index
MSAVI	Modified soil-adjusted vegetation index
MSAVI-2	Modified secondary soil-adjusted vegetation index
NDVI	Normalized difference vegetation index
NDWI	Normalized difference water index
NRVI	Normalized ratio vegetation index
RVI	Ratio vegetation index
SAVI	Soil-adjusted vegetation index
SR	Simple ratio

(continued)

Table 1. (*continued*)

Index	Description
TTVI	Transformed triangular vegetation index
TVI	Triangular vegetation index
WDVI	Weighted difference vegetation index

3 Results

Of the 130 available Sentinel-2 L2A scenes for our study area and time period, only 24 had cloud coverage of less than 10% within the study area (Table 2). These scenes were subsequently used for calculating the NDVI, which serves as example here (Fig. 3). Additional results for the other 16 indices can be found in Appendix A2.

Table 2. Sentinel-2 Data scenes with less than 10% cloud coverage in the study area, which were used for exemplarily calculating the NDVI.

Date	NDVI	Clouds (study area)	Clouds (scene)
2017-02-08	0.78	0.00	0.01
2017-03-10	0.76	0.00	0.45
2018-03-05	0.65	0.06	0.08
2018-07-28	0.64	0.05	0.06
2018-12-25	0.72	0.04	0.23
2019-01-19	0.84	0.00	0.08
2019-02-03	0.77	0.00	0.00
2019-02-08	0.73	0.06	0.24
2019-02-28	0.78	0.00	0.01
2019-03-15	0.61	0.07	0.03
2019-03-20	0.73	0.01	0.02
2019-06-23	0.76	0.00	0.12
2019-07-23	0.74	0.00	0.27
2019-09-01	0.68	0.00	0.34
2019-12-20	0.83	0.00	0.25
2019-12-30	0.82	0.00	0.31
2020-01-14	0.74	0.01	0.37
2020-02-08	0.84	0.00	0.15

(*continued*)

Table 2. (*continued*)

Date	NDVI	Clouds (study area)	Clouds (scene)
2020-06-02	0.64	0.09	0.50
2020-06-17	0.72	0.03	0.55
2020-06-22	0.71	0.00	0.39
2020-07-02	0.75	0.00	0.65
2020-08-11	0.73	0.00	0.22
2020-08-31	0.59	0.09	0.19

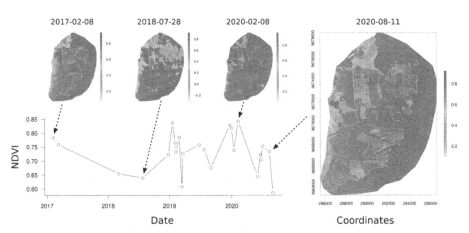

Fig. 3. Changes in vegetation greenness (NDVI) derived from Sentinel-2 data in the study area between January 2017 and September 2020. Note that on July 28th 2018, a decent amount of cloud coverage is present, which can be screened with the graphical outputs of the R scripts provided.

4   Discussions and Conclusions

Sentinel-2 data as used here provide the opportunity to carry out consistent monitoring at high spatial and temporal resolutions with various opportunities for applications in biodiversity and ecosystem monitoring [12]. This is because remote sensing allows measurements of large regions in high temporal resolution, thereby providing continuous information about vegetation status. The reflectance and emission of light from the Earth's surface can be directly related to the physiological, morphological and structural composition of plants [13].

Several studies have proven for instance a significant correlation between species richness and spectral indices [14]. The most common used index is the NDVI, capturing the greenness and chlorophyll content [15]. NDVI is often used in research related to regional and global vegetation assessments, and was shown not only to be related to canopy structure and leaf area index, but also to canopy photosynthesis [16]. The most common validation process is through direct or indirect correlation between the indices obtained and vegetation characteristics measured in-situ, including vegetation cover and leaf area index [16], of which Sentinel-2 data as utilized in this study come to play.

Using optical remote sensing for biodiversity monitoring in tropical areas like the Kilimanjaro National Park is very challenging because of the high cloud coverage throughout the year. The techniques and workflows presented here could mitigate this challenge by focusing on a well-defined study area instead of utilizing the normal procedure of relying on the full satellite scenes. By only considering full scenes for obtaining image data, one could miss a lot of information by discarding full scenes of overall bad quality. However, by considering the focal area of interest, more scenes and thus information can be obtained for calculating indices, analyzing vegetation trends, and thus better monitoring of the study area over time. This approach goes in line with the fact that biodiversity and ecosystem monitoring in protected areas like the Mount Kilimanjaro National Park should be complemented with remote sensing methods as demonstrated in this study. Our provided scripts in the R-environment can furthermore be applied in any other study area for customized workflows and automatic generation of similar results.

Time series of vegetation indices derived from Sentinel-2 data provide a bird's eye view snapshot of the required indicators for monitoring vast areas such as Kilimanjaro Mountain National Park [2], while contributing to the global biodiversity conservation agenda especially needed in achieving the Aichi Conservation Targets (2011–2020) for developing essential biodiversity variables from remote sensing data [18, 19]. Figure 3 shows for instance that trends in greenness derived here were consistent in that all the values were above the NDVI value of 0.59, which indicates stable green vegetation throughout the study period, i.e. from 2017 until today. This is not surprisingly since our study area is in the total protection zone of the ecosystem, having included the Half-mile strip inside the park (annexation in 2008), where anthropogenic activities are prohibited and other illegal activities are checked by park staff through routine surveillances. Detailed results from the different indices in this study (a total of 17 including the NDVI, Appendix A2) is a confirmation that consistent Sentinel-2 data acquisition can supplement the small-scale ground in-situ observations carried out by park staff.

In order to overcome limitations in obtaining sufficient continuous image data from scenes that are cloud free, our developed workflow and scripts in the R-environment provide an automation for the selection of available and suitable scenes as well as for obtaining final products for further studies. It is anticipated that remote sensing techniques and their application for biodiversity conservation and monitoring in the Kilimanjaro National Park will enhance efforts undertaken by park staff on a daily basis and ultimately provide a long-term database for the conservation of the cloud-montane forest ecosystem.

Acknowledgements. This work was supported by the German Research Foundation (DFG) through the KiLi1-Project (2010–2018), as part of the post-project synthesis phase, 2018–2020, for monitoring key biodiversity aspects in the Kilimanjaro Mountain Ecosystems. F. Msoffe was supported by a postdoc scholarship of the "Katholischer Akademischer Ausland Dienst" (KAAD), in the Lab of Environmental Informatics at the University of Philipps-Marburg, Germany.

Appendix

A1: Downloading Sentinel-2 Data

```
#title: "Download sentinel scenes with sen2R for a particular study area and time
period"
#authors: "Dirk Zeuss, Fortunata Msoffe"
#date: "1 September 2020"
# Praeambel ----------------------------------------------------------------
rm(list = ls()) # clean workspace
# Load packages
library("sen2r")
library("rgdal")
library("sf")
# sen2r() # Use the gui to enter your scihub credentials, which will then be saved in
the package.
# Set working directory
wd <- "/home/sentinel_processing"
setwd(wd)
# Set data directory for sentinel scenes
path_sentinel_data <- "/home/data/sentinel/kili"
# Set study area for querying available Sentinel scenes
studyarea <- readOGR("studyarea/kinapahalfmile.shp") # Vector polygon defining the
study area within the sentinel tile set above. Check, if the projection is defined and the
same as the sentinel tiles.
## Download -----------------------------------------------------------
# Get list of available Sentinel scenes
sen_list <- s2_list(spatial_extent = sf::st_as_sf(studyarea), # could be omitted if the
tile name is known
            tile = "37MBS", # choose sentinel tile name. Be careful here to provide
only five characters.
            time_interval = as.Date(c("2017-01-01", "2020-09-01")), # choose time
interval
            level = "L2A",
            max_cloud = 100) # get all scenes independent of overall cloud coverage
# Download scenes
s2_download(s2_prodlist = sen_list,
        downloader = "builtin",
        apihub = NA,
        service = NA,
        outdir = path_sentinel_data,
        order_lta = TRUE,
        overwrite = FALSE)
## END -------------------------------------------------------------------------------
```

A2: Vegetation Indices Calculated from 130 Sentinel-2 L2A Scenes for Our Study Area ("the Half-Mile Strip").

Scene	Date	CTVI	DVI	EVI	EVI2	GEMI	GNDVI	MSAVI	MSAVI2	NDVI	NDWI	NRVI	RVI	SAVI	SR	TTVI	TVI	WDVI	Clouds (study area)	Clouds (scene)

A3: Processing Sentinel-2 Data

```
#title: "Extraction of vegetation indices from Sentinel L2A scenes for a particular
study area considering cloud coverage"
#authors: "Dirk Zeuss, Fortunata Msoffe"
#date: "1 September 2020"
#---Praeambel -------------------------------------------------------------
rm(list = ls(all = TRUE)) # clean workspace
library("raster")
library("RStoolbox")
library("rgdal")
# Set working directory
wd <- "/home/sentinel_processing"
setwd(wd)
## Choose sentinel tile name -----------------------------------------------
# Set sentinel tiles to process (all scenes matching the string below in the sentinel data
folder will be processed)
sentinel_tile <- "T37MBS"
# Set study area -----------------------------------------------studyarea <- read-
OGR("studyarea/kinapahalfmile.shp") # Vector polygon defining the study area with-
in the sentinel tile set above
# plot(studyarea)
## Set and get paths -------------------------------------------------------
# Set path to the directory with sentinel scenes
path_sentinel_data <- "/home/data/sentinel/kili"
# Get paths to folders of sentinel scenes
paths_sentinel_tiles <- list.files(path_sentinel_data, pattern = sentinel_tile, full.names
= TRUE, recursive = FALSE)
# length(paths_sentinel_tiles) # number of scenes matching the tile name set above in
the data folder

paths_sentinel_tiles <- grep(".SAFE", paths_sentinel_tiles, value = TRUE) # remove
potential non-sentinel paths in the data folder
## Batch processing --------------------------------------------------
# Loop over all scenes in the sentinel data folder to calculate vegetation indices and
cloud coverage for the study area
result <- list() # create empty list for collecting the results later
for(i in paths_sentinel_tiles)try({ # iterate over all sentinel scene folders in the senti-
nel data folder
    # Show some output on the status of the batch processing
    cat("Processing:", basename(i), "\n")
    # Select bands -------------------------------------------------    # Set the search
pattern for bands to process. In this case only the 10m bands are selected.
    searchPattern_10m <- "_10m.jp2$"
    # Get paths with images containing "searchPattern_10m"
    paths_bands_10m <- list.files(file.path(i, "GRANULE"), pattern = searchPat-
tern_10m, full.names = TRUE, recursive = TRUE)
    # Create stack of bands
```

```
bands_10m <- stack(paths_bands_10m)
# Rename bands to band name and resolution (only for long names)
regs_matched <- gregexpr("_..._.*$", names(bands_10m))
tempname <- as.character(regmatches(names(bands_10m), regs_matched))
names(bands_10m) <- substr(tempname, 2, nchar(tempname))
# Reproject, crop and clip -------------------------------------------------
# Reproject study area to Sentinel CRS
studyarea <- spTransform(studyarea, projection(bands_10m))

# Crop and clip Sentinel tile with study area polygon
bands_10m <- crop(bands_10m, studyarea)
bands_10m <- mask(bands_10m, studyarea)
# Index calculation --------------------------------------------------------
# Choose indices for calculation
# indices_to_process <- c("RVI", "NDVI") # Manually choose indices here. If you
like to process indices which need the 20m resolution bands, these bands must be
added to the search pattern above.
indices_to_process <- NULL # "NULL" in this case means the calculation of all
available indices in RStoolbox::spectralIndices()
# Create layer of indices
Index_layer         <-         RStoolbox::spectralIndices(bands_10m,      #      see
?RStoolbox::spectralIndices for available indices and the required bands   blue =
"B02_10m", # add additional bands here if they are required for other vegetation indi-
ces
                              green = "B03_10m",
                              red = "B04_10m",
                              nir = "B08_10m",
                              indices = indices_to_process,
                              scaleFactor = 1,
                              skipRefCheck = TRUE) # see ?RStoolbox::spectralIndices
for details.
# Create raster stack of index layers
Index_layer <- stack(Index_layer)
# Calculate summary statistics for each index layer
indices_res <- sapply(names(Index_layer), function (x) cellStats(Index_layer[[x]],
stat = "mean")) # Note that the mean vegetation index over the whole study area is
calculated here. Change, if you need other summary statistics.
# Cloud coverage in study area   ----------------------------------------------   #
Get path to cloud mask
path_cloud_mask      <-      list.files(file.path(i,    "GRANULE"),    pattern     =
"MSK_CLOUDS_B00.gml", full.names = TRUE, recursive = TRUE)

# Import cloud mask
cloud_mask <- readOGR(path_cloud_mask, disambiguateFIDs = TRUE, verbose =
FALSE)
# Mask clouds in study area for coverage calculation
clouds <- mask(bands_10m[[1]], cloud_mask, updatevalue = NA)
# Calculate cloud coverage
```

```r
all_pixels_study_area <- length(na.omit(raster::values(bands_10m[[1]]))) # number
of all pixels in the study area
cloud_pixels_study_area <- length(na.omit(clouds@data@values)) # number of
cloud pixels in the study area
cloud_coverage <- cloud_pixels_study_area / all_pixels_study_area
names(cloud_coverage) <- "cloud_coverage"
  # Cloud coverage in full scene  -------------------------------------------------------
  # Get path to metadata
path_overall_cloud_coverage <- list.files(file.path(i, "HTML"), pattern =
"UserProduct_index.html", full.names = TRUE, recursive = TRUE)
  # Read in metadata
metadata                   <-              readChar(path_overall_cloud_coverage,
file.info(path_overall_cloud_coverage)$size)
  # Extract cloud coverage of the full scene
search_pattern <- ".*(Cloud Coverage Assessment: )"
temp_string <- sub(search_pattern, "", metadata)
cloud_cover_full_scene <- as.numeric(substr(temp_string, 1,5)) / 100
  # Visual checks  ---------------------------------------------------   # Visually check
cloud coverage calculation
  # graphics.off()
  # plotRGB(bands_10m, r = 4, g = 3, b = 2, stretch = "lin")
  # plot(studyarea, add = TRUE)
  # plot(cloud_mask, add=TRUE)
  # plot(clouds, add=TRUE, col="red")
  # Visually check index layer
  # plot(Index_layer)
  # title(main=i)
  # Write out visual checks to disk
dir.create(file.path(wd, "output/graphics/indices"), recursive = T, showWarnings =
FALSE)
dir.create(file.path(wd, "output/graphics/cloud_coverage"), recursive = T, show-
Warnings = FALSE)
jpeg(filename = paste0(file.path(wd, "output/graphics/indices", basename(i)),
".jpg"),
    width = 1600, height = 1400, pointsize = 24)
plot(Index_layer)
dev.off()
jpeg(filename = paste0(file.path(wd, "output/graphics/cloud_coverage", base-
name(i)), ".jpg"), width = 800, height = 600)
plotRGB(bands_10m, r = 4, g = 3, b = 2, stretch = "lin")
plot(studyarea, add = TRUE)
plot(cloud_mask, add=TRUE)
plot(clouds, add=TRUE, col="red")
dev.off()
  # Collect results  --------------------------------------------------
# Show some output on the status of the batch processing
cat(names(indices_res), ":", indices_res, ",",
```

```
    "cloud coverage:", cloud_coverage, ",",
    "cloud coverage full scene:", cloud_cover_full_scene,
    "\n")
  # Concatenate index results and corresponding Sentinel scene
  result[[basename(i)]] <- c(indices_res, cloud_coverage, cloud_cover_full_scene =
cloud_cover_full_scene)

  # Clean up
  #rm(cloud_mask, clouds, bands_10m); gc() # if you run into memory issues, try this
line.
  })
# Postprocessing -----------------------------------------------------------
# Create a data.frame ("table") for the results
result_df <- data.frame(Tile = names(result),
             Date = as.Date(substr(names(result), 12, 19), format = "%Y%m%d"),
             sapply(names(indices_res), function (x) sapply(result, function (y)
 y[x])),

             cloud_coverage = sapply(result, function (x) x["cloud_coverage"]),
             cloud_cover_full_scene   =   sapply(result,   function   (x)
x["cloud_cover_full_scene"]),
             row.names = NULL)
# Order results by date of the processed sentinel scenes
result_df <- result_df[order(result_df$Date),]
result_df
# Save results as csv file in the "output" directory -----------------------------------
# Creates the folder "output" in your working directory, if it does not already exist.
dir.create(file.path(wd, "output"), showWarnings = FALSE)
# Set name of the output result file with number of scenes processed, indices calculat-
ed and processing date
name_output_file <- paste("results_",
             sentinel_tile, "_",
             length(paths_sentinel_tiles),
             "scenes_",
             collapse="_",
             Sys.Date(),
             sep = "")
# Write to file
write.csv(result_df, file = paste0(file.path(wd, "output", name_output_file), ".csv"),
row.names = FALSE)
## Plot change in indices over time --------------------------------------------------
pdf(file = paste0(file.path(wd, "output", name_output_file), ".pdf"), width = 20,
height = 12, pointsize=18)
par(mfrow=c(4,5))
for (j in names(indices_res)){
  plot(result_df[,j] ~ result_df$Date, type = "b", xlab = "", ylab = j, main = j)}
dev.off()
## END ------------------------------------------------------------------------
```

References

1. Peters, M., et al.: Predictors of elevational biodiversity gradients change from single taxa to the multi-taxa community level. Nat. Commun. **7**, 13736 (2016)
2. Msoffe, F.; Nauss, T., Zeuss, D.: Use of current remote sensing methods for biodiversity monitoring and conservation of Mount Kilimanjaro National Park ecosystems. In: Proceedings of the 6th International Conference on Geographical Information Systems Theory, Applications and Management, vol. 1. GISTAM, 2020. pp. 175–183 (2020) (ISBN: 978-989-758-425-1. https://doi.org/10.5220/0009357701750183
3. Hemp, A.: Climate change-driven forest fires marginalize the impact of ice cap wasting on Kilimanjaro. Glob. Change Biol. **11**, 1013–1023 (2005). https://doi.org/10.1111/j.1365-2486. 2005.00968.x
4. Hemp, A., Hemp, C.: Broken bridges: the isolation of Kilimanjaro's ecosystem. Glob. Change Biol. **24**, 3499–3507 (2018)
5. Thompson, L.G., et al.: Kilimanjaro ice core records: evidence of holocence climate change in tropical Africa. Science **298**, 589–593 (2002)
6. ESA-Corpenicuswebsite (2020) https://sentinels.corpenicus.eu/sentinel-data-access/registration/. Accessed Sept 2020
7. Drusch, M., et al.: Sentinel-2: ESA's optical high-resolution mission for GMES operational services. Remote Sens. Environ. **120**, 25–36 (2012)
8. Rouse, J.W., Haas, R.H., Schell, J.A., Deering, W.D.: Monitoring vegetation systems in the Great Plains with ERTS. In: Third ERTS Symposium, NASA SP-351, pp. 309–317 (1973)
9. Appelhans, T., Mwangomo, E., Otte, I., Detsch, F., Nauss, T., Hemp, A.: Eco-meteorological characteristics of the southern slopes of Kilimanjaro Tanzania. Int. J. Climatol. **36**, 3245–3258 (2016)
10. Detsch, F., Otte, I., Applhans, T., Nauss, T.: A glimpse at short-term controls of evapotranspiration along the southern slopes of Kilimanjaro. Environ. Monit. Asses. **189**, 465 (2017)
11. Ranghetti, L., et al.: sen2r - an R-Toolbox for automatically downloading and pre-processing Sentinel-2 satellite data. Comput. Geosci. (2020). https://doi.org/10.1016/j.cageo.2020. 104473
12. Rocchini, D., et al.: Satellite remote sensing to monitor species diversity: potential and pitfalls. Remote Sens. Ecol. Conserv. **2**, 25–36 (2016). https://doi.org/10.1002/rse2.9
13. Jetz, W., et al.: Monitoring plant functional diversity from space. Nat. Plants **2**(3), 1–13 (2016)
14. Frampton, W.J., Dash, J., Watmaugh, G., Milton, E.J.: Evaluating the capabilities of Sentinel-2 for quantitative estimation of biophysical variables in vegetation. ISPRS J. Photogram. Remote Sens. **82**, 83–92 (2013)
15. Xue, J., Su, B.: Significant remote sensing indices: a review of developments and applications Hindawi. J. Sens. (2017). https://doi.org/10.1155/2017/1353691.17pp.2017
16. Gamon, J.A., et al.: Relationships between NDVI, canopy structure, and photosynthesis in three California vegetation types. Ecol. Appl. **5**(1), 28–41 (1995)
17. QGIS-Version: 3.4.9-Madeira. General Public Licence. https://www.gnu.org/licences
18. Alleaume, S., et al.: A generic remote sensing approach to derive operational essential biodiversity variables (EBVs) for conservation planning. Methods Ecol. Evol. **2018**(9), 1822–1836 (2018)
19. Skidmore, A.K., et al.: Environmental science: agree on biodiversity metrics to track from space. Nature **523**, 403–405 (2015)

3D Urban Growth Simulation Using Human Settlement Capacity SLEUTH Model (HSCS)

Rani El Meouche[1]([⊠]), Mojtaba Eslahi[1]([⊠]), Anne Ruas[2],
and Muhammad Ali Sammuneh[1]

[1] Institut de Recherche en Constructibilité (IRC), ESTP Paris, 94230 Cachan, France
{relmeouche,meslahi,msammuneh}@estp-paris.eu
[2] LISIS/IFSTTAR, Université de Marne-la-Vallée, 77420 Champs-sur-Marne, France
anne.ruas@ifsttar.fr

Abstract. In recent years, the growth of urbanization in the world is increasing. This almost leads to irreversible changes that affect biodiversity, ecosystems, and climate change. The aim of this research is to provide different urban growth scenarios that can be considered for sustainable urban development strategies. We have proposed the HSCS (Human Settlement Capacity SLEUTH) model which is based on SLEUTH urban growth simulation. This model leads to the acquisition of new urban areas in the form of a number of pixels on which urbanization is supposed to take place. We have defined a building classification and have estimated population growth, and by adding these two parameters to our model, we have improved the simulation results. These parameters also helped us to define different growth scenarios and to calculate the height of the buildings as the third dimension according to each scenario. In parallel, the footprints of buildings have been created in the new urban pixels by considering some urban constraints, such as the direction of the buildings, the distance to urban entities and geographical features. These building footprints take height values according to the defined scenarios, and so we have simulated a three-dimensional model of the city. This model has been applied on a small city called Saint Sulpice la Pointe which has a significant rate of population growth and urban sprawl during the last two decades. The 3D representation of the urban growth provides disparate images of city of tomorrow for its application in urban.

Keywords: HSCS (Human Settlement Capacity SLEUTH) model · CA (Cellular Automata) modelling · Urban growth modelling · 3D model · GIS (Geographic Information System)

1 Introduction

1.1 Urban Growth Modelling

Urbanization refers to the process of increasing the size of cities, which occurs due to several factors, including population growth and rural exodus. The phenomenon of urban sprawl is a major challenge for city officials and urban planners. Urban simulation

C. Grueau et al. (Eds.): GISTAM 2020, CCIS 1411, pp. 46–65, 2021.
https://doi.org/10.1007/978-3-030-76374-9_4

techniques tend to solve various problems of urban growth modelling. Today many scientists work on simulating urban growth using a variety of modelling methods. Almost all urban growth models are based on historical data and simulate growth similar to today's trends. CA (cell automation) modelling is one of the most widely used urban simulation models that can be integrated with GIS and RS (remote sensing) data [1–4].

SLEUTH is a pattern-based model that uses cell automation and land mapping and is widely used to simulate urban growth [5–7]. **SLEUTH** is derived from the acronym of its input maps including **S**lope, **L**and use, **E**xcluded, **U**rban, **T**ransportation and **H**illshade. SLEUTH model calibration requires several historical maps such as urban and transportation maps. In SLEUTH modeling, the growth rhythm is considered using historical data and it produces prospective simulations with the same current trend. Therefore, the effects of population growth and urban tissue are not explicitly considered in the simulations. In addition, the SLEUTH results are raster data on which urban planning is supposed to occur. This makes it difficult for decision makers to interpret the results. In this research, we have integrated more parameters including the estimation of the population growth and building type to overcome SLEUTH limitations and to optimize the model simulation. Furthermore, we have provided a three-dimensional view of the model, taking into account some constraints such as the direction of buildings to roads, and the distance from urban entities and geographical features. The proposed model is called **HSCS** (**H**uman **S**ettlement **C**apacity **S**LEUTH) urban growth model that aims to study the housing capacity for the population forecast in the growth model. In addition, it is a scenario-based urban growth model that can compare and evaluate land use and urban configuration in different urban fabric scenarios. In the proposed HSCS model, we have extended our previous works by considering the environmental protection scenario in urban growth simulations, making some modifications in modelling of 3D representation of the grown city, and applying the model on a larger study area [8].

1.2 3D Urban Modelling

In recent years, modelling of virtual 3D cities has been in demand by governments, municipalities and companies. The three-dimensional city models are used in various aspects of urban planning and management such as smart city mobility, operating cost savings, increased resilience, sustainability improvement, emergency response and evacuation planning, seismic damage and flooding [8–11]. They are also used in estimations of solar radiation, energy demand and energy efficiency, cast shadows with urban features, noise emission in a restricted environment, and lighting simulations as well as in management of urban heritage, urban planning projects, and simulation modelling in terms of pollution, climate changes, and urban sprawl [12–17].

There are various techniques for producing a three-dimensional model of the city, such as creating three-dimensional urban footprints [18–20] and three-dimensional reconstruction and data integration used in photogrammetry or laser scanning with GIS data [21–27]. Factors such as data availability, performance accuracy, efficiency, speed, human capital and costs should be considered to select the most appropriate 3D modelling technique.

In this research, by giving a third dimension to the building footprint, a 3D geo-visualization of the building in new urban areas is presented. The third dimension represents the height of a building, which is obtained according to urban fabric scenarios commensurate with the type of building and population density.

Our goal is to develop a model that can provide different scenarios for future urban growth resulting from today's urban planning, which conforms with different land priorities and constraints, so that it can influence future strategies for sustainable urban development. Therefore, we aim to find the effects of population growth and types of buildings in the urban growth simulation model. This leads to the preparation of urban fabric scenarios that help to compare the determinants of urbanization and measure it in different scenarios of urban dispersion.

The study area is presented in the next section. In Sect. 3, the process and methodology are defined. The results of urban growth simulation are shown and discussed in Sect. 4. In Sect. 5, a three-dimensional geo-visualization of the urban growth model is presented. This research is concluded in Sect. 6.

2 Study Area

The model has been applied to three different study areas with different sizes and scales in terms of geographical extent and population, including a metropolis, a city and a rural area to test its effectiveness. In all three study areas, over the past two decades, a significant amount of population growth and urban expansion has been observed. In this article, for ease of visualization, we have presented a small town called Saint Sulpice la Pointe (43° 46′ 30″ N, 1° 41′ 14″ E). Saint Sulpice la Pointe is a peri-urban located in the Tarn department of France (see Fig. 1). The extent of the study area is 3600 ha. The city had a population of 8934 in 2016 and the average population growth rate between 2009 and 2016 was 1.73 percent per year (Legal populations, INSEE - National Institute of Statistics and Economic Studies, France, 2016).

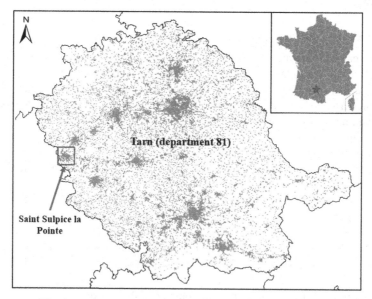

Fig. 1. Location of Saint Sulpice la Pointe study area, France.

We have used geospatial database and geographic information systems to create the input maps for the simulations by SLEUTH model. Input maps contain raster data with a size of 200 × 200 pixels that feature a cell size of 30 m × 30 m (~900 m^2). We have created urban, land use, excluded and transportation maps from the BD TOPO and BD ORTHO databases from IGN (National Institute of Geographic and Forestry Information) database of 2017. Slope and hillshade maps have been created from the Digital Elevation Model (DEM) of RGE ALTI, provided by IGN. We have also calculated the average population for the coming years and defined the classification of the building as complementary parameters to make the model more reliable. Using the HSCS urban growth model, we have defined the different urban fabric scenarios based on socio-demographic data that have been integrated into the model during simulations.

3   Simulation Modelling and Methodology

In the proposed model, we have first simulated the prospective urban growth using SLEUTH. As discussed, the 2017 data has been used and the 2050 forecasts have been simulated. In this model, we have added other parameters such as population estimation and type of buildings as socio-geographical features. These two parameters have been considered in the HSCS model as well as in the definition of urban fabric scenarios for the 3D model of urban growth. The focus of this paper is on creating a representation of 3D buildings from new pixels simulated by the HSCS model. In creating the 3D representation of the buildings, first, their footprints are created, then the model gives the appropriate height to these footprints according to the scenario of the urban fabric, neighbourhood and district in which they are located. In the urban planning system, there are certain distances between a building and its neighbours, as well as to roads, rivers, forests, and so on. We have defined some constraints such as buildings, rivers, exclusion zones, and existing buildings to consider the distance of new pixels from each other or from urban features and topographic objects. Figure 2 illustrates the procedure of generating the 3D city representation from the new pixels obtained from model.

SLEUTH output maps are the GIF format images that are composed of pixels and have no information about the height of the simulated urban areas. In fact, they are made up of pixels on which urbanization is about to occur, which is difficult for decision makers to interpret the results. In addition, like many other methods of urban growth simulation, SLEUTH considers only historical data without taking into account changes in population growth rates or types of buildings. Therefore, the aim of this research is to diversify the simulations by explicitly integrating various factors such as the type of buildings and population growth and to provide visual methods for representing the results of the urban growth scenario in 3D.

To optimize the results, we have first considered certain factors in defining excluded areas in our simulations so that the model can meet some limitations in terms of geographical features and environmental protection (see Sect. 4.1). We have defined different types of buildings and have classified the existing buildings (see Sect. 4.2). In parallel, we have extracted the demographic information of the study area and calculated the compound annual population growth rate and average estimate of population for the target year (see Sect. 4.3).

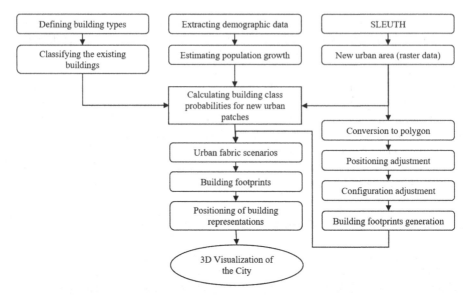

Fig. 2. Method procedure to generate a 3D geo visualization of the urban growth.

The estimation of the population growth and the building classification will help to calculate the building class probabilities for the new urban areas obtained from model. Therefore, different probabilities of height have been achieved for each pixel. We have defined different urban fabric scenarios based on socio-demographic data (see Sect. 4.4). Later, according to the urban fabric scenarios, each footprint of building is given an appropriate height to simulate a 3D city model.

The SLEUTH output maps consist of some raster data that should be transformed into polygons that indicate the building footprints. To transform a pixel to a polygon, the SLEUTH results need to be georeferenced and converted to vector data (see Sect. 5.1). Vector data makes polygons that should be oriented along their nearest road sections (see Sect. 5.2). As discussed earlier, the urban objects define some constraints for a polygon. These constraints adjust the polygon configuration. We have defined two types of constraints, including continuous constraints such as the roads, rivers, and railways, and discrete constraints that define the spaces such as cemeteries, airports, and industrial, residential and commercial buildings (see Sect. 5.3). In the next step, the surfaces are adjusted according to the scenarios to obtain the desired footprint for each building (see Sect. 5.4). Finally, we have given the appropriate height to each building footprint and we have created a 3D representation of the prospective city (see Sect. 5.5).

4 Urban Growth Simulation

4.1 SLEUTH Model

SLEUTH is an urban growth model that used the cellular automation techniques. The SLEUTH model fits in well with simulation of a dynamic urban expansion and it is compatible with the morphological model of urban configuration. This model is based on a probabilistic and self-modification process that corresponds with two states of the urban or non-urban.

SLEUTH includes three processes of calibration, prediction and self-modification. This urban growth simulation model is based on four growth rules including spontaneous growth, new spreading centre growth, edge growth and road-influenced growth in which the five coefficients of dispersion, breed, spread, slope and road gravity coefficients control these rules. SLEUTH coefficients are determined in calibration process.

As mentioned earlier, SLEUTH input maps include slope, land use, excluded, urban, transportation and hillshade maps. Each pixel of the excluded map has a value between 0 and 100, where 100 indicates 100% protection and the zero specified areas that are not protected from urbanization. By changing the pixel values in the excluded maps, we have defined different levels of protection according to the environmental areas and land use of the study area. In creating excluded maps, areas include remarkable buildings, cemeteries, airfields and sport grounds, railways stations, activity areas, water surfaces, national parks and closed forests areas (wood land, closed coniferous forest, closed deciduous forest, mixed closed forest and tree area) are given a value of 100. Open forests, hedges, woody heath, poplar grove, orchard and vineyards are taken value 50, which means they provide 50% protection. These classifications have been made based on the IGN data. Figure 3 shows the excluded map. Historical transport and urban maps of 2000, 2008, 2012 and 2017 have been used to calibrate the model.

In the calibration mode, we have extracted the best-fit coefficients for the simulation. Given the appropriate coefficients, the model has been implemented first to produce urban growth maps for 2017 for accuracy assessment and then for 2050 using the forecast mode.

The model has been tested with the input maps of 2000 for simulating the prospective maps of 2017. The results have been compared to the observed maps on 2017. The overall accuracy for the goodness-of-fit is calculated to measure the overall proportion of the pixels that change correctly, to the total number of cells. The evaluation of the model shows that its accuracy is acceptable according to the scale of the study area and the size of the pixels. Figure 4 illustrates the simulated result for 2050.

4.2 Building Type Classification

To simulate new buildings, current buildings can provide a perspective view for the future building. Therefore, we have defined building classes based on observations and we have classified current buildings. For building classification, residential building information has been taken from BD TOPO from IGN. For each type of building, numbers and heights have been extracted and an average height has been calculated for each type. Classification of building type has been done with regards to land use and urban tissue. According to the observations of the study area, three classes of the building have been defined, including single dwellings, low-rise housing and shop top housing. Later, considering the height of the neighbouring buildings, the appropriate height has been given to the new simulated area to display the new buildings on 3D. This process is based on the classification of building types and helps us to define urban fabric scenarios.

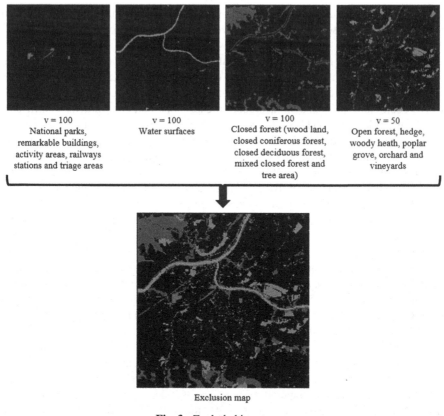

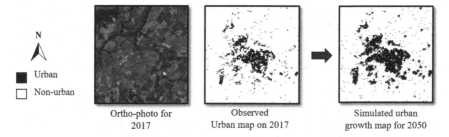

<table>
<tr><td>v = 100</td><td>v = 100</td><td>v = 100</td><td>v = 50</td></tr>
<tr><td>National parks, remarkable buildings, activity areas, railways stations and triage areas</td><td>Water surfaces</td><td>Closed forest (wood land, closed coniferous forest, closed deciduous forest, mixed closed forest and tree area)</td><td>Open forest, hedge, woody heath, poplar grove, orchard and vineyards</td></tr>
</table>

Exclusion map

Fig. 3. Excluded input map.

N

■ Urban
□ Non-urban

Ortho-photo for 2017 | Observed Urban map on 2017 | Simulated urban growth map for 2050

Fig. 4. Urban growth simulated results for 2050.

4.3 Population Growth Estimation

We have used the INSEE database to obtain the demographic information. We have generated a population map that gives the ratio of individuals per pixel. Given the total population of the study area, the number of inhabitants of each building class has been calculated by integrating the number of individuals per pixel, the building classes and the number and kinds of the existing buildings. Table 1 shows the number, occupancy level and the heights of buildings in Saint Sulpice la Pointe according to the building classification.

Table 1. Number, area and height of residential buildings according to building classification, 2016, Saint Sulpice la Pointe.

Building class	Number of buildings	Total area		Average height (m)
		m^2	%	
Single dwellings	2 782	420 239	69,80%	4
Low-rise housing	1 189	179 156	29,76%	8
Shop top housing	6	2 674	0,44%	15

After calculating the number of inhabitants for each type of building, population growth has been estimated to calculate the amount of buildings required, and urban fabric scenarios have been defined accordingly.

The average population growth rate during the years 2009 and 2016 is equal to 1.73% per year. This growth rate has been used to estimate population growth forecasts. Then, given the population and compound annual population rate, we have estimated the average population in the coming years. The compound annual population growth rate has been calculated for the simulated urban growth of 2050 in 33 growth cycles from 2017. Given the actual number of 8934 inhabitants in 2017, the estimated rate shows that the population will increase 79% on 2050. To create urban fabric scenarios, we have estimated the number of buildings that are needed to accommodate the projected population. Therefore, we have calculated the number of occupants of each building and the space used by each occupant. We have assumed the same housing rate per person for the forecast date, according to the type of building. Table 2 shows the estimate of the number of inhabitants in each type of building for undifferentiated buildings in Saint Sulpice la Pointe.

Table 2. Estimation of the average number of inhabitants for each type of buildings in Saint Sulpice la Pointe.

Building class	Estimated average number of inhabitants
Single dwellings	2
Low-rise housing	3
Shop top housing	6

4.4 Urban Fabric Scenario

To create urban fabric scenarios, some primary scenarios have been first assumed to better understand the type of buildings and their residential capacities. Later, the final urban fabric scenarios have been defined according to the results of the initial scenarios. In our model, we have categorized and integrated the type of buildings into the model to know what types of buildings might be built in the grown area. Integrating population growth can help us see how many residents can be accommodated in an urban growth simulation area, as well as how much housing is needed to meet the estimated population increase. These scenarios are based on the expansion of the city and are defined as follow:

1. Sprawl urban: In this scenario we assume that all new urban areas are covered by single dwellings.
2. Medium dense urban: The medium dense scenario considers 50% of single dwellings and 50% of shop top housing.
3. Medium/high dense urban: This scenario covers 30% of single dwellings and 70% of shop top housing.
4. High dense urban: High dense scenario assumes 100% shop top housing.

Primary scenarios are fictitious, however can help define the final scenarios based on the number of residents who can live in the simulated areas. Table 3 illustrates the increased population in primary urban fabric scenarios.

Table 3. Estimation of the increased population in primary urban fabric scenarios for 2050.

Population per urban fabric scenarios in 2050	Sprawl urban fabric scenario		Medium dense urban fabric scenario		Medium/high dense urban fabric scenario		High dense urban fabric scenario	
	100% single dwelling		50% single dwelling & 50% shop top housing		30% single dwelling & 70% shop top housing		100% shop top housing	
	4 684	52%	9 368	105%	11 242	126%	14 052	157%

As mentioned in Sect. 4.3, the estimation of population growth indicates that the population will increase by 79% in 2050, while the housing capacities in the primary scenarios, as shown in Table 3, are far from this. Table 3 shows 52% of the population housing capacity for the sprawl urban fabric scenario, which cannot reach a growth rate of 79%. This rate exceeds 79% for the other three scenarios. Therefore, to achieve reliable results, we define the final scenarios.

In SLEUTH, a simulation is made of a series of growth cycles in which each growth cycle represents one year of growth. Considering the classification of the type of buildings, the simulated urban growth and the average estimated population, we evaluate the appropriate growth cycle to achieve the desired urban fabrics. For the final urban fabric scenarios, we defined four scenarios, including low, medium, medium/high and high dense urban fabrics, with growth cycles of 33, 28, 23, and 18, respectively, that can nearly accommodate expected population growth (see Table 4).

Table 4. Estimation of the increased population in final urban fabric scenarios for 2050.

	Low dense urban fabric scenario		Medium dense urban fabric scenario		Medium/high dense urban fabric scenario		High dense urban fabric scenario	
Population per urban fabric scenarios in 2050	45% single dwelling & 45% low-rise & 10% shop top housing		50% single dwelling & 50% shop top housing		30% single dwelling & 70% shop top housing		100% shop top housing	
	33th growth cycle		28th growth cycle		23th growth cycle		18th growth cycle	
	6 675	75%	7 924	89%	6 456	72%	7 470	84%

The differences in scenarios also indicate the amount of environmental protection that could affect urban planning for the coming years. Figure 5 shows the simulated urban area in each growth cycle for each scenario. We have maintained 79% population growth, while land uses ranged from 110 hectares to 210 hectares. The differences indicate the loss of natural and environmental resources which shows that changing urban fabric scenarios has a very significant effect on limiting urban development, thus saving natural landscapes.

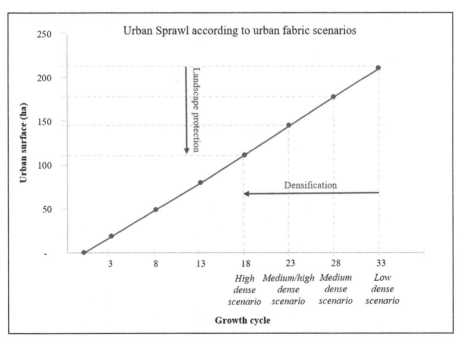

Fig. 5. Urban sprawl obtained from different urban fabric scenarios to accommodate 79% urban population growth.

5   3D Representation of Prospective Urban Growth Simulation

In this section, the aim is to create a 3D geo-visualization of simulated urban growth by creating 3D building representations from the new simulated pixels. To do this, the pixels have been first converted from raster data to building footprints. Given the excluded areas such as buildings, rivers, exclusion zones, and current buildings, we have defined some urbanization constraints. Later, building footprints have been produced based on these constraints. The height of the building for the building footprint has been calculated based on the probability of the height of the adjacent neighbours according to the probabilities estimated in the urban fabric scenarios.

5.1   Transform Pixels into Polygons

SLEUTH outputs include a non-referenced raster data that contains three types of pixels i.e. current urban patches, the new urban patches, and blank pixels. We have first geo-referenced the raster data according to our database vector data and then have converted it to vector data. In the process of geo-referencing a polynomial transformation has been performed which provides the mean square root deviation (RMS) as a control indicator. RMS should generally be less than size of a pixel.

5.2   Positioning the Building Footprints

As shown in Fig. 6, the generated polygons rotate along their nearest section of road. Orientation is done according to the size of the polygon and its central coordinates (X_c, Y_c).

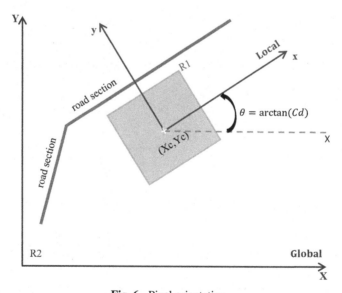

Fig. 6. Pixel orientation.

In this process, first the roads are divided into small sections, then their coefficient of orientation (Cd) is calculated by the following equation:

$$Cd = \frac{Ye - Ys}{Xe - Xs} \tag{1}$$

(Xs, Ys) and (Xe, Ye) are the start and end coordinates, respectively. Later, the orientation angle of the road section is calculated according to the horizontal axis in two cases. When Xe − Xs = 0 (section parallel to the vertical axis):

$$\theta = \pi/2 \tag{2}$$

If no:

$$\theta = \text{arc tan (Cd)} \tag{3}$$

The squares are oriented by considering the coordinates of the corners of the polygons in the general reference, by connecting any polygon to a local coordinate system using this angle. Therefore, we will have one rotation plus two translations. Equation 4 describes the rotations according to Z:

$$R_z = \begin{bmatrix} \cos\theta & -\sin\theta & 0 \\ \sin\theta & \cos\theta & 0 \\ 0 & 0 & 1 \end{bmatrix} \tag{4}$$

The coordinates change according to Eq. 5:

$$\begin{cases} X = Xc + x\cos\theta - y\sin\theta \\ Y = Yc + x\sin\theta + y\cos\theta \end{cases} \tag{5}$$

Where (x, y) are the coordinates of the corners in the local coordinate system and (X, Y) their counterparts in the global coordinate system.

$$\begin{cases} X = Xc + \left(\frac{R}{2}\right)(\cos\theta - \sin\theta) \\ Y = Yc + \left(\frac{R}{2}\right)(\sin\theta + \cos\theta) \end{cases} \tag{6}$$

Next, we change the cosine and sine sign to quadrilateral coordinates to reach to the four corners.

5.3 Building Footprints Configuration

Adjusting and locating new buildings follows the layout of old buildings. Hence, it is necessary to define the distance between a polygon that represents the representation of new buildings and the various land occupation entities. Here, the situation of existing buildings into the polygons is used to create new buildings that take into account the distance between buildings as well as vegetation, roads, rivers, and so on. We defined two types of restrictions:

- Continuous constraints: Constraints on linear distribution in space, including vegetation, water, roads, and railroads.
- Discrete constraints: Discrete constraints that can be modelled by small points or areas, such as the remarkable buildings, cemeteries, airfields, sports fields, activity areas, industrial or commercial areas, and existing buildings.

These restrictions are based on finding the nearest neighbour and applying similar distances. They differ in their definition of the concept of "closest".

For continuous constraints we have applied a dual geo-processing buffer. First, we have measured the distance from the nearest existing building to them, then we have created a buffer ten times this distance. We assume that all buildings close to them are at this distance (i.e. the second buffer). Then the average distance of these buildings from the continuous constraint located in the second buffer has been calculated. This average for new buildings is considered as the minimum distance to the continuous constraint. In fact, to apply continuous constraints to a polygon, the algorithm creates a second buffer at a distance equal to the average distance and eliminates the intersection of this buffer with the polygon.

Discrete constraints have been defined by undifferentiated buildings, industrial buildings, and some special spaces such as remarkable buildings, cemeteries, airfields, and activity areas. To consider the distance of a polygon from discrete constraints, it is necessary to measure the distance of current buildings from each other and from other discrete constraints. After obtaining the average distance for the current buildings, the same distance has been applied to the nearest discrete constraints to each of the polygons. Thus, a medium-distance buffer has been created that defines the constraint of a particular building or location.

5.4 Building Footprints Generation

So far, we have created a layer that defines the distance constraints of new polygons from land occupation entities (e.g., existing buildings, roads, rivers, plants, railways, etc.). We have superposed this layer on the polygon layer that we have already created from the HSCS output. This gives us a new urban area that respects the urban constraints of our study area.

The urban fabric scenarios are based on one or the combination of the building types considering the density of the population. We have defined maximum surfaces (Smax) for new building footprints in terms of building type and polygon size. According to the urban fabric scenarios, three types of buildings have been considered for the study area, which include a Single dwelling, a low-rise housing and a shop top housing with Smax of 120 m^2, 250 m^2 and 400 m^2, respectively (see Table 5). To make the footprints of buildings, we must first consider the smaller polygons, while examining that the entire area exceeds the maximum defined area for each scenario (Smax). The polygons whose surface is larger than Smax are divided into smaller polygons. Therefore, we will obtain the desired surface for the building footprints while respecting the Smax and the distances between the new buildings.

Table 5. Area of the new building footprints buildings classified based on the building types.

	Smax (m^2)		
Study area	Single dwelling	Low-rise housing	Shop dutop housing
Saint Sulpice la Pointe	120	250	400

Next, different footprints have been used to create a three-dimensional display of a prospective urban model. Calculating the appropriate height for the footprints of buildings according to the urban fabric scenario, which includes urban sprawl due to population growth and types of buildings, leads to the production of a 3D visualization of a prospective urban model.

We have calculated the different probabilities of the type of building for each polygon according to its neighbourhood. This gives information about the possible height of new buildings. We have used an algorithm that combines a random aspect and a statistical interpolation according to the scenarios that have mixed height values.

According to the urban fabric scenarios, we have three types of buildings with three different heights. In our algorithm, we have arranged the buildings in ascending order of their surface (SB1 < SB2 < SB3). For each type of building B1, B2 and B3, the percentage of their combination in the scenarios has been defined by Prs, Prs2 and Prs3, respectively. P1, P2 and P2 each show the average height probability for each building, which has been calculated from the nearest available building height. Therefore, we have classified new buildings according to the distance of the nearest neighbours. Figure 7 shows this classification based on the nearest neighbour. In the classification process, the first class consists of new buildings that have at least one neighbour that is part of the current buildings on a circle (r1). The next class is new buildings that have at least one neighbour that is part of the current building and is located on a boundary ring between the small circle (r1) and the large circle (r2). The last class includes new buildings that have no neighbours that are part of the current buildings on a circle (r2).

The two radii with values r1 and r2 have been calculated based on the distance of the nearest neighbor from each existing building using the quintile classification. Next, the distance between the new building and the current building (DIS) is calculated. Finally, the inverse distance (IDIS) and the sum of the inverse distance (SIDIS) have been calculated.

5.5 3D City Visualization

The impact of each type of building has been calculated, which affects the type of new building with a height equal to Hi. Then, the total probability of each type associated with each building has been inferred, leading to a new Pi, which represents the probability of a building of height Hi. The initial percentage (Pri) of each type of building has been calculated for the variable percentage (Pr). Figure 8 shows the algorithm of calculating the probability of the height for each building according to the types of buildings and urban fabric scenarios.

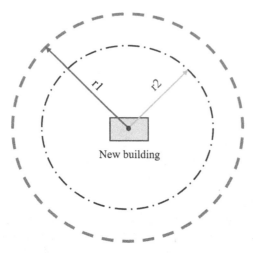

Fig. 7. Searching for the nearest neighbor for each building footprints.

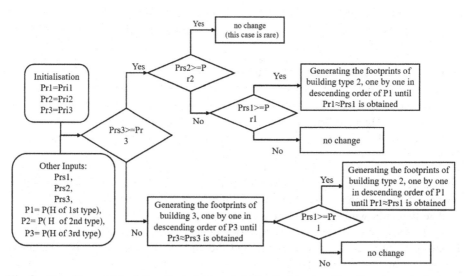

Fig. 8. Algorithm of calculating the height probability. In this algorithm Pr represents the percentage of the variable, Pri indicates the initial percentage, Prs represents the percentages of combination in the scenarios and P indicates the probability of the average height (H).

The last step is to display a three-dimensional representation of the urban growth model. To do this, a Digital Elevation Model (DEM) has been created using the BD TOPO (IGN) data altitudes. Using the calculated heights, an extrusion of the various layers including new buildings has been applied. The results are displayed in ArcScene. Figures 9 and 10 shows a 3D view of Saint Sulpice la Pointe for 2050.

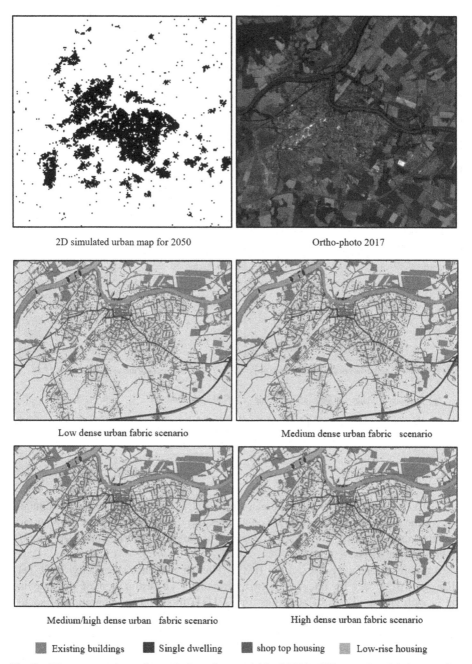

2D simulated urban map for 2050

Ortho-photo 2017

Low dense urban fabric scenario

Medium dense urban fabric   scenario

Medium/high dense urban   fabric scenario

High dense urban fabric scenario

Existing buildings   Single dwelling   shop top housing   Low-rise housing

Fig. 9. 2D representations of prospective urban model for 2050 in different urban fabric scenarios.

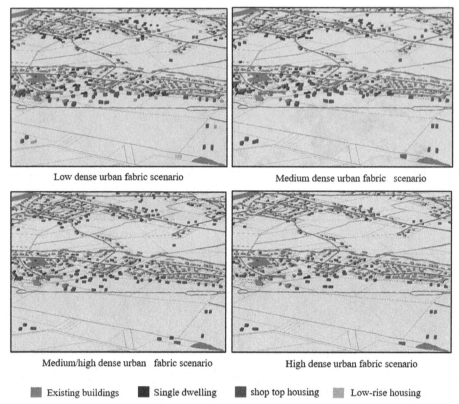

Low dense urban fabric scenario   Medium dense urban fabric scenario

Medium/high dense urban fabric scenario   High dense urban fabric scenario

■ Existing buildings   ■ Single dwelling   ■ shop top housing   ■ Low-rise housing

Fig. 10. 3D representations of prospective urban model for 2050 in different urban fabric scenarios.

6 Conclusion

The SLEUTH urban growth model creates prospective 2D maps. These maps contain some of the pixels on which urbanization is supposed to take place. These 2D maps are limited to raster data that is difficult to interpret and they need to be converted into 3D urban representations.

In this research, we proposed the HSCS (Human Settlement Capacity SLEUTH) urban growth model by integrating two parameters i.e. estimation of the population growth and the types of buildings to SLEUTH model. The integration of socio-demographic features and classification of residential buildings according to their height and configuration makes it possible to assess the capacity of human settlement in different scenarios for the future city.

Different urban fabric scenarios are defined to understand the difference between scattered and dense growth. These scenarios can help us see the impact of our model on environmental protection and conservation of natural landscapes, which could affect urban planning for years to come. As shown, for a small town the size of Saint Sulpice la Pointe, the amount of natural lands protected from urbanization in different scenarios varies by 100 hectares over 33 years.

In this research, we proposed an algorithm that transforms our HSCS results to 3D representations of buildings by considering the population density, urban fabric, and some urban constraints, including direction of the footprints and the distances to the urban entities. The 3D representation of the model can facilitate the interpretation of the simulation, the understanding of the simulation results and the differentiate of scenarios in order to support the scientists and authorities in charge of urban planning and management. In addition, the numerical model of 3D urban growth scenarios can be used in a variety of applications such as pollution calculation, energy demand and energy efficiency, cast shadows, solar radiation estimation, traffic management and other applications, and compare them in different scenarios. To create the 3D model, we first create the footprints of the buildings and then apply some constraints such the direction of buildings to roads, and the distance from urban entities and geographical features on them to respect some adjustments of the local urban plan. The 3D representations are created by giving an appropriate height to the footprints of buildings according to urban fabric scenarios. The height of each building depends on the probability of the height of the adjacent buildings according to the urban fabric scenarios.

The proposed 3D model and the defined scenarios use the potential of 3D modelling to assist urban planners in sustainable urban development, as well as to better understand the simulation results and facilitate the interpretation of SLEUTH simulations.

References

1. Schiff, J.L.: Cellular Automata: A Discrete View of the World, p. 40. Wiley, New York. ISBN 978-111-80-3063-9 (2011)
2. Clarke, K.C., Gaydos, L.J.: Loose-coupling of a cellular automaton model and GIS: long-term growth prediction for the San Francisco and Washington/Baltimore. Int. J. Geogr. Inf. Sci. **12**, 699–714 (1998)
3. Antoni, J.P., Vuidel, G., Omrani, H., Klein, O.: Geographic cellular automata for realistic urban form simulations: how far should the constraint be contained? (2019). https://doi.org/10.1007/978-3-030-12381-9_7
4. Eslahi, M., El Meouche, R., Ruas, A.: Using building types and demographic data to improve our understanding and use of urban sprawl simulation. Proc. Int. Cartogr. As-soc. **2**, 28 (2019). https://doi.org/10.5194/ica-proc-2-28-2019
5. Clarke, K.C.: A decade of cellular urban modeling with SLEUTH: unresolved issues and problems. In: Brail, R.-K. (ed.) Planning Support Systems for Cities and Region, pp. 47–60. Lincoln Institute of Land Policy, Cambridge (2008)
6. Project Gigalopolis (2018). http://www.ncgia.ucsb.edu
7. Jantz, C.A., Goetz, S.J., Donato, D., Claggett, P.: Designing and implementing a regional urban modeling system using the SLEUTH cellular urban model. Comput. Environ. Urban Syst. **34**(1), 1–16 (2010). https://doi.org/10.1016/j.compenvurbsys.2009.08.003
8. El Meouche, R., Eslahi, M., Ruas, A., and Sammuneh, M.: From pixels to 3D representations of buildings: a 3D geo-visualization of perspective urban respecting some urbanization constraints. In: Proceedings of the 6th International Conference on Geographical Information Systems Theory, Applications and Management, GISTAM, vol. 1, pp. 199–207 (2020). https://doi.org/10.5220/0009408901990207

9. Eslahi, M.: Urban growth simulations in order to represent the impacts of constructions and environmental constraints on urban sprawl - Constructibility and application to urban sprawl, Ph.D. diss., University of Paris Est (2019)

10. Tashakkori, H., Rajabifard, A., Kalantari, M.: A new 3D indoor/outdoor spatial model for indoor emergency response facilitation. Build. Environ. **89**, 170–182 (2015)

11. Christodoulou, S.; Vamvatsikos, D.; Georgiou, C.: A BIM-based framework for forecasting and visualizing seismic damage, cost and time to repair. In: Proceedings of the European Conference on Product and Process Modelling, Cork, Ireland, 14–16 September 2011

12. Varduhn, V.; Mundani, R.P.; Rank, E.: Multi-resolution models: recent progress in coupling 3D geometry to environmental numerical simulation. In: Breunig, M., Al-Doori, M., Butwilowski, E., Kuper, P., Benner, J., Haefele, K. (eds.) 3D Geoinformation Science. Lecture Notes in Geoinformation and Cartography. Springer, Cham. https://doi.org/10.1007/978-3-319-12181-9_4

13. Shiode, N.: 3D urban models: recent developments in the digital modelling of urban environments in three-dimensions. GeoJournal **52**, 263–269 (2000). https://doi.org/10.1023/A:101 4276309416

14. Kolbe, T.H. and Gröger, G.: Towards unified 3D city models. In: Proceedings of the ISPRS Commission IV Joint Workshop on Challenges in Geospatial Analysis, Integration and Visualization II, Stuttgart, Germany, 8–9 September 2003 (2003)

15. Zhu, Q., Hu, M., Zhang, Y., Du, Z.: Research and practice in three-dimensional city modeling. Geo-spatial Inf. Sci. **12**, 18–24 (2009). https://doi.org/10.1007/s11806-009-0195-z

16. Billen, R., Zaki, C., Servières, M., Moreau, G., Hallot, P.: Developing an ontology of space: application to 3D city modeling. 02007 (2012). https://doi.org/10.1051/3u3d/201202007

17. Billen, R., et al.: 3D city Models and urban information: current issues and perspectives (2014). https://doi.org/10.1051/tu0801/201400001

18. Biljecki, F., Stoter, J., Ledoux, H., Zlatanova, S., Çöltekin, A.: Applications of 3D city models: state of the art review. ISPRS Int. J. Geo-Inf. **2015**(4), 2842–2889 (2015). https://doi.org/10.3390/ijgi4042842

19. Ledoux, H., Meijers, M.: Topologically consistent 3D city models obtained by extrusion. Int. J. Geogr. Inf. Sci. **2011**(25), 557–574 (2011)

20. Pedrinis, F., Gesquière, G.: Reconstructing 3D building models with the 2D cadastre for semantic enhancement (2017). https://doi.org/10.1007/978-3-319-25691-7_7

21. Chaturvedi, K., Yao, Z., Kolbe, T.H.: Integrated management and visualization of static and dynamic properties of semantic 3D city models. Int. Arch. Photogramm. Remote Sens. Spatial Inf. Sci. **XLII-4/W17**, 7–14 (2019). https://doi.org/10.5194/isprs-archives-XLII-4-W17-7-2019

22. Haala, N., Kada, M.: An update on automatic 3D building reconstruction. ISPRS J. Photogram. Remote Sens. **65**, 570–580 (2010). https://doi.org/10.1016/j.isprsjprs.2010.09.006

23. Kapoor, M., Khreim, J.F., El Meouche, R., Bassit, D., Henry, A., Ghosh, S.: Comparison of techniques for the 3D modeling and thermal analysis. In: x Congreso Internacional Expresión Gráfica aplicada a la Edificación Graphic Expression applied to Building International Conference, APEGA 2010 (2010)

24. Hervy, B., et al.: A generalized approach for historical mock-up acquisition and data modelling: towards historically enriched 3D city models 02009 (2012). https://doi.org/10.1051/3u3d/201202009

25. El Meouche, R., Rezoug, M., Hijazi, I., Maes, D.: Automatic reconstruction of 3D building models from terrestrial laser scanner data. ISPRS Ann. Photogram. Remote Sens. Spat. Inf. Sci. **II-4**(W1), 7–12. https://doi.org/10.5194/isprsannals-ii-4-w1-7-(2013)

26. Tomljenovic, I., Höfle, B., Tiede, D., Blaschke, T.: Building extraction from airborne laser scanning data: an analysis of the state of the art. Remote Sens. **7**, 3826–3862 (2015). https://doi.org/10.3390/rs70403826
27. Pepe, M., Fregonese, L., Crocetto, N.: Use of SfM-MVS approach to nadir and oblique images generated through aerial cameras to build 2.5D maps and 3D models in urban areas. Geocarto Int. 1–17 (2019). https://doi.org/10.1080/10106049.2019.1700558

Quality Assessment of Worldview-3 Stereo Imagery Derived Models Over Millennial Olive Groves

Ante Šiljeg, Fran Domazetović$^{(\boxtimes)}$, Ivan Marić, and Lovre Panđa

Department of Geography, University of Zadar, Trg kneza Višeslava 9, 23 000 Zadar, Croatia
{asiljeg,fdomazeto,imaric1,lpanda}@unizd.hr

Abstract. Worldview-3 (*WV-3*) stereo-extracted very high resolution (*VHR*) *DSM*s represent state-of-the-art products in the domain of satellite-based digital surface modelling.

The main goal of our research was a quality assessment of *WV-3* stereo imagery derived *DSM*s of olive groves. Quality assessment was based on extraction of olive trees by geographic object-based image analysis (*GEOBIA*) and point cloud-based assessment of vertical accuracy.

The quality of *WV-3* extracted *DSM*s was assessed at the test area (31 870,6 m^2) which represents the core of the Olive Gardens of Lun (Pag Island, Croatia). Areal accuracy of olive trees extracted by *GEOBIA* from *WV-3* multispectral image was evaluated for three different commonly used classification methods (*Support Vector Machine - SVM, Random Trees- RT and Maximum Likelihood - ML*) using the following indicators *CORrectness, COMpleteness* and *Overall Quality*. Vertical accuracy was evaluated through comparison of reference point cloud and *WV-3* derived point cloud, using the *M3C2* tool within *CloudCompare*.

RT classifier has achieved the highest areal classification accuracy. Classification matching between reference data and *WV-3* is 92.4%. The vertical accuracy of individual olive trees from *WV-3* stereo imagery deviates from the reference model (*STD* = 2.57 m). *STD* values are lower for single, individual olive trees, than for grouped, dense olive tree canopies, as it is further confirmed with *STD* value for the whole test area.

Performed quality assessment has shown that *WV-3* stereo imagery can be used for the successful application of *GEOBIA* and mapping of olive trees. Creation of high-accuracy *WV-3* derived models would allow efficient large-scale management and protection of this valuable agricultural resource.

Keywords: Worldview-3 stereo imagery · UAV photogrammetry · VHR DSMs · Quality assessment · GEOBIA

1 Introduction

The emergence of very high resolution (*VHR*) optical satellite stereo imagery allowed extensive extraction of digital surface models (*DSM*s) with application in a broad range of scientific fields [1]. Advance of commercial satellites (e.g. *IKONOS*, *Pleiades*, *GeoEye*,

C. Grueau et al. (Eds.): GISTAM 2020, CCIS 1411, pp. 66–84, 2021.
https://doi.org/10.1007/978-3-030-76374-9_5

Worldview) have promoted stereo satellite imagery as cost and time effective method for the creation of *DSM*s over large areas [2, 3]. Although such *DSM*s lack the detail and resolution of models created with field geospatial methods like *LiDAR* or *UAV* photogrammetry, they require minimal field deployment [4], thus shortening the overall modelling process. If the spatial extent of created *DSM*s is considered, satellite stereo imagery represents a relatively inexpensive data collection method, where a single collected stereo-pair image covers large swaths of Earth's surface [3].

The development of satellites from the *Worldview* constellation has significantly advanced the capabilities of capturing multispectral and stereo satellite imagery with sub-meter ground sampling distance (*GSD*) [5, 6]. Currently, most advanced commercial satellite is Worldview-3 (*WV-3*), launched in August, 2014. *WV-3* provides the highest commercially available spatial resolution (0.31 m panchromatic band and eight 1.24 m multispectral bands) of collected satellite images, along with a very large daily collection capacity (up to 1 200 000 km^2) [7]. Stereo imagery is collected by *WV-3* on the daily basis, where images of specific locations of interest are being collected from different angles, along the in-track orbit, within minimal time interval [8]. Short collection interval between two stereo images ensures that changes (e.g. atmospheric conditions, land-cover change, moving targets, etc.) at the target location are minimal, thus minimalizing the potential image matching error.

As *WV-3* stereo-extracted *DSM*s represent state-of-the-art products in the domain of satellite-based digital surface modelling, the main goal of our research was to evaluate the vertical accuracy of such *DSM*s over olive groves. Assessment of vertical accuracy for *DSM* produced from *WV-3* stereo-pair image (DSM_{WV3}) was based on comparison with reference VHR *DSM* (DSM_{UAV}) produced with the unmanned aerial vehicle (*UAV*) photogrammetry. *UAV* photogrammetry was chosen for the creation of reference *DSM*, as a practical and cost-effective geospatial method that allows the creation of accurate and reliable, high-quality *VHR DSM*s over terrains with noticeable vegetation presence [9–11].

Although the overall quality of *DSM*s derived from Worldview stereo imagery was already evaluated in some previous researches, their main focus was mostly on comparison with reference *LiDAR* data [1–3, 12, 13] and on the accuracy of extraction of various man-made structures (e.g. buildings [14], plastic greenhouses [1, 12], etc.).

In our research, we have decided to concentrate on the assessment of *DSM* quality over olive groves, as an important specific land cover type of Mediterranean area which serves as one of the main agricultural sources of income and development [15]. Detailed *DSM*s of olive groves are the basis for efficient management and protection of this valuable agricultural resource, as they can provide unprecedented insight into all spatio-temporal changes that are occurring within the groves [16]. Therefore, the possibility of the application of *WV-3* stereo imagery for the creation of high-quality *DSM*s would significantly improve large scale management and protection efforts.

While vertical accuracy of *WV-3* stereo derived *DSM* was successfully evaluated earlier within two different test areas [17], this paper is focused on *the evaluation of areal representation of olive trees extracted from WV-3 multispectral image by geographic object-based image analysis (GEOBIA)* (1) and on *point cloud-based assessment of vertical accuracy* (2).

2 Study Area

Quality of *WV-3* extracted *DSM* was assessed at test area within Olive Gardens of Lun (*OGL*), located on Lun peninsula at the most northern part of Pag Island, Croatia (Fig. 1A). *OGL* represents a large, protected olive grove that contains some of the oldest millennial olive trees in the World (Fig. 1B). As such it is protected as Sites of Community Importance (*SCI*), under the Natura 2000 network of European nature protection areas [18].

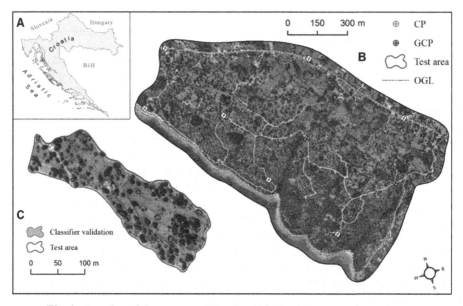

Fig. 1. Location of the test area (TA) (C) within the OGL (B) and Croatia (A).

Test area (*TA*) (Fig. 1C) covering 31 870.6 m^2, represents the core of the *OGL*, where most millennial olive trees are located. This area was chosen for quality assessment because of the high concentration of millennial olive trees with a well-developed and maintained canopy. The location of the test site (*TA*) within the study area can be seen on Fig. 1B. Acquisition of both *WV-3* imagery and *UAV* aerial imagery was conducted before the seasonal pruning of the olive trees [19], so that possible human-induced changes in height of olive trees are eliminated.

3 Materials and Methods

3.1 Data Acquisition and Specifications

3.1.1 Acquisition of Worldview-3 Imagery

Worldview-3 stereo imagery covering the study area was collected on December 4th, 2018, at ideal conditions, with 0% cloud cover and with optimal off-NADIR angles

($<30°$) [12], thus achieving claimed 5 m $CE90^1/LE90^2$ absolute horizontal accuracy specification with 2.3 m Root Mean Square Error (*RMSE*) [8]. Collected stereo *WV-3* images covering the study area have been provided to Authors as part of the funding of *DigitalGlobe Foundation* as *OrthoReady Stereo imagery (OR2A)*. *OR2A* is radiometrically and sensor corrected imagery, with no terrain corrections applied, and as such it is suitable for further orthorectification and elevation extraction [8]. Detailed specifications of acquired *WV-3* stereo imagery are given in Table 1.

Table 1. Specifications of acquired *WV-3* stereo imagery. (Source: [17])

Image ID	*WV-3*A	*WV-3*B
Image type	Stereo OR2A	Stereo OR2A
Acquisition date	04.12.2018.	04.12.2018.
Acquisition time	14:20:46	14:28:40
Off-NADIR (°)	12.1	27.1
Cloud cover (%)	0	0
GSD (m)	0.30	0.30
Scan direction	Forward	Backward
Sun azimuth (°)	157.1	157.6
Sun elevation (°)	62	62.1
Product pixel size (PAN)	0.3 m	0.3 m
Product pixel size (MS)	1.2 m	1.2 m

3.1.2 Aerial Survey with *UAV* Photogrammetry

The aerial survey was carried out on March 10th, 2019., with an advanced repeat aerophotogrametric system (*RAPS*), composed of professional-grade *DJI Matrice 600 PRO* drone, *Gremsy T3* gimbal, *Sony Alpha A7RII* (42 MP) *DSLR* camera equipped with 20 mm lens, and *Reach M+ GNSS* module for *UAV* mapping. Advanced capabilities of *RAPS* have allowed detailed aerial survey, which resulted with a collection of VHR aerial imagery.

Flight missions were planned and automated in *Universal Ground Control Software* (*UgCS*), which allowed adjustment of flight parameters (double-grid flight profiles, *GSD* (cm), flight speed (m/s), side and forward overlap (%), etc.), according to the suggestions given in [20]. Flight height was set to 165 m above ground, side and forward overlap were set to 80%, and *GSD* was 2.6 cm. The overall accuracy of *DSM* created from *UAV*

---

[1] CE90 - circular error at the 90th percentile, where a minimum of 90 percent of the points measured has a horizontal error less than the stated CE90 value.

[2] LE90-90th percentile linear error, where a minimum of 90% of vertical errors fall within the stated LE90 value.

aerial images was improved with 6 fixed ground control points (*GCPs*) and 3 check points (*CPs*) distributed uniformly within the study area. *GCPs* and *CPs* were marked before the aerial survey with red paint and their precise coordinates were collected with *Stonex S10* Real-Time Kinematic (*RTK*) *GPS*.

3.2 Data Processing and *DSM* Production

3.2.1 Creation of *DSM* from *WV-3* Stereo Imagery

OrthoEngine 2018 suite of *Geomatica* 2018 software was used for the creation of *DSM* of study area from *WV-3* stereo imagery. Workflow for *DSM* creation within *OrthoEngine* can be divided into the following substeps: *math model selection* (1), *the introduction of ground control points (GCPs), check points (CPs) and tie points (TPs) required for image orientation* (2), *bundle adjustment* (3), *epipolar image creation* (4) and *automatic DSM extraction* (5).

The first step of DSM_{WV3} extraction includes the selection of corresponding math model (1) that serves as mathematical relationship used for correlation of two-dimensional (2D) image pixels with correct three-dimensional (3D) locations on the ground (X, Y, Z) [21]. *Optical Satellite modelling* based on provided rational polynomial coefficients (*RPC*) and zero-order polynomial adjustment was selected as one of the most commonly used math models for *DSM* extraction from *WV* stereo imagery [1, 3, 5]. In order to produce a highly accurate *DSM*, the introduction of *GCPs* (2) is required for systematic compensation of *RPC* induced errors and improve overall image geo-referencing accuracy [3, 5]. Therefore, seven *GCPs* and five *CPs* scattered throughout the study area and surveyed with the *Stonex S10 RTK-GPS* were introduced, along with 187 *TPs* automatically detected from *WV-3* stereo-pair. Reported *RMSE* for used *GCPs*, *CPs* and *TPs* is given in Table 2.

Table 2. *RMSE* for *GCPs*, *CPs* and *TPs* used for the creation of *WV-3* stereo-derived *DSM* (Source: [17]).

Point type	N_0	*RMSE* X (m)	*RMSE* Y (m)	*RMSE* Z (m)	*MEAN RMSE* (m)
GCP	7	0.369	0.197	0.504	0.356
CP	5	0.320	0.517	0.737	0.525
TP	187	0.071	0.017	0.001	0.029

Introduced *GCPs* and *TPs* were then used for bundle adjustment (3) which in combination with *RPC*-derived sensor geometry calculates the exact position of the satellite at the time of image collection. The next step covers the creation of epipolar image (4), that represents a stereo-pair image, where left and right images are reprojected to have common orientation and matching features distributed along the common x-axis [22].

The final step in the creation of DSM_{WV3} was automated *DSM* extraction (5). Recent research conducted by [3] demonstrated that frequently used semi-global matching

(*SGM*) is not suitable for the creation of *DSM*s over forested areas, since it significantly underestimates tree presence and height. Therefore, in order to produce the best possible quality *DSM* of our research area, we have tested both *SGM* and normalized cross-correlation (*NCC*) technique (both implemented within *Geomatica Orthoengine 2018*) for automated *DSM* extraction. Pixel sampling interval was set to 1 for both *NCC* and *SGM* derived *DSM*s, meaning that image correlation was performed at full image resolution, thus enabling extraction of fine details (e.g. bushes, trees, buildings, etc.) in created *DSM*s [22].

Final created DSM_{WV3} was used for orthorectification of pansharpened 8-ban multispectral *WV-3* image (Fig. 5a2) of the study area with 0.3 m spatial resolution that was later used for extraction of vegetation cover through *GEOBIA* approach. As dense point cloud was required for evaluation of vertical accuracy (Sect. 3.4), created *DSM* was converted to point cloud using the *Extract vector grid from DSM* tool in *Orthoengine* software. Every pixel of DSM_{WV3} was converted into one height point of the dense point cloud. Dense point cloud (DC_{WV-3}) was extracted exclusively for *TA*, which allowed point-based evaluation of vertical accuracy.

3.2.2 Creation of *DSM* from *UAV* Photogrammetry

Aerial imagery acquired by *RAPS* was used for the creation of the *VHR* reference *DSM* of the study area in *Agisoft Metashape* 1.5.1. software. This software is currently one of the most advanced and precise image-based 3D modelling software that uses structure-from-motion (*SfM*) algorithm and multi-view 3D reconstruction technology for the creation of high-quality models [23]. Workflow for extraction of *VHR DSM* from aerial images collected by *RAPS* followed the recommendations given in [24]. Processing of collected aerial imagers allowed the creation and extraction of sub-decimeter spatial resolution *DSM* and digital orthophoto image (*DOP*) (Fig. 5a1). Along with *DOP* and *DSM* dense point cloud (DC_{UAV}) was extracted from *Agisoft Metashape* software.

3.3 *GEOBIA* Extraction of Olive Groves

Extraction and mapping of olive trees within *OGL* was performed by *GEOBIA* in *ArcGIS* software. Olive trees were extracted from both *WV-3* multispectral imagery and digital orthophoto (*DOP*) derived by aerial imagery acquired by *RAPS*.

The workflow was divided into the following sub steps: *derivation and segmentation of a multispectral image* (1), *marking and adding samples - data augmentation* (2), *selecting the classifier (Support Vector Machine - SVM, Random Trees - RT, Maximum Likelihood - ML)* (3), *image classification* (4) and *estimation of the olive tree classification accuracy* (5) (Fig. 2).

The first step of olive trees extraction was *derivation and segmentation of multispectral image* (1), through the image segmentation based on the *Mean Shift* approach [25]. The characteristics of image segments depend on three parameters: *spectral detail*, *spatial detail* and *minimum segment size*. The iterative process was performed in which 64 possible combinations of parameters were examined with the aim of optimizing the mentioned parameters and generating better quality models. Selection of the best parameters combination was performed based on visual interpretation of resulting image segments.

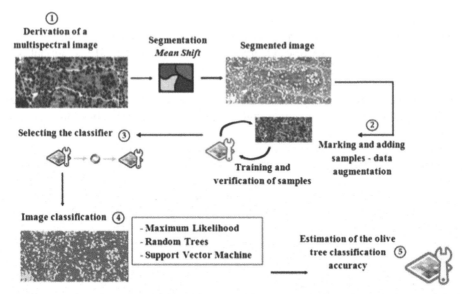

Fig. 2. *GEOBIA* workflow applied for extraction of olive trees from *DOP* and *WV-3* multispectral image.

The second step, *marking and adding samples* (2) refers to the collection of polygon test samples and verification of test samples using the cross-validation method. Data *augmentation* (2), is used to artificially increase the number of samples in a test set by applying specific input distortions. These deformations include: rotation, translation, cutting, and change in pixel brightness. In total 13 classification samples were selected and used for the classification of image segments within the *TA* (*ArcGIS*).

The third step was *selection of the classifier* (3). Three most commonly used methods (*Support Vector Machine - SVM, Random Trees- RT and Maximum Likelihood - ML*) [26–29] were selected for the classification of olive trees from the *DOP* acquired by *RAPS* and from the *WV-3* multispectral imagery. The fourth step included *image classification* (4) which was performed using all three mentioned classifiers based on 13 classification samples (Fig. 3).

The last step was *the estimation of the olive tree classification accuracy* (5). Classification results were compared using the following areal accuracy indicators [30]: correctness (*COR*), completeness (*COM*) and overall quality (*OQ*). By applying different accuracy indicators, it is possible to quantify the correspondence between reference data and generated objects and to assess the accuracy and success of the performed segmentation [31]. Calculation of these indicators was performed by comparing seven reference olive trees polygons (R_o) with polygons representing olive trees (C_i) generated by three different classifiers. Reference polygons were selected based on randomly selected pixels using the *Create accuracy assessment points* tool within *ArcGIS* software. Olive trees on which the pixels were located, or to which the pixels were nearest, were selected as reference samples for assessing the best classifier. Seven olive tree canopies were manually vectorized from the *DOP* and from the *WV-3* multispectral imagery at a

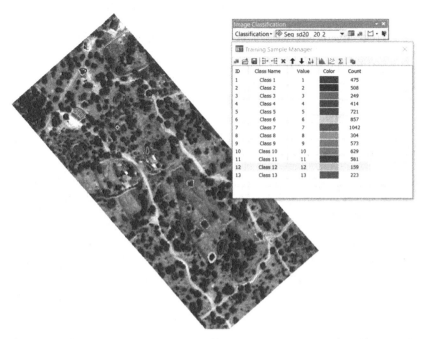

Fig. 3. 13 classification samples used for classification of *DOP* and *WV-3* multispectral image.

scale of 1:25. Overlap polygons were obtained using the *Intersect* tool within *ArcGIS*. These polygons represent the reference for the determination of the areal accuracy of olive trees derived by three different classifiers. Overlap area (A_p) of the reference and classified olive trees was calculated, as well as the over-estimated area (A_o) and under-estimated area (A_u)(Fig. 5d). The calculated values were used to calculate the selected areal accuracy metrics, according to the following formulas:

COR calculation formula [30]:

$$COR = \frac{A_p}{A_{C_i}}$$

Where is:

A_p - overlap area of reference and classified area, A_{C_i} - total area of *GEOBIA* olive tree

COM calculation formula [30]:

$$COM = \frac{A_p}{A_{R_o}}$$

Where is:

A_p - overlap area of reference and classified area, A_{R_o} - total area of the reference olive tree

OQ calculation formula [30]:

$$OQ = \frac{A_p}{A_{R_o} + A_{C_i} - A_p}$$

Where is:

A_p - overlap area of reference and classified area, A_{R_o} - total area of the reference olive tree

A_{C_i} - total area of *GEOBIA* olive tree

The values of *COR*, *COM* and *OQ* indexes vary from 0 to 1. Higher values indicate a greater match between the reference and classified objects, that is, higher accuracy of the performed classification [32].

3.4 Model Vertical Accuracy Assessment

The vertical accuracy of *WV-3* derived models was evaluated from two unfiltered dense point clouds. Dense clouds of *WV-3* derived *DSM* (DC_{WV-3}) and *UAV* photogrammetry derived *DSM* (DC_{UAV}) were compared by *Cloud to Cloud* tool (*C2C*) [33] within the *CloudCompare* software. DC_{UAV} was set as the reference point cloud because of its higher point density, while DC_{WV-3} was set as the compared cloud. In the *Distance computation* option, parameters were set to create a model of the absolute distances between compared clouds. *Octree level* was set to automatic and *max thread count* to 12/12. The *Maximum distance* was set to 4.88245 m which was checked in the *Approximate distances* option (Table 3).

Table 3. Approximate distances of points of compared dense clouds DC_{UAV} and $DC_{WV-3.}$

	Distance values (m)
Min dist.	0
Max dist.	4.88245
Avg dist.	0.773797
Sigma	1.18259
Max error	1.22061

The *M3C2* (*Multiscale Model to Model Comparison*) plugin by [34] allows the generation of positive and negative distance values based on which the standard deviation (*STD*) was calculated [35]. DC_{UAV} was set as the reference cloud and the registration error was set to 0.1 m because of the model error of reference data. *STD* was used as the main statistical method to check the vertical accuracy of the DC_{WV-3}.

4 Results and Discussion

4.1 Created *DSMs* and Point Clouds of Study Area

4.1.1 *WV-3* Derived Models

WV-3 Derived DSM

As the spatial resolution of initial *WV-3* stereo imagery was 0.3 m and pixel sampling interval for *NCC* and *SGM* was set to 1, the spatial resolution of final created *DSM*_WV3 was 0.6 m. Although *NCC* and *SGM* approaches were based on identical input *WV-3* stereo imagery and *GCPs*, resulting *DSMs* were very dissimilar. Significant differences between *DSMs* of study area created by *NCC* and *SGM* approaches are obvious even from a basic visual comparison of created models (Fig. 4). *DSM* created by the *SGM* approach was much smoother and it lacks most of single, individual trees, thus confirming what was stated by [3]. On the other hand, *NCC* also failed to represent all individual olive trees, but representation was much better than with the *SGM* approach.

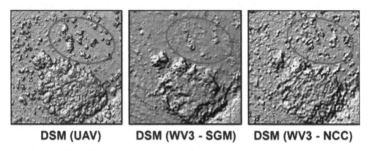

DSM (UAV)   **DSM (WV3 - SGM)**   **DSM (WV3 - NCC)**

Fig. 4. Visual comparison of *DSMs* created by *NCC* (right) and *SGM* (middle) approaches with *DSM* created from *UAV* photogrammetry (left); red ellipse – the area covered by individual, dispersed olive trees. (Source: [17]) (Color figure online)

While *SGM* was very straightforward and easy-to-use, *NCC* allowed higher autonomy for adjustment of user-defined parameters for *DSM* extraction to the local characteristics of our study area. Namely, high individual olive trees rise several meters above the surrounding terrain, significantly rising overall surface roughness. *SGM* technique neglected the high surface roughness and created a rather smooth *DSM*, with a very poor representation of individual olive trees. To solve this problem, we set the smoothing filter and terrain type parameters of the *NCC* technique to fill holes only and mountainous, respectively. Fill holes only parameter interpolates all holes in created *DSM*, but does not apply any additional filtering and smoothing, which is important for preservation and representation of individual olive trees in the created model. Although terrain within our study area is represented by gentle hills, we decided to set terrain type parameter to mountainous, in order to preserve individual trees, that would be filtered with the other two terrain type parameters (flat, hilly). As a result, *DSM* produced by *NCC* had a much better representation of individual olive trees than *DSM* produced by *SGM*, and thus this *DSM* was chosen as the final DSM_{WV3}.

WV-3 Derived Multispectral Image
Orthorectification of pansharpened 8-ban multispectral *WV-3* image based on generated DSM_{WV3}, resulted in the creation of a single terrain-corrected multispectral image with spatial resolution of 30 cm. Created *WV-3* multispectral image has very-high spatial resolution and versatility of spectral information, that served as the basis for extraction and classification of olive trees.

WV-3 Derived Dense Point Cloud

Final created DSM_{WV3} served as the basis for conversion of individual pixels to height points and creation of dense point cloud DC_{WV-3}.

4.1.2 UAV Photogrammetry Derived Models

VHR reference DSM_{UAV} with 10 cm spatial resolution and digital orthophoto image (*DOP*) with 3 cm spatial resolution were created, as well as high-density point cloud. Created models are used as reference models since the spatial resolution of both created *DSM* and *DOP* are significantly higher than the one of *WV-3* derived models.

4.2 Selected Parameters and Classifier

Mean Shift parameters were set to equal values for both *WV-3* multispectral image and *DOP* segmentation. In order to minimize generalization in the process of segmentation by an iterative process, the following values proved to be optimal:

a) *Spectral detail* was set to 20/20 which enabled detailed vegetation differentiation.
b) *Spatial detail* was set to 20/20 which enabled highlighting small compact features.
c) *Minimum segment size* was set to 2/20 which enabled merging segments smaller than this size.

The proximity of the olive canopies conditioned the high values of selected spectral and spatial parameters, as lower values resulted in merged canopies and larger vegetation generalization. The distribution of seven reference polygons, used for validation of three tested classifiers, within the *TA* is given in Fig. 5 (b1 and b2). The results of comparing the three classifiers (*SVM, RT* and *ML*) using the three accuracy indicators (*COR, COM* and *OQ*) are shown in Tables 4, 5 and 6.

Table 4. Results of *COR* validation of classifiers for *DOP* and *WV-3*.

Reference sample	DOP			WV-3		
	COR_{ML}	COR_{RT}	COR_{SVM}	COR_{ML}	COR_{RT}	COR_{SVM}
1	0.709	0.694	0.717	0.827	0.872	0.862
2	0.957	0.963	0.962	0.852	0.854	0.853
3	0.814	0.818	0.818	0.926	0.921	0.923
4	0.622	0.633	0.620	0.164	0.505	0.503
5	0.671	0.689	0.689	0.913	0.912	0.907
6	0.531	0.545	0.541	0.250	0.301	0.247
7	0.277	0.274	0.267	0.155	0.151	0.151
Result	**0.654**	*0.660*	**0.659**	**0.584**	*0.645*	**0.635**

Table 5. Results of *COM* validation of classifiers for *DOP* and *WV-3*.

Reference sample	DOP			WV-3		
	COM_{ML}	COM_{RT}	COM_{SVM}	COM_{ML}	COM_{RT}	COM_{SVM}
1	0.974	0.985	0.980	0.965	0.922	0.928
2	0.929	0.938	0.917	0.808	0.837	0.860
3	0.946	0.926	0.933	0.900	0.881	0.883
4	0.985	0.980	0.971	0.978	0.988	0.989
5	0.976	0.979	0.979	0.850	0.921	0.939
6	0.990	0.982	0.981	0.968	0.974	0.982
7	0.910	0.932	0.931	0.951	0.951	0.951
Result	**0.959**	*0.960*	**0.956**	**0.917**	**0.925**	*0.933*

Table 6. Results of *OQ* validation of classifiers for *DOP* and *WV-3*.

Reference sample	DOP			WV-3		
	OQ_{ML}	OQ_{RT}	OQ_{SVM}	OQ_{ML}	OQ_{RT}	OQ_{SVM}
1	0.702	0.687	0.707	0.803	0.812	0.808
2	0.891	0.905	0.885	0.708	0.732	0.750
3	0.779	0.767	0.773	0.839	0.819	0.823
4	0.616	0.625	0.609	0.164	0.502	0.500
5	0.660	0.679	0.679	0.786	0.845	0.857
6	0.528	0.530	0.535	0.248	0.298	0.246
7	0.270	0.259	0.262	0.153	0.150	0.150
Result	**0.635**	*0.636*	**0.636**	**0.529**	*0.594*	**0.591**

From the obtained values of the *COR* indicator (Table 4), it can be seen that the accuracy of classification of olive trees based on *DOP* is 0.660 for the RT method, which is higher than for the other two tested methods ($ML_{DOP} = 0.654$; $SVM_{DOP} = 0.659$). Furthermore, based on the *WV-3* image, the *COR* indicator also confirmed that *RT* (0.645) classifier performed better than the other two methods ($ML_{WV-3} = 0.584$; $SVM_{WV-3} = 0.635$). Based on this indicator, it is possible to conclude that a significant part of the surface of the olive trees classified by the *GEOBIA* approach is inside the reference olive trees.

The next calculated areal indicator is *COM* (Table 5), which represents the ratio between the overlap of reference and classified area (A_p) with the total area of the reference olive trees (A_{R_o}) [30]. The average representation is 0.960 for the *RT* method on *DOP* and 0.933 for the *SVM* method on *WV-3*. As indicated by this metric, the optimal classifier for *WV-3* image is *SVM* method, although *COM* value for *RT* is not significantly lower (0.925). High values of this metric indicate that classification results for both *DOP* and *WV-3* have very high matching (>0.9) with total reference area, for all three tested classifiers.

The *OQ* indicator (Table 6) considered more accurate than *COR* and *COM*, as it depends less on the area of reference and classified objects [30]. As *COR* and *COM*, calculated values of *OQ* also indicate that *RT* (0.636 for *DOP*; 0.594 for *WV-3*) classification method performed better than the other two classifiers ($ML_{DOP} = 0.635$; $SVM_{DOP} = 0.636$; $ML_{WV-3} = 0.529$; $SVM_{WV-3} = 0.591$). As all three indicators confirmed that *Random Trees* classifier achieved the highest areal accuracy (Fig. 6), olive trees extracted by this method have been selected as test areas for further evaluation of vertical accuracy.

The total area of the olive trees classified by *RT* method from the *DOP* is $10\,360.45\ \text{m}^2$ (Fig. 5c1), while from *WV-3* total area is $11\,201.25\ \text{m}^2$ (Fig. 5c2). Although the same classifier and user-defined parameters were used, the extracted area is not identical. If higher spatial resolution *DOP* is considered as a reference dataset, then *WV-3* derived areas represent a slight overestimation of the total area classified as olive trees. This is further confirmed through the overlap of extracted olive tree areas. Classification matching between reference *DOP* and *WV-3* is 92.4% (Fig. 5d), which is a very high

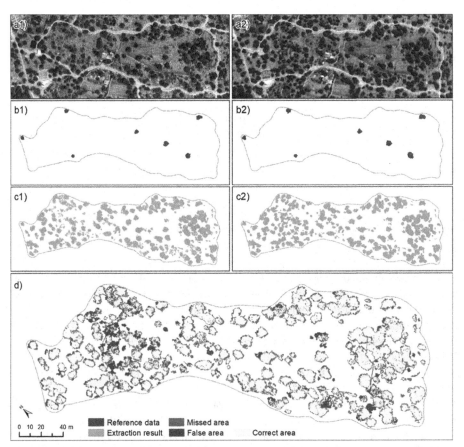

Fig. 5. Extraction of olive trees using the *GEOBIA* from *DOP* (a1) and *WV-3 MS* (a2), (b1 and b2 - reference olive trees; c1 and c2 - olive trees extracted by *RT*; d - overlap between olive trees classified from *WV-3* and *DOP*).

value considering the difference between the two data resolutions. A high percentage of overlap between *DOP* and *WV-3*confirms the quality of areal representation of *WV-3* extracted olive trees.

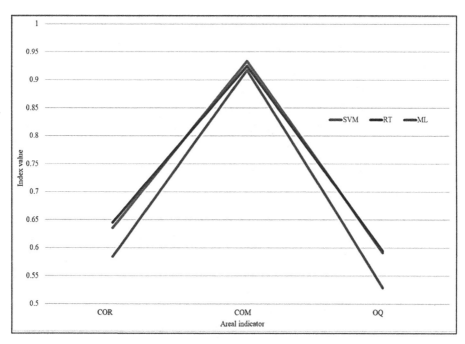

Fig. 6. Graphical representation of three areal indicators of horizontal accuracy.

4.3   Vertical Accuracy of *WV-3 DSM*

Vertical accuracy is expressed as distance between reference point cloud (DC_{UAV}) and evaluated point cloud (DC_{WV-3}), where higher distance values represent higher vertical errors. Results of the *C2C* tool represent absolute distances between two clouds, calculated in meters (Fig. 7A). The *C2C* model shows that the smallest vertical differences are located at the edges of the olive tree canopy, while distances are growing towards the canopy centre. Such distribution of distances is the result of vertical inaccuracy of canopy shape and height representation in DC_{WV-3}, compared to the canopies represented in DC_{UAV}. In comparison to the reference canopy, DC_{WV-3} significantly underestimates the canopy height. This is further confirmed by the 3D representation of two point clouds (Fig. 8).

Unlike *C2C* that represents only absolute distances, *M3C2* calculated both positive and negative distance, thus providing a better insight into the actual deviations between two point clouds. Calculated distances clearly indicate that negative distances are prevailing in the majority (over 90%) of points from DC_{WV-3} (Fig. 7B). Such representation of negative distances further confirms that DC_{WV-3} underestimates the height of the olive tree canopy, in comparison to reference DC_{UAV}.

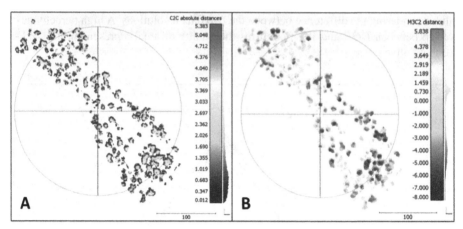

Fig. 7. Distances between DC_{WV-3} and reference DC_{UAV} calculated by $C2C$ tool (A) and $M3C2$ tool (B).

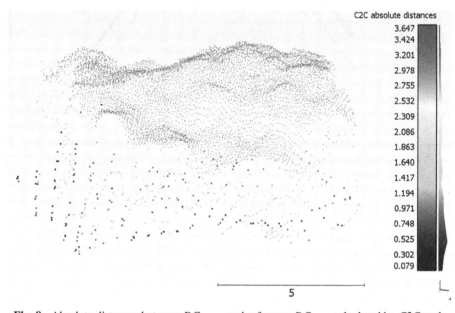

Fig. 8. Absolute distances between DC_{WV-3} and reference DC_{UAV} calculated by $C2C$ tool.

Figure 9 represents the spatial distribution (A) and histogram (B) of STD values, calculated based on a comparison of reference DC_{UAV} and evaluated DC_{WV-3} in the $M3C2$ tool. STD calculated for all olive trees within TA based on vertical distances determined by the $M3C2$ tool is 2.58 m. Generally, STD values are lower for single, individual olive trees, than for grouped, dense olive tree canopies. This demonstrated that although produced DSM_{WV3} managed to reproduce individual olive trees, the vertical accuracy of such representation is relatively low, as it is further confirmed with STD value for whole TA.

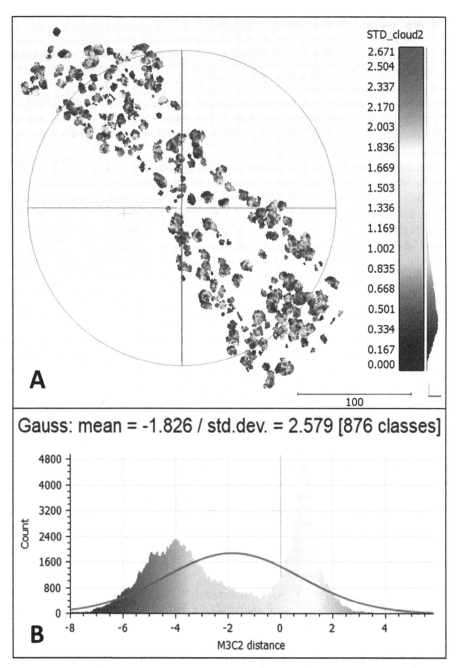

Fig. 9. Spatial distribution (A) and histogram (B) of calculated STD for calculated by *M3C2* tool.

5   Conclusion

The main aim of our study was the quality assessment of *WV-3* derived *DSM*s for potential application over olive groves. The first aim was to test two different approaches (*NCC* and *SGM*) for creation of *WV-3* derived *DSM*. While *SGM* was very straightforward and easy-to-use, *NCC* allowed higher autonomy for adjustment of user-defined parameters for *DSM* extraction to the local characteristics of the study area. As a result, *DSM* produced by *NCC* had a much better representation of individual olive trees than *DSM* produced by *SGM*.

The second aim was to test the areal accuracy of olive trees extracted from *WV-3* multispectral image through three different *GEOBIA* approaches. According to the calculated areal indicators (*COR, COM, OQ*) *Random Trees* classifier has achieved the highest areal classification accuracy from all three tested approaches (*RT, SVM, ML*). While there were some minor differences between olive trees classified by *RT* from *DOP* and *WV-3* multispectral image, the overall overlap was very high (92.4%). Thus, it can be concluded that an orthorectified *WV-3* multispectral image can be used for accurate extraction and mapping of olive trees on large areas.

Overlap area of extracted olive trees was used as a test area for evaluation of DC_{WV-3} vertical accuracy. Vertical accuracy is expressed as distance between reference point cloud (DC_{UAV}) and evaluated point cloud (DC_{WV-3}), where higher distance values represent higher vertical errors. Calculated distances are clearly indicating that negative distances are prevailing in the majority (over 90%) of points from DC_{WV-3}. Such representation of negative distances further confirms that DC_{WV-3} underestimates the height of the olive tree canopy, in comparison to reference DC_{UAV}

In overall, performed quality assessment has shown that *WV-3* stereo imagery can be used for successful application of *GEOBIA* and mapping of olive trees, as well as for creation of dense point clouds and high-resolution *DSM*s.

Acknowledgements. This research was performed within the project UIP-2017-05-2694 financially supported by the *Croatian Science Foundation*. The authors would like to thank *Digital-Globe Foundation* (Maxar Technologies), *Hexagon Geospatial* and *SPH Engineering* for provided necessary *VHR Worldview* satellite imagery and software (UgCS, *Erdas Imagine 2018*).

References

1. Aguilar, M.A., Nemmaoui, A., Aguilar, F.J., Qin, R.: Quality assessment of digital surface models extracted from WorldView-2 and WorldView-3 stereo pairs over different land covers. GIScience Remote Sens. **56**(1), 109–129 (2019)
2. Shean, D.E., et al.: An automated, open-source pipeline for mass production of digital elevation models (DEMs) from very-high-resolution commercial stereo satellite imagery. ISPRS J. Photogram. Remote Sens. **116**, 101–117 (2016)
3. Goldbergs, G., Maier, S.W., Levick, S.R., Edwards, A.: Limitations of high-resolution satellite stereo imagery for estimating canopy height in Australian tropical savannas. Int. J. Appl. Earth Observ. Geoinf. **75**, 83–95 (2019)
4. Wang, S., et al.: DEM generation from Worldview-2 stereo imagery and vertical accuracy assessment for its application in active tectonics. Geomorphology **336**, 107–118 (2019)

5. Aguilar, M.Á., del Mar Saldaña, M., Aguilar, F.J.: Generation and quality assessment of stereo-extracted DSM from GeoEye-1 and WorldView-2 imagery. IEEE Trans. Geosci. Remote Sens. **52**(2), 1259–1271 (2013)
6. Aguilar, M.A., Bianconi, F., Aguilar, F.J., Fernández, I.: Object-based greenhouse classification from GeoEye-1 and WorldView-2 stereo imagery. Remote Sens. **6**(5), 3554–3582 (2014)
7. Maxar Technologies: Worldview-3 datasheet (2019). https://www.digitalglobe.com/company/about-us. Accessed 03 Dec 2019
8. Maxar Technologies: Stereo Imagery datasheet (2019). https://www.digitalglobe.com/resources. Accessed 03 Dec 2019
9. Mohan, M., et al.: Individual tree detection from unmanned aerial vehicle (UAV) derived canopy height model in an open canopy mixed conifer forest. Forests **8**(9), 340 (2017)
10. Tomaštík, J., Mokroš, M., Saloň, Š., Chudý, F., Tunák, D.: Accuracy of photogrammetric UAV-based point clouds under conditions of partially-open forest canopy. Forests **8**(5), 151 (2017)
11. Krause, S., Sanders, T.G., Mund, J.P., Greve, K.: UAV-based photogrammetric tree height measurement for intensive forest monitoring. Remote Sens. **11**(7), 758 (2019)
12. Nemmaoui, A., Aguilar, F.J., Aguilar, M.A., Qin, R.: DSM and DTM generation from VHR satellite stereo imagery over plastic covered greenhouse areas. Comput. Electron. Agric. **164**, (2019)
13. Rizeei, H.M., Pradhan, B.: Urban mapping accuracy enhancement in high-rise built-up areas deployed by 3D-orthorectification correction from WorldView-3 and LiDAR Imageries. Remote Sens. **11**(6), 692 (2019)
14. Qin, R.: Change detection on LOD 2 building models with very high resolution spaceborne stereo imagery. ISPRS J. Photogram. Rem. Sens. **96**, 179–192 (2014)
15. Orlandi, F., Aguilera, F., Galan, C., Msallem, M., Fornaciari, M.: Olive yields forecasts and oil price trends in Mediterranean areas: a comprehensive analysis of the last two decades. Exp. Agric. **53**(1), 71–83 (2017)
16. Jiménez-Brenes, F.M., López-Granados, F., de Castro, A.I., Torres-Sánchez, J., Serrano, N., Peña, J.M.: Quantifying pruning impacts on olive tree architecture and annual canopy growth by using UAV-based 3D modelling. Plant Methods **13**(1), 55 (2017)
17. Domazetović, F., Šiljeg, A., Marić, I., Jurišić, M.: Assessing the Vertical Accuracy of Worldview-3 Stereo-extracted Digital Surface Model over Olive Groves. In: GISTAM, pp. 246–253 (2020)
18. European Environment Agency: Natura 2000 End 2018 – Shapefile (2019). https://www.eea.europa.eu/data-and-maps/data/natura-10/natura-2000-spatial-data/natura-2000-shapefile-1. Accessed 12 Dec 2019)
19. Gucci, R., Cantini, C.: Pruning and training systems for modern olive growing. Csiro Publishing (2000)
20. Pepe, M., Fregonese, L., Scaioni, M.: Planning airborne photogrammetry and remote-sensing missions with modern platforms and sensors. Eur. J. Remote Sens. **51**(1), 412–436 (2018)
21. Barazzetti, L., Roncoroni, F., Brumana, R., Previtali, M.: Georeferencing accuracy analysis of a single worldview-3 image collected over Milan. The International Archives of the Photogrammetry, Remote Sensing and Spatial Information Sciences, vol. XLI-B1 (2016)
22. PCI Geomatics Enterprises: GeomaticaOrthoEngine Course Exercises (2018). https://www.pcigeomatics.com/pdf/TrainingGuide-Geomatica-OrthoEngine.pdf. Accessed Jan 2020
23. Mancini, F., Dubbini, M., Gattelli, M., Stecchi, F., Fabbri, S., Gabbianelli, G.: Using unmanned aerial vehicles (UAV) for high-resolution reconstruction of topography: the structure from motion approach on coastal environments. Remote Sens. **5**(12), 6880–6898 (2013)
24. James, M.R., et al.: Guidelines on the use of structure-from-motion photogrammetry in geomorphic research. Earth Surface Processes and Landforms (2019)

25. Comaniciu, D., Meer, P.: Mean shift: a robust approach toward feature space analysis. IEEE Trans. Pattern Anal. Mach. Intell. **24**(5), 603–619 (2002)
26. Nitze, I., Schulthess, U., Asche, H.: Comparison of machine learning algorithms random forest, artificial neural network and support vector machine to maximum likelihood for supervised crop type classification. In: Proceedings of the 4th GEOBIA, vol. 35 (2012)
27. Myburgh, G., Van Niekerk, A.: Effect of feature dimensionality on object-based land cover classification: a comparison of three classifiers. S. Afr. J. Geomat. **2**(1), 13–27 (2013)
28. Myburgh, G., Van Niekerk, A.: Impact of training set size on object-based land cover classification: a comparison of three classifiers. Int. J. Appl. Geospat. Res. (IJAGR) **5**(3), 49–67 (2014)
29. Li, M., Ma, L., Blaschke, T., Cheng, L., Tiede, D.: A systematic comparison of different object-based classification techniques using high spatial resolution imagery in agricultural environments. Int. J. Appl. Earth Obs. Geoinf. **49**, 87–98 (2016)
30. Cai, L., Shi, W., Miao, Z., Hao, M.: Accuracy assessment measures for object extraction from remote sensing images. Remote Sens. **10**(2), 303 (2018)
31. Eisank, C., Smith, M., Hillier, J.: Assessment of multiresolution segmentation for delimiting drumlins in digital elevation models. Geomorphology **214**, 452–464 (2014)
32. Whiteside, T.G., Maier, S.W., Boggs, G.S.: Area-based and location-based validation of classified image objects. Int. J. Appl. Earth Observ. Geoinf. **28**, 117–130 (2014)
33. Bronzino, G.P.C., Grasso, N., Matrone, F., Osello, A., Piras, M.: LASER-visual-inertial odometry based solution for 3D heritage modeling: the sanctuary of the blessed virgin of Trompone. International Archives of the Photogrammetry, Remote Sensing & Spatial Information Sciences (2019)
34. Lague, D., Brodu, N., Leroux, J.: Accurate 3D comparison of complex topography with terrestrial laser scanner: application to the Rangitikei canyon (NZ). ISPRS J. Photogram. Rem. Sens. **82**, 10–26 (2013)
35. Midgley, N.G., Tonkin, T.N.: Reconstruction of former glacier surface topography from archive oblique aerial images. Geomorphology **282**, 18–26 (2017)

Integration of New Data Layers to Support the Land Cover and Use Information System of Spain (SIOSE): An Approach from Object-Oriented Modelling

Benito Zaragozí[1]([✉]) [ID], Jesús Javier Rodríguez-Sala[2] [ID], Sergio Trilles[3] [ID], and Alfredo Ramón-Morte[4] [ID]

[1] Departament de Geografia, Universitat Rovira i Virgili, C/Joanot Martorell, Vilaseca, Spain
benito.zaragozi@urv.cat
[2] Centro de Investigación Operativa, Universidad Miguel Hernandez de Elche, Av. de la Universidad, Elche, Spain
[3] Institute of New Imaging Technologies, Universitat Jaume I, Av. Vicente Sos Baynat s/n, Castellón de la Plana, Spain
[4] Instituto Interuniversitario de Geografia, Universidad de Alicante, C/San Vicente s/n, Alicante, Spain

Abstract. Land use and land cover (LULC) information is essential in territorial planning for the study of natural risks and landscape science. Given the importance of LULC data, increasing efforts are being focused on producing quality and easily accessible databases. In Spain, the Land Use and Cover Information System (SIOSE) is a clear example of these efforts. The SIOSE database was one of the first to be built following an object-oriented data model and a set of specifications that facilitates the integration of data from different sources. However, the SIOSE information alone is so accurate and complete that there is a *usability gap* that means that this data is not used to its full potential in some contexts, nor is the possibility of integrating other data sources considered. In this work, we examine the circumstances of this *usability gap*, its causes and consequences, and we introduce an extension of the SIOSE object-oriented data model that will enable enriching the LULC data including new useful data for different types of studies. Finally, an example of implementation of this extended model serves to encourage the user community to propose and disseminate new extended LULC datasets that facilitate various types of landscape studies.

Keywords: Land use · Land cover · Object-oriented · Geodatabase · SIOSE

1 Introduction

The geographical and cartographic nature of the information on Land Use and Land Cover (LULC) makes it essential in works of territorial planning and natural risks, as

This work was supported by grants from the Spanish Ministry of Economy and Competitiveness, project SIOSE-INNOVA (CSO2016-79420-R AEI/FEDER UE). Sergio Trilles has been funded by the Juan de la Cierva - Incorporación postdoctoral programme of the Ministry of Science and Innovation - Spanish government (IJC2018-035017-I).

© Springer Nature Switzerland AG 2021
C. Grueau et al. (Eds.): GISTAM 2020, CCIS 1411, pp. 85–101, 2021.
https://doi.org/10.1007/978-3-030-76374-9_6

well as for landscape science [2, 22]. Geographical information on land use integrates biophysical information on the territory and human activities, and shows the socio-economic use of the natural environment from a cartographic or spatial perspective. For these reasons, LULC data have a strategic role in any study on natural resources management, environmental conservation, and territorial planning [27].

1.1 LULC Data Official Repositories in the EU

Information on land use in most European countries has been associated with map production for the many national map series that have been published since cartography became a modern science, with works related to the preparation of official maps, as well as with topographic and cadastral maps. This responsibility continues to depend mainly on those official and public organisations who are responsible for the production and management of maps at the national level. For example, in Spain, the National Geographic Institute (Instituto Geográfico Nacional; IGN) is the leading organisation for the production of maps, and has produced national topographic maps since the nineteenth century.

Since the second half of the last century, official repositories of digital geographic information have been created, in part, thanks to the development of the Geographic Information Systems (GIS) and the increasing importance of remote sensing applications (which have enabled us to obtain large amounts of information and provided useful tools for its processing). It is worth highlighting the Coordination of Information of the Environment Programme (CORINE) of the European Environment Agency (EEA), which since the end of the last century has represented a coordinated effort in the compilation of this type of information on a regular and structured basis, and with a detailed reference scale (1:100,000). This European-level project has served as a model for extending the initiative worldwide [7].

A global approach has allowed us to perceive the environmental consequences of climate change and the recent development of human activities; and LULC information has become increasingly demanded for decisive issues in the United Nations Framework Convention on Climate Change (1992) and the revision of the Kyoto Protocol (1998) [11]. There are increasing numbers of users of this type of information; both in the public sector and private companies – and these users are using this data for different interests. This heterogeneous demand is being satisfied by the Copernicus Land Monitoring Service (CLMS), part of the Global Monitoring for Environment and Security (GMES) of the European Environment Agency (EEA), which at the same time reports to the Copernicus Land Observation Programme of the European Space Agency (ESA) [9].

More specifically, in Spain, this environmental affiliation in the usefulness of LULC information is the reason why the Ministry of Ecological Transition and Demographic Challenge, through the Secretary of State for the Environment, encourages the production of this type of information, in coordination with European organisations, and within the legal framework of the INSPIRE Directive (2007/2/EC) [8]. IGN (IGN in Spanish) is responsible for the production of LULC data under the National Plan for the Occupation of the Territory (PNOT), which since 2005 centralises storage and updates in a national database named SIOSE. CORINE Land Cover Programme (CORINE LC) data on Spain is currently produced through the cartographic generalisation of the SIOSE [17]. The raw data from this database, as well as its derived products, is freely distributed using open standard formats and a non-commercial license. According to the IGN, between 2012 and 27 July 2017, PNOT datasets have been downloaded 5.2 million times, demonstrating the importance of this information. The principal users are the state administrations and regional or provincial governments. Frequent uses include agrarian policy, environmental management, urban development, or mapping. Also noteworthy are the downloads of this information for other purposes, such as university research, research office centres, companies, and consultancies.

1.2   Hierarchical vs. Object-Oriented LULC Classifications

During the last years of the twentieth century, the LULC classification paradigm used by CORINE LC was also adopted by other similar programmes, such as the Geological Survey of Land Use and Coverage of the Geological Survey of the United States [1]. This paradigm lasted for several decades and is still being used, but at the beginning of the current century, it revealed deficiencies coinciding with the spread of the massive use of geographic databases. These limitations consisted in the fact that mutually exclusive LULC classes were not oriented to an adequate diagnosis of reality, they were not designed for diverse and complicated use; instead, they were designed for the elaboration of thematic cartography, subject to the limitation of a reference scale. In the twenty-first century, more complex and voluminous datasets are being used, and this has led to the emergence and need for an object-oriented paradigm [29].

The European Union created the EAGLE group, within the European Network for Information and Observation on the Environment (EIONET), to establish the procedures for optimising the integration and homogenisation of LULC data from the official repositories of each country on a pan-European scale [3]. EAGLE proposed a solution based on an object-oriented data model that was based on standards or reference code lists, such as Corine LC and technical specifications directed by INSPIRE (2007/2/CE) and ISO 19144-2 (LCML-Land Cover Meta Language). An excellent example of this approach was the development of the SIOSE Spanish database (information system on land occupation in Spain), created in 2005 with an integrated object-oriented model as an initiative of the EIONET Network [10]. As already explained, the SIOSE database was developed in Spain under the coordination of the IGN and the National Centre for Geographical Information (CNIG). SIOSE is supported by a data model that meets INSPIRE technical specifications, and its composition reflects the indications of the EAGLE group, ensuring compatibility and comparability with pre-existing databases such as Corine (CLC90 and CLC00), Murbandy/Moland, and the Land Cover Classification System (LCCS) of the Food and Agriculture Organisation of the United Nations.

In Fig. 1, we show the geometric difference between a CORINE LC polygon (brown outer line) and a SIOSE polygon (yellow), which is contained by the CORINE polygon. The comparison clearly shows the difference in size and scale, with Corine LC at a 1:100,000 scale, while SIOSE is built at a 1:25,000 scale. On the map, we can see how the thematic classification of the CORINE polygon (*discontinuous urban fabric*) hides other realities that are more detailed in the SIOSE classification – roads, car parks, hotel buildings, leisure areas, swimming pools, and gardens – that do not appear spatially

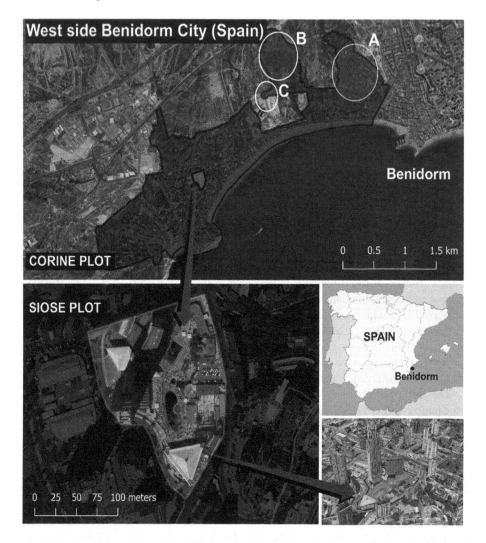

Fig. 1. Benidorm city surroundings (Spain). Comparison of geographic information on LULC data between Corine LC plot and SIOSE plot. Source: Corine LC, SIOSE, aerial orthophotography flight from National Geographic Institute (PNOA) and Google Earth.

delimited but are included in the SIOSE database with detailed information (e.g. coding, description, surface). The CORINE LC classification and model exclude these complex realities. Inside the CORINE polygon, we see the three areas marked with white circles (A, B and C). In these areas, single-family housing (circle A), unbuilt areas, or isolated buildings (circle B) and large communication infrastructures appear (circle C) under the same thematic label: *discontinuous urban fabric*.

An object-oriented LULC data model diminishes the loss of information during the thematic labelling process because there are no mutually exclusive classes. This is possible thanks to the storage of LULC statistical observations (e.g. percentages of an occupied area) at levels of detail that hierarchical classification models cannot achieve because of their dichotomous nature [23]. In the case of SIOSE, this had a significant influence on the economic savings in the production of datasets because deepening the information and expanding the scale of application would not have been possible with a hierarchical system. The components or variables of the landscape are unique in their meaning, and this enables personalised thematic results, according to the demands of the user. As a result, the object-oriented approach enables dynamic and extensible classifications to be generated to meet future needs. Furthermore, new types of parameters can be inserted into the database without creating conflicts with previous database versions [28].

Following the example of Fig. 1 and zooming in on the SIOSE and CORINE polygons, we can better see the difference in the wealth of information offered by the SIOSE object-oriented model versus the CORINE LC hierarchical classification model. The CORINE model keeps less information, as can be seen in the examples in Fig. 2. The SIOSE model offers a higher level of detail, describing the type of buildings and the areas occupied within the polygon. The SIOSE database indicates that the area is a *Hotel Zone* with a surface presence of 50% of roads, parking areas, and pedestrian areas, 35% isolated buildings, 10% swimming pools, and 5% gardens, all distributed within the polygon. This thematic richness is lost in the Corine LC polygon as its hierarchical model excludes the variety of information that exists within the polygon's graphical boundary, while the SIOSE object-oriented system preserves the information in the database.

1.3   Opportunities for the SIOSE Database

The SIOSE data model has enabled saving costs and effort in the production of the database, facilitating periodic updates, and the integration of national and international information, as well as increased data detail and a derivation of products for very diverse purposes. The notable benefits of using the object-oriented model also come with certain drawbacks; this model is usually challenging to learn for less experienced users, due to variations from traditional hierarchical classifications that could be considered familiar for users of desktop GIS programmes. Hierarchical data models, such as CORINE LC, reduce the thematic resolution of the data that make the data easier to understand. On the other hand, the object-oriented model usually needs to be adapted to a relational database management system with spatial capabilities, and this forces database managers to address this incompatibility at the conceptual level. This is a case of object-relational impedance mismatch that has been recognised in the literature as a data structure problem due to paradigm differences [18,20]. Another disadvantage generated by the complexity of the system is in the study of land use and land cover changes (LULCC), which must be performed not only in geometry but also in semantics [27]. Problems like these have been addressed in previous studies that pointed out the great value of the data collected by SIOSE, but also the difficulty in handling the database. It is an excellent example of a handy tool that is limited to experts. Several studies highlight the drawbacks of the effort required to use SIOSE LULC in applied research, and these range from climate change [21,25], flood risk mapping [19], farmland abandonment [24], wildfires [4] or purely cartographic studies [16,17].

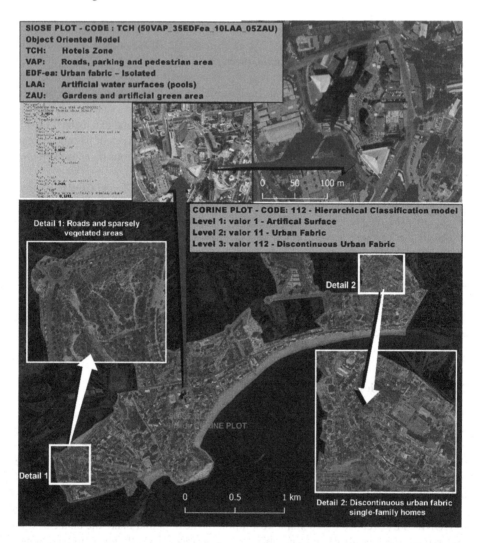

Fig. 2. Detail of same area of Benidorm (SE of Spain). Example of the treatment of the thematic LULC information between Corine LC hierarchical model and SIOSE object-oriented model. Source: Corine LC, SIOSE and aerial orthophotography flight from National Geographic Institute (PNOA) and Google Earth.

The drawbacks mentioned above are mainly related to the lesser ease of use of the information by ordinary users. However, these can be compensated by the great versatility and usefulness of the information contained in the SIOSE database. The versatility of the database is not only related to the information richness, but also with the extensible object-oriented model. Another strength of SIOSE goes beyond the object-oriented data model, and resides in a coordinated and participative production model that integrates data from all interested public administrations. This results in an economy of effort and an increase in the quality of the outputs that earned the 2013 United Nations

Public Service Award. Considering both strengths, it is logical that SIOSE developers are considering how the database could benefit integrating data coming from volunteer geographic information (VGI) projects such as OpenStreetMap (OSM), or how to take advantage of the VGI contributions to better plan the need for updating in different territories. Several studies have addressed different topics regarding VGI and LULC data and have concluded that exciting contributions could come from these synergies [12].

In this scenario, we present the SIOSE-INNOVA project (http://siose-innova. es/) funded by the Spanish Ministry of Economy and Competitiveness. This project addresses the study of these questions: the technical aspects derived from the SIOSE object-oriented data model and the above-mentioned *usability* drawbacks. Within the scope of this project, the main objectives of this research are developed in the following sections. In the next section (Sect. 2), we analyse the ecosystem where SIOSE data are used (i.e. actors, applications, use scenarios, and case studies) in order to accurately define the *usability gap* of the SIOSE database. Once this usability gap is well defined, in Subsect. 2.2, we introduce an extension to the SIOSE data model showing how to integrate new data layers in tailored distributions of SIOSE. Finally, in Subsect. 2.3, we provide an example of the implementation of the extended model. In the last section (Sect. 3), we discuss the benefits of this approach for providing enriched LULC datasets. This proposal has already been addressed at the conceptual level [30]. However, in this work, more explicit examples and implementation details are provided.

2 Extending the SIOSE Data Model

As explained in the previous section, there are several issues related to the SIOSE database model that could be improved. However, proposing changes to an already functioning system is difficult and must be done carefully and at the conceptual level to better understand what such changes may entail. In this section, we follow the complete process of describing the current system, proposing amendments and showing an example of implementation.

2.1 Describing the SIOSE Usability Gap

The concept of usability has been widely used for many years in the field of software and information system design [26]; it is a measure of the quality of a user's experience when interacting with this type of tool. In the SIOSE-INNOVA project, we consider usability as an indicator to determine the ease with which the SIOSE database can be used, but also to refer to the methods that serve to improve usability in the design process. In the end, usability is nothing more than the sum of several factors that control how users interact with a system; among these factors are speed of use, ease of learning, accessibility, navigability, user efficiency, and error rates in use [5].

Usability can also be seen as a characteristic of any system built to be used: (1) by a specific type of user; (2) to perform a series of tasks allowed by the system; and (3) in a specific context in the interaction [5]. It is especially important to describe in detail these three elements in the SIOSE system: the actors; the tasks; and the various contexts.

To better explain how the SIOSE database is used, we are going to use a series of concepts and graphical tools from the field of software engineering that are part of the Unified Modelling Language (UML) [6]. A use case diagram is a graphical tool that shows the different actors (user types or user roles) that interact with the system and what functions or operations can be performed, as well as those tasks or functions that an actor can invoke on it. Systems are called use cases. Additionally, in systems of a specific size, the subsystems that make up the global system are also distinct.

According to the proposed definition of usability and the concepts introduced of *actor* and *use case*, it is possible to identify specific types of users for whom making use of the SIOSE database tends to be more complicated. If we set ourselves the objective of improving the user experience of the different actors who can interact in the system and the various scenarios in which this interaction can occur, we will have to deal with various extensions of the system itself from the design phase. Fortunately, the SIOSE database has been designed following the object-oriented paradigm, and this feature makes its extensibility possible [28]. The SIOSE system consists of three main subsystems or modules, each of which represents one of the phases required for the use of LULC data. Initially, there is the *data production* module, in charge of the initial data capture with which the system is fed. The second module or phase is *data integration*, in which the collected data is incorporated in an organised way into the system for publication. Moreover, we have the *usage* phase, in which the end-users of SIOSE consult and process the data to carry out their analysis and reports. Each of these three modules encompasses the most important tasks or *use cases*. Figure 3 shows the use case diagram of the SIOSE *data integration* module. The elliptical figures represent the different use cases included in this module. Each use case is linked with a continuous line to the actor (user role) who can invoke it in this context.

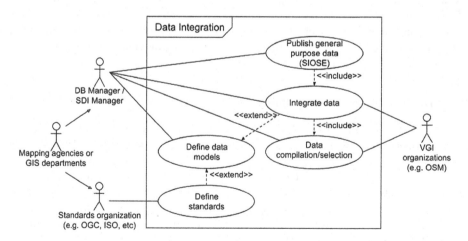

Fig. 3. Sample use case diagram corresponding to the *data integration* module of SIOSE. Adapted from [30].

Among the use cases, it is seen that there are certain types of relationships (dashed arrows) marked with the $<< include >>$ and $<< extend >>$ tags. A relation of type

$<<$ *include* $>>$ means that the use case from which the arrow starts includes in its behaviour the use case to which it points, for example, if the user *VGI organisations* performs the task *integrate data*. This operation must necessarily perform the *data compilation/selection* task. On the other hand, the relation $<<$ *extend* $>>$ indicates that the use case from which the relation starts could be called, although not necessarily, by the use case to which it points. In Fig. 3, the use case *define data models*, if certain conditions were met, could incorporate the functionality of the *define standards* use case.

Finally, in the diagram use case, we can find inheritance relationships between actors, and these are represented by solid arrows that go from one actor to another. In our example in Fig. 3, the actor *mapping agencies or GIS departments* inherits the behaviour of *DB manager/SDI manager* and *standards organisation*, and this means that the first of these three actors can invoke the same tasks or use cases as the other two.

Figure 4 shows the global use case diagram of the SIOSE system, including its three main modules (the three phases for LULC data compilation or management): (1) data production; (2) data integration (sampled in Fig. 3); and (3) usage. In this way, we can identify all the elements of the system and how they are organised. Description of use cases obeys a model that may not be applicable in all cases, but according to our experience and knowledge, this model draws most of the uses that can be made with the SIOSE system, most of which are present in the scientific literature. In the lower-left, the role *GIS producers or contractors* represents the actors that produce the most data for the SIOSE database, which need to make an official request (see Sect. 1) to carry out their tasks. The user *VGI* (bottom right) represents the providers of volunteered information; they are professionals who are encouraged to include in the SIOSE system the data that they collect on the ground (which allows improving the overall quality of the system data). At the other end of the diagram, in the *usage* module, some users want to use SIOSE for specific particular purposes (some having little or no knowledge about managing spatial databases, while others may have some experience in using the SIOSE database).

The diagram in Fig. 4 shows, for each context, the types of user with access to use cases more or less linked to that context. For example, the role of *GIS technician* represents the class of users who might have an interest in processing or transforming data from the SIOSE system to carry out an analysis or mapping, but in general, either due to lack of interest, resources, or sufficient knowledge, it will not be their role to develop new tools. On the other hand, the *non-GIS consultant* role would be that of users who want to report certain information, but who do not have previous knowledge or experience in the use of geospatial data, therefore, to achieve their objective they need the help of an actor with the role *GIS analyst*.

Note that when the database administrator (role *DB manager/SDI manager*) invokes the use case for which the SIOSE data is published, for both the general-purpose (context *data integration*) and the explicitly processed data according to specific requirements (*usage* context), there is no specific user role that provides new tools or facilitates access to these new datasets (e.g. providing predefined equivalence maps and operating environments with custom re-classifications). To represent this peculiarity, the *provide tools* use case has been conceived and is located outside of the three primary SIOSE use contexts. This use case could be invoked both by the *DB manager/SDI manager* role and by an eventual type user name *GIS develops*.

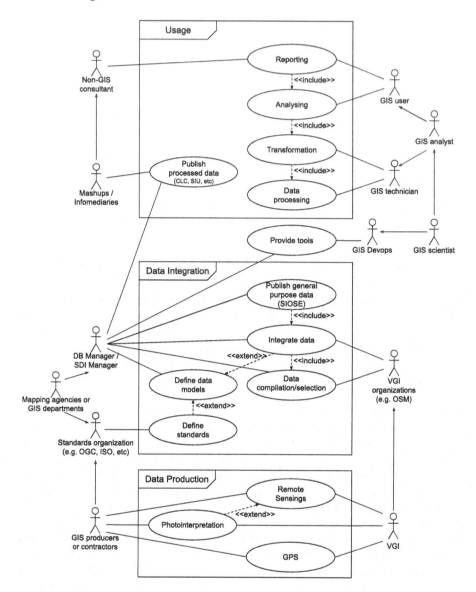

Fig. 4. Use case diagram showing the actors, applications and contexts where the SIOSE is developed [30].

2.2 Proposed Design

As in the previous section, we introduced the use case diagrams to represent the different actors, use cases (tasks), and subsystems that intervene in the SIOSE system, and we are now going to resort to class diagrams to define the internal components of this system. This type of diagram is also part of the UML standard [6] and is very useful when a software system has been designed with the object-oriented paradigm. A class is a form of extended data type (we all have an intuitive idea of what integer data is), integer data can take a specific type of value (e.g. 1, 2, 3) and enables specific operations, (e.g. add, subtract). More specifically, a class is a software component that, in general, can contain one or more properties defined by a series of attributes (values), and it can also have associated a specific behaviour determined by a series of methods that can be invoked (operations). Once a class has been defined, it can be instanced as an *object*. Graphically, a class is represented by one of the shapes shown in Fig. 5.

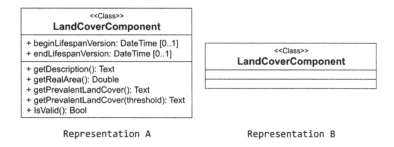

Representation A   Representation B

Fig. 5. LandCoverComponent class representations. Adapted from [30].

In the *A* representation of the *LandCoverComponent* class, its name is indicated in the upper part, its attributes or possible values in the central part, and the methods or operations that define its behaviour in the lower part. Eventually, there may be classes that only have properties but no behaviour and vice versa, and in such a case, the non-existent part (properties or behaviour) would be empty. Additionally, when a problem is well known to its designers, or when certain details are not especially important and can be ignored, a class may be represented without indicating its properties and/or its methods (even if it has them) to simplify the diagram. The presentation *B* of Fig. 5 is an example of how the same class *LandCoverComponent* would be represented, ignoring both its attributes and its methods.

The SIOSE data model, like other similar ones that have been referenced in the introduction, can be represented with an object-oriented design. From these designs, a LULC description can be enriched by adding new elements without affecting previously represented information.

In the class diagram in Fig. 6, we show our proposal for the extensibility of the SIOSE model. The design pattern that handles a group of instances that are the same as a single object of the same class is called a *composite pattern* [15]. The SIOSE data model uses this composite pattern, and the three core classes (*LandCoverComponent*, *LandcoverComposite* and *LandCoverLeaf*) along with their relationships are displayed according to this composite pattern. The *attribute* interface represents the land use portion of each land cover element or unit. Through this interface, the model can be easily extended by adding new attributes to both the *LandCoverUnit* class and the *LandCoverComponent*.

The SIOSE polygon described in Fig. 2 can be used as an example to interpret this class diagram. The area described in Fig. 2 contains LULC information from the

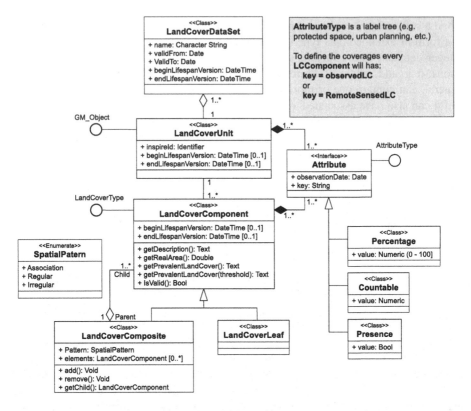

Fig. 6. Class diagram for extending the SIOSE data model [30].

SIOSE-2011 database version, which is the *LandCoverDataSet* of this example. The red polygon can be instantiated as an object of the *LandCoverUnit* class, and this class inherits its properties from a geometry object (*GM_Object*). The surface of this polygon represents a *Hotel zone* land cover composed of 50% of roads, parking areas and pedestrian areas, 35% of isolated buildings, 10% swimming pools, and 5% gardens. The current SIOSE data model already comprises a shortlist of attributes for describing land uses. With our proposal, we can describe the characteristics of the polygon much more precisely. For example, we could explain if there is a single hotel in that area, or if several different hotels coexist (presence). If there are several hotels, we could explain which is the most important (percentage) or, in the case of having a buildings count (e.g. point in polygon), what is its exact number (countable). With our model we do not need the geometry to be necessarily a polygon, we could use, among other options, geometries such as points to indicate the presence of trees, or lines to represent power lines.

Our model differs fundamentally from the current one in that it provides a superior semantic richness of attributes, which until now, depending on the scale of production, have been less critical. We also need this application of the model (or some analogous modification) to incorporate new data from other sources. For example, we could create OpenStreetMap thematic information, or save and distribute a particular re-classification without losing the link to SIOSE.

2.3   Example of Implementation

In this subsection, we show the implementation details of the proposed extended model. They are made by developing the *composite pattern* into a JavaScript object notation (JSON) data structure, which is one of several possibilities for implementing this pattern in a relational database (i.e. through PostgreSQL JSON data type or SQLite's JSON1 extension). In this example, we demonstrate how to integrate the maximum number of building floors – extracted from OSM thematic data – as *numeric attributes* of the SIOSE database (see Fig. 6).

The example in Fig. 7 represents the same area shown in the examples in Sect. 1. This implementation example shows how new attributes could be preprocessed and joined for creating tailored SIOSE distributions for different purposes. In this case, the top heights of the buildings contained by the SIOSE polygon are added, but the number of hotels contained in a SIOSE polygon or other attributes available through OSM data, could also be integrated in the process. These new attributes could be added at different semantic levels inside the composite pattern, even if it is a *LandCoverUnit*, *LandCoverComposite*, or a *LandCoverComponent*. Of course, it seems easier to assign these values at the *LandCoverUnit* level, as they represent a geometry and a *one-to-one* relationship can be established. However, other criteria could be applied for assigning attributes at the thematic level. In this area we find a hotel zone composed of 50% roads, parking areas and pedestrian areas, 35% isolated buildings, 10% swimming pools and 5% gardens, distributed within the polygon. The maximum building height in that area could be assigned to the hotel complex label, or even to the label of the isolated building. In the second case, it is evident that not all the isolated buildings covering 35% of the *LandCoverUnit* are described by the "45 floor" figure, but at least the area estimation would not include the 50% of surfaces covered by roads and parking areas (which would make sense in other scenarios). A more concise example would be applying the number of orange trees to a *LandCoverUnit* of agricultural land, composed of 80% fruit trees and 20% roads. In that case, the purpose of assigning the number of trees to the first *LandCoverComponent* (fruit trees) would be completely clear.

As already pointed out, OpenStreetMap can provide valuable data specially for describing artificial surfaces [12]. Following the first example, we downloaded the OpenStreetMap data set for the area of interest, extracting all the geometries for Benidorm – a Spanish city shaped by tourism (SE Spain) – and spatially joined the number maximum building heights to the SIOSE database as numeric *attributes*. Figure 7 shows how the extended SIOSE model would look when implemented in a JSON data structure. Three options are shown using letters indicating (compatible) alternatives. The new attribute describes: A) the whole polygon; B) *LandCoverComposite*; or C) and a *LandCoverComponent*, in this case, the only land cover referred to any type of buildings. Evidently, these type of assignations require a reclassification strategy specific to the studied area.

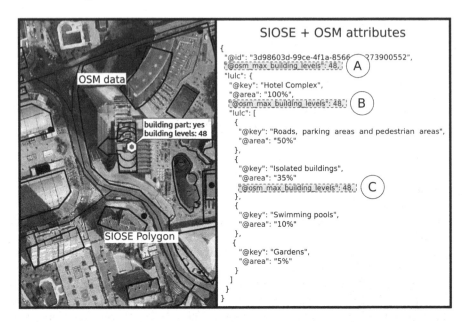

Fig. 7. Example of implementation of the extended SIOSE data model. The image shows a light JSON implementation of the extended model with some possibilities of enriching the SIOSE polygon description at different semantic levels: (A) LandCoverUnit level; (B) LandCoverComposite level; or (C) LandCoverComponent level.

3 Final Thoughts and Future Applications

The CORINE LC database has a greater historical perspective than SIOSE and this factor, together with its relatively higher *usability*, makes it more attractive for many users. The SIOSE is also an indispensable source, with a greater spatial and thematic resolution, and a growing temporal resolution (2005–2017). However, the object-oriented data model means that many users with little training in SQL (or other similar querying tools) prefer to directly use aerial photography when the CORINE LC is unsuitable due to scale problems, or when the areas to be studied are small. Hence, *usability* is an essential factor in determining the preference for a geographic dataset, and it weighs more on the decision of users than the versatility and richness of the information – since neither by scale, nor for information efficiency, does CORINE offer advantages in comparison with SIOSE. It is mandatory to ensure that we provide all the tools for using SIOSE at its full potential, or many sub-products and re-classifications will be necessary.

As explained in Subsect. 2.1, SIOSE presents some usability problems and one way to deal with these could be to offer specific training to these users in the use of this tool as based on their needs. However, this option does not seem practical since it would affect a large number of users and, in a context where most of the official GIS data is already offered in a way that is ready to use for most users, it does not seem necessary. On the other hand, we could address these usability problems by developing novel tools so that less experienced users could obtain useful custom classifications from LULC information. To date, the scientific community has not made much effort to address this line of action. From various perspectives, very few works present a solution – some propose the development of interoperable web services [14], the use of non-conventional databases [20], or the design of ArcGIS extensions to reclassify the LULC information hierarchies [13]. All of these are technical solutions that involve developing a software layer on top of the SIOSE system that would act as an intermediary between the system and the end-user, and allow the latter to bypass the driest parts of the system. A third approach to address the usability problem consists in reinterpreting the SIOSE data model to enable new and more specific information to be added to the database. With this perspective, we have (1): tried to determine what are the primary uses of SIOSE data in a general context; and (2) designed a mechanism that enables us to add new thematic information to the database, or useful re-classifications, so that the community can reuse them. In this work, we have proposed a method to add new information to the SIOSE database without forgetting that different users may have very different needs. The implementation example in the previous section shows how the model enables this and introduces the need for defining the rules for transparently joining new attributes. This model seems a good starting point for developing a tool for interactively defining SIOSE reclassifications and writing new attributes for enriching the SIOSE database. Considering the central importance of LULC data it is natural for the SIOSE to be the frame for integrating geographic data from different sources.

In this work we have introduced a *soft solution* for extending the model, but other possibilities could be assessed that would not imply changes or amendments in the data model. We consider that the modifications on the database model are minimal and would produce several positive effects that would not be achieved otherwise: (1) the users would see the effort required to use SIOSE data better rewarded; and (2) there would be further opportunities in the distribution of geographic information (e.g. distribution of thematic re-classifications of interest in some fields). Most importantly, it would be possible to create and share specific datasets for various purposes (such as regional planning, natural risks, and tourism). This contribution only solves the first part of the usability problem. From this point, new highly usable tools are needed for evaluating the information contained by SIOSE and to help users create tailored queries on an object-oriented database. After proposing this model extension, any new tool for working with this kind of data should follow the same model and definitions, and these tools could also include web services, GIS desktop extensions, and database extensions.

References

1. Anderson, B.J.R., Hardy, E.E., Roach, J.T., Witmer, R.E.: A land use and land cover classi-fication system for use with remote sensor data. Technical report, U.S. Geological Survey, Washington (1976)
2. Antrop, M.: Sustainable landscapes: contradiction, fiction or Utopia? Landscape Urban Plann. **75**(June 2005), 187–197 (2006). https://doi.org/10.1016/j.landurbplan.2005.02.014
3. Arnold, S., Kosztra, B., Banko, G., Smith, G., Hazeu, G., Bock, M.: The EAGLE concept – a vision of a future European land monitoring framework. In: EARSeL Symposium Proceed-ings 2013, Towards Horizon 2020, pp. 551–568 (2013)

4. Badia, A., Pèlachs, A., Vera, A., Tulla, A.F., Soriano, J.M.: Land use and land cover change and the effects on vulnerability to forest fire of counties in the mountains of Catalonia : from managing the land to managing a threat. Pirineos. Revista de Ecología de Montaña **169**, 1–13 (2014). https://doi.org/10.3989/Pirineos.2014.169001

5. Ben Ramadan, A.A., Jackson-Thompson, J., Boren, S.A.: Geographic information systems: usability, perception, and preferences of public health professionals. Online J. Public Health Inf. **9**(2) (2017). https://doi.org/10.5210/ojphi.v9i2.7437

6. Booch, G.: UML in action. Commun. ACM **42**(10), 26–28 (1999)

7. Büttner, G., Feranec, J., Jaffrain, G.: Corine land cover update 2000. Technical report, European Environment Agency, Copenhagen (2002)

8. Commission, E.: Directive 2007/2/EC of the European parliament and of the council of 14 March 2007 establishing an infrastructure for spatial information in the European community (inspire). Official J. European Union **50**, 1–14 (2007)

9. Congedo, L., Sallustio, L., Munafò, M., Ottaviano, M., Tonti, D., Marchetti, M.: Copernicus high-resolution layers for land cover classification in Italy. J. Maps **12**(5), 1195–1205 (2016)

10. Del Bosque González, I., Arozarena Villar, A., Villa Alcázar, G., Valcárcel Sanz, N.: Creación de un Sistema de Información Geográfico de Ocupación del Suelo en España. PROYECTO SIOSE. In: XI Congreso Nacional de Teledetección, pp. 255–262. Universidad de La Laguna, Puerto de la Cruz, Tenerife (2005). http://hdl.handle.net/10261/28697

11. Dymond, J.R., Shepherd, J.D., Newsome, P.F., Gapare, N., Burgess, D.W., Watt, P.: Remote sensing of land-use change for Kyoto protocol reporting: the New Zealand case. Environ. Sci. Policy **16**, 1–8 (2012)

12. Estima, J., Painho, M.: Investigating the potential of openstreetmap for land use/land cover production: a case study for continental Portugal. In: Jokar Arsanjani, J., Zipf, A., Mooney, P., Helbich, M. (eds.) OpenStreetMap in GIScience. LNGC, pp. 273–293. Springer, Cham (2015). https://doi.org/10.1007/978-3-319-14280-7_14

13. Fernández Noguerol, S.: Desarrollo de herramientas para el tratamiento de la información y el análisis con SIG de los usos del suelo utilizando el SIOSE. Una aproximación al caso de Asturias. GeoFocus Revista Internacional de Ciencia y Tecnología de la Información Geográfica **20**(20), 233–251 (2017). https://doi.org/10.21138/GF.573, http://www.geofocus.org/index.php/geofocus/article/view/573/449

14. Fernández Villarino, X., Delgado Hernández, J., Valcárcel Sanz, N., Caballero, M.E., Benito Saz, M.A., Porcuna Fernández-Monasterio, A.: Geoservicios web SIOSE: un sistema de información como servicio público. In: VI Jornadas de SIG Libre. p. 8. Servei de Sistemes d'Informació Geogràfica i Teledetecció (SIGTE). Universitat de Girona, Girona (2012). http://www.sigte.udg.edu/jornadassiglibre2012/uploads/articulos_12/art17.pdf

15. Gamma, E., Helm, R., Johnson, R., Vlissides, J.M.: Design Patterns: Elements of Reusable Object-Oriented Software. Addison-Wesley Professional, Boston, 1 edn. (1994). http://www.amazon.com/Design-Patterns-Elements-Reusable-Object-Oriented/dp/0201633612/ref=ntt_at_ep_dpi_1

16. García-Álvarez, D., Olmedo, M.T.C.: Changes in the methodology used in the production of the Spanish Corine: uncertainty analysis of the new maps. Int. J. Appl. Earth Observ. Geoinf. **63**, 55–67 (2017)

17. García-Álvarez, D., Olmedo, M.T.C., Paegelow, M.: Sensitivity of a common land use cover change (LUCC) model to the minimum mapping unit (MMU) and minimum mapping width (MMW) of input maps. Comput. Environ. Urban Syst. **78**, 101389 (2019)

18. Ireland, C., Bowers, D., Newton, M., Waugh, K.: A classification of object-relational impedance mismatch. In: Proceedings - 2009 1st International Conference on Advances in Databases, Knowledge, and Data Applications, DBKDA 2009, pp. 36–43 (2009). https://doi.org/10.1109/DBKDA.2009.11

19. Morte, A.R., Carrión, J.T.N., Botella, E.G.: Objective assessment of land use in hydrographical studies. WIT Trans. Ecol. Environ. **234**(2019), 41–51 (2019). https://doi.org/10.2495/RBM190051

20. Navarro-Carrión, J.T., Zaragozí, B., Ramón-Morte, A., Valcárcel-Sanz, N.: Should EU land use and land cover data be managed with a NOSQL document store? Int. J. Design Nature Ecodyn. **11**(3), 438–446 (2016). https://doi.org/10.2495/DNE-V11-N3-438-446, http://www.witpress.com/elibrary/dne-volumes/11/3/1215, http://www.witpress.com/doi/journals/DNE-V11-N3-438-446

21. Olaya-Abril, A., Parras-Alcántara, L., Lozano-García, B., Obregón-Romero, R.: Soil organic carbon distribution in Mediterranean areas under a climate change scenario via multiple linear regression analysis. Sci. Total Environ. **592**, 134–143 (2017). https://doi.org/10.1016/j.scitotenv.2017.03.021, http://dx.doi.org/10.1016/j.scitotenv.2017.03.021

22. Olwig, K.R.: The Meanings of Landscape: Essays on Place, Space. Routledge, Environment and Justice (2019)

23. Omrani, H., Abdallah, F., Charif, O., Longford, N.T.: Multi-label class assignment in land-use modelling. Int. J. Geograph. Inf. Sci. **29**, 1023–1041 (2015). https://doi.org/10.1080/13658816.2015.1008004, http://www.tandfonline.com/doi/full/10.1080/13658816.2015.1008004

24. Peña-Angulo, D., Khorchani, M., Errea, P., Lasanta, T., Martínez-Arnáiz, M., Nadal-Romero, E.: Factors explaining the diversity of land cover in abandoned fields in a Mediterranean mountain area. Catena **181**(May), 104064 (2019). https://doi.org/10.1016/j.catena.2019.05.010

25. Ropero, R.F., Rumí, R., Aguilera, P.A.: Bayesian networks for evaluating climate change influence in olive crops in Andalusia. Spain. Nat. Resource Model. **32**(1), 1–18 (2019). https://doi.org/10.1111/nrm.12169

26. Shneiderman, B.: Software Psychology: Human Factors in Computer and Information Systems (Winthrop Computer Systems Series). Winthrop Publishers, Cambridge (1980)

27. Valcarcel, N., Castaño Fernández, S. (eds.): Cartografía de Ocupación del Suelo en España. Proyecto SIOSE. No. May 2014, Centro Nacional de Información Geográfica (CNIG), Madrid (2013). https://doi.org/10.7419/162-6882

28. Valcarcel, N., et al.: SIOSE, a successful test bench towards harmonization and integration of land cover/use information as environmental reference data. In: Remote Sensing and Spatial Information Sciences, Beijing, vol. XXXVII, pp. 1159–1164. (2008). http://www.isprs.org/proceedings/XXXVII/congress/8_pdf/11_WG-VIII-11/28.pdf

29. Villa, G., Valcarcel, N., Caballero, M.E., Porcuna, A., Domenech, E., Peces, J.J.: Land cover classifications: an obsolete paradigm. In: ISPRS Archives, Beijing, vol. XXXVII Part B4, pp. 619–614 (2008)

30. Zaragozí, B., Navarro-Carrión, J., Rodríguez-Sala, J., Trilles, S., Ramón-Morte, A.: Improving the usability of the land cover and use information system of Spain (SIOSE): a proposal to distribute new thematic layers and predefined reclassifications. In: Proceedings of the 6th International Conference on Geographical Information Systems Theory, Applications and Management, pp. 294–301. SCITEPRESS - Science and Technology Publications (2020). https://doi.org/10.5220/0009579502940301, http://www.scitepress.org/DigitalLibrary/Link.aspx?doi=10.5220/0009579502940301

Analysis of Public Transport Mobility Data: A System for Sharing and Reusing GIS Database Queries

Benito Zaragozí[1,2]($\boxtimes$) [iD], Aaron Gutierrez[1,2] [iD], and Sergio Trilles[1,2] [iD]

[1] Departament de Geografia, Universitat Rovira i Virgili,
C/Joanot Martorell, Vilaseca, Spain
`benito.zaragozi@urv.cat`
[2] Institute of New Imaging Technologies, Universitat Jaume I,
Av. Vicente Sos Baynat s/n, Castellón de la Plana, Spain

Abstract. Data from automated fare collection systems have become almost essential in the study of the mobility of people using public transport. Among other advantages, the data collected enable longitudinal studies to be carried out with a detail that other sources cannot approximate. However, despite the great potential of these data, the data collecting systems are usually intended for purely accounting purposes and not for carrying out mobility studies. Largely for this reason, these data are not always used to their full potential, and so it is necessary to propose strategies that allow the preparation and exploitation of these data, especially in those cases where the usefulness and value of the data have not yet been proven. This study proposes a workflow that seeks to prevent duplication of efforts when querying this type of data. The implementation of a generic database model and a protocol for sharing meaningful queries and results greatly facilitates an initial analysis of these data. This strategy has been applied within a specific project, but it could be the basis for sharing methods between different studies.

Keywords: Public transportation · Automated fare collection system · Smart card data · Domain-specific language · File naming convention

1 Introduction

In recent decades, automated fare collection systems (AFCSs) around the world have been generating vast amounts of data. In many cities and metropolitan

Research funded by the Spanish Ministerio de Ciencia e Innovación [grant number CSO2017-82156-R], the AEI/FEDER,UE, the Departament d'Innovació, Universitats i Empresa, Generalitat de Catalunya [grant number 2017SGR22] and the Escola d'Administració Publica de Catalunya, Generalitat de Catalunya [grant number 2018 EAPC 00002]. Sergio Trilles has been funded by the Juan de la Cierva - postdoctoral programme of the Ministry of Science and Innovation - Spanish Government (IJC2018-035017-I).

© Springer Nature Switzerland AG 2021
C. Grueau et al. (Eds.): GISTAM 2020, CCIS 1411, pp. 102–118, 2021.
https://doi.org/10.1007/978-3-030-76374-9_7

regions, the public use smart transport cards or similar technologies each time they board public transport (bus, train, or metro) and the AFCS collects data from its validation. The main aim is for accounting purposes, and so the data is not organised for analysis, nor are there specific tools for exploring the data to its full potential. Despite not being its main purpose, these data have been analysed to create relevant knowledge for understanding the behaviour of users and generating better quality services [15]. These types of analysis are widespread in the scientific literature [2,20]. Some works use smart transport card validations to achieve huge flexibility for studying any temporal and geographical aspect [19]. An example is the use of smart travel card data to detect different profiles of public transport users [18], build origin-destination matrices [1], and investigate user mobility patterns [17].

Many authors agree on the opportunities that smart travel card data provide for transport and mobility studies [15,20]. However, these data are challenging to handle and costly to analyse. Smart transport cards gather all transactions, and so the size of data may become huge after a relatively short period. The managers of public transport systems in large cities or regions may have the resources and the will to analyse such data to obtain some value. However, in regions or cities with fewer resources, analysing this data may not be a priority, especially if the value of analysing the data has yet to be demonstrated. In these cases, collaboration between public transport authorities and mobility research groups in universities has become an interesting strategy to start analysing data from AFCSs [25].

There are no standard solutions for analysing data from an AFCS. During the last decade, many research works have applied differing technologies or approaches to analyse different amounts of data generated by an AFCS. For example, the authors in [21] used *big data* technologies to analyse 160 million records from the Jakarta's Bus Rapid Transit in Indonesia, and another study analysed nearly 200 GB of data logs from the AFCS in the city of Montevideo in Uruguay [7]. Other studies were more focused on real-time analysis and developed tailored solutions such as the data mining frameworks for bus service management [3]. Some studies did not need to analyse such volumes of data and used better-known software for working (e.g. MS Excel, SPSS, QGIS, Rstudio) [8,9]. Finally, there are examples of other studies that did not indicate the use of any specific technology to perform the analysis [22]. Among this diversity of options, it can be highlighted that SQL databases are widely used to analyse this data, alone or in combination with other tools. In a recent systematic literature review, seven out of nine of the documents that reported the tools chosen for the analysis of smart travel card data used an SQL database [16].

1.1   A Collaboration for Analysing Data from an AFCS

This research work is the result of a research project carried out jointly by a research group at the Universitat Rovira i Virgili (Tarragona, Spain) and the Territorial Mobility Authority of the Camp de Tarragona (ATMCdT, according to its acronym in Catalan). The ATMCdT has been running an AFCS for more than ten years, while serving an area of 2,998 km^2 and a population of 626,277 residents [14]. The area includes 132 municipalities and 457 interurban bus stops. Figure 1 shows how the population is unequally distributed over the study area. This region is shaped by coastal tourism, which further increases the pressure on public services in the largest cities and municipalities where tourism plays a prominent role. This drives an unbalanced public transport demand, especially during the summer season.

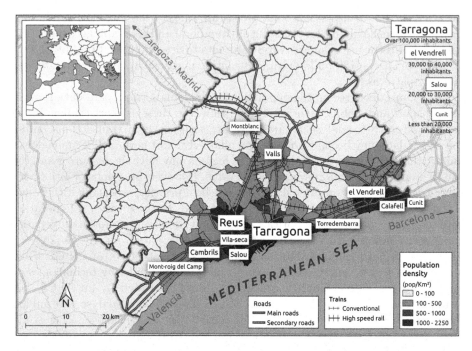

Fig. 1. Reference map and context of the Territorial Mobility Authority of Camp de Tarragona (ATMCdT) service area.

During the last decade, ATMCdT has been using the data from its AFCS for creating reports for different needs (such as network planning, accounting, and management of public grants). These tasks are performed through tailored queries directly exploding the raw data logs. In this way, the fundamental purpose of the data collected by the AFCS is fulfilled. More recently, in 2017 the collaboration mentioned above started several studies for analysing the effectiveness and spatial coverage of the public transport system [5], and the use of public transport by tourists [6,11,12]. A subsequent study has found evidence of the different patterns of public transport use by tourists in the summer [10]. These studies also demonstrated that smart card data collected by the ATMCdT has much to offer.

Together with the wide variety of technical options discussed above, the design of a well-defined workflow and the choice of flexible free and open software tools can make the initial exploitation of this data less expensive and avoid duplicating efforts [27]. However, although the studies mentioned in the previous paragraph faced data management problems, documenting these problems was far from their main goals, and so data preparation was not documented in detail.

In an initial effort to document the management and analysis of these data, a system was proposed to uniquely name the AFCS data queries. This system enables the creation of a repository to store the code together with the results, thereby facilitating collaboration within the same research team and opening the possibility of contributing to a public repository where these methods can be shared [26]. Figure 2 shows a diagram that describes the communication between the different roles of the team, the encapsulated access to a structured database, and the need for a results repository containing spreadsheets or geographic information system (GIS) files with specific and descriptive names. The main advantages of this approach are that nobody need repeat the same query and the database manager will hold a useful base of code for building new queries [26].

1.2 Objectives

As mentioned above, the duplication – or multiplication – of efforts and the strategy adopted to tackle this was first described in [26]. However, this work describes the proposed framework (database schema and naming convention) and provides more detailed examples in which the advantages of sharing methods and SQL queries become more evident.

The main aim of this work is to offer the lessons learned in this project when the data from an AFCS was analysed for the first time. To achieve this, this chapter develops the following objectives:

1. Study the data gathered by the ATMCdT and design a simple but adequate GIS database model. This model includes only the most basic mobility data that could be collected by any AFCS.
2. Propose a domain-specific language (DSL) to be used as a file naming convention that enhances code reuse and time saving. This should allow the description of the largest possible number of queries of this domain.
3. Extend a previous mobility grammar presented in [26] to add the capability to store GIS results.
4. Apply and evaluate the proposed strategy, showing detailed examples that demonstrate the value of code sharing in this area.

This chapter is organised as follows. The next section describes the proposed framework, which includes a logical database model and a naming convention for unambiguously storing the database queries. Section 3 shows how the framework can be used to store database queries and reuse them to avoid duplicating efforts. Three compelling examples are described. Finally, Sect. 4 presents some concluding remarks and indicates issues that will be addressed in future works.

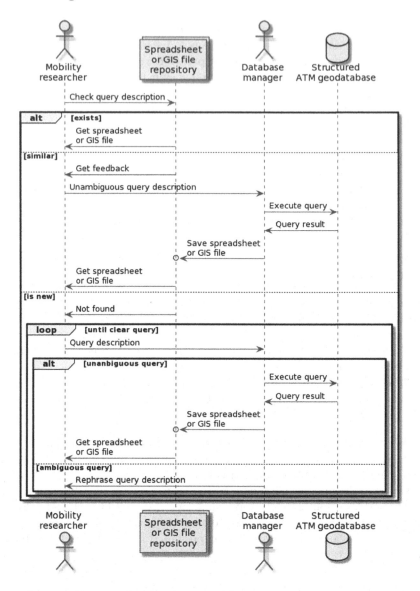

Fig. 2. Sequence diagram showing the proposed workflow. The spreadsheet or GIS file repository works on the basis of a file naming convention. Adapted from [26].

2   Proposed Framework

2.1   GIS Database Schema

The analysis of the ATMCdT data logs reveals some heterogeneity in the structure and attributes that are meaningless for research purposes. Avoiding this complexity is essential so that the different analyses can be reproducible and extrapolated to other similar projects. This can be achieved by adding an abstraction layer for querying the data more quickly, and this can be done by using a common data model. Depending on the type of bus tickets, the data collected by the ATMCdT includes between 22 and 60 different attributes (columns). Many of these attributes are of no interest for analysing mobility patterns but, as said before, they fulfil an accounting purpose. Considering the needs of the project, only a few attributes are beneficial for analysing mobility patterns and user profiles in the region: the exact day and time of travel; the id of the stop where the passenger boarded; the company and carrier that operate the transport; the municipality; and the type of fare used in each transaction. The destination stop can sometimes also be registered. The main advantage of these data is that the information has a spatio-temporal dimension, and it enables us to perform cross-sectional studies as well as longitudinal analysis [10]. These databases do not store much data on the socio-economic profile of travellers, and these data cannot be used due to legal constraints.

The design of the database is quite generic and is given by the characteristics of the raw data collected by the ATMCdT (see Fig. 3). This model does not include other transactions that are also systematically recorded (such as card sales, recharges, or cancellations). For clarity, the tables were named following the main elements of the general traffic feed specification (GTFS) and the columns were named predictably. The level of specificity of this model enables collecting the most basic information for analysing the mobility of users. This information is presumably available in all AFCSs, and it would take a relatively simple extract-transform-load (ETL) process to structure the data in this way. Figure 3 shows that, in addition to the ATMCdT data, the database was enriched with some layers of geographical information (such as municipalities, roads, shoreline, population, and land uses). The stop locations and routes were manually geolocated and digitised. However, in a geospatial database, there is room for increasing the list of support data layers by applying spatial join operations.

2.2 *MobilityFNC* Definition

One of the most significant difficulties detected in the proposed workflow (Fig. 2) is the query definition process between the mobility researcher and the database administrator. The lack of a common language can cause loss of information and context, which increases the probability of needing more iterations before obtaining the desired query. An approach to resolve this problem is to define a domain-specific language (DSL) for this type of application need. A DSL is considered a programming language and defines a set of notations and abstractions to cover a particular problem domain [23]. The main advantage of designing and using a DSL is that they offer more significant optimisation and adaptation to the particular domain and systematic reuse [4,23]. DSLs have been used previously in different application domains (HTML, Unix shell scripts, and GraphViz are widely used examples). A DSL does not always fit a specific application domain. For example, SQL is recognised as a DSL for managing databases, but it remains a very general and comprehensive language [13].

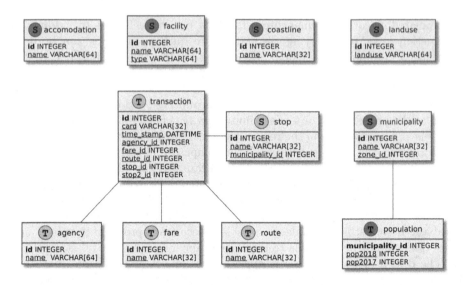

Fig. 3. Entity-relationship data model derived from the ATMCdT smart card log data. The diagram distinguishes between regular attribute tables (*T*), spatial tables (*S*) and the colours indicate if the data comes from ATMCdT (red) or an external source (orange). Based on [26]. (Color figure online)

In this work, the previous mobility file naming convention (*MobilityFNC*) introduced in [26] is expanded. *MobilityFNC* is used as a convention to represent and define queries accurately. The main objective is to improve the communication between the two most important roles: mobility researcher and database manager. This DSL specifies a structured and understandable method for mobility specialists to make a database query without any previous experience in database languages. *MobilityFNC* is used for encoding the name files of the SQL scripts. A mobility researcher who uses this DSL can immediately recognise if the query has been made previously or if there is a similar query with useful code to create a new one. Although *MobilityFNC* can be extended to several kinds of public mobility, such as cars, trains, or planes, based on the ATMCdT scenario, *MobilityFNC* has been applied to public bus mobility. In the same way as SQL, *MobilityFNC* is used to represent the *shape* and main parts of a query result. Thus, the main intention is to maximise its compatibility and improve this proposal so that it can be translated into valid SQL, at least for a previously known database model (like the model shown in Fig. 3).

The query definition and results are stored in two different files and both files are named using this DSL. In this way, the query definition and query result guarantee consistency – the SQL query defined by the database experts and the results file – are inseparable. This repository should be checked before developing a new query.

Figure 2 presents the workflow enhanced by using *MobilityFNC*. The largest difference compared to the version presented in [26] is the option to return and store the results as GIS files. *MobilityFNC* can act as a queries repository and joins SQL scripts and results following a filename nomenclature. Figure 2 shows these three situations: 1) the query exists when a query description was previously encoded, a mobility expert can obtain the results without any other procedure; 2) a similar query exists if the query to encode is similar to another other previously executed, the database manager can adapt it and obtain the results; and 3) in other cases (when similar queries do not exist) the database specialist follows the query description encoded using *MobilityFNC* and creates and executes the SQL query and both files are incorporated into the catalogue.

Lexicon. As previously described, a *MobilityFNC* expression is used to encode file names that store SQL queries or their corresponding results. In this way, filenames present restrictions based on the operating system. For example, depending on the operating system, some of these characters are not permitted for naming files: *NULL*, \, /, :, %, ?, *, ", <, > or |. In compliance with these conditions, *MobilityFNC* does not admit any of these characters. Following the same logic, another restriction imposes a limit of 255 characters per query description, and so the DSL avoids redundancies. Based on these character limitations, the list of possible operators is as follows:

- Principal blocks (source, filter, dimension and operations) are separated using the "+" symbol.
- A new component at the same level is added using the "−" symbol
- A new level and add a component is started using the "_" symbol
- Rows and columns are separated using the "~" symbol
- A range in the canonical form is defined using the "[␣]" symbol
- A function or method are established using the "{␣}" symbol
- An array of variables are defined using the "[␣,␣]" symbol

In addition to this set of operators, there is a collection of restricted terms to encode queries. Six different classes with an assortment of reserved words are defined as a word-list to formulate queries (see Table 1).

Syntax and Semantics. Once the structure and terms of the DSL are defined, Grammar 1 shows how these elements are combined. This grammar is described using the extended Backus-Naur notation [24] and is also summarised in a more visual manner in Fig. 4.

The query definition following this DSL is composed of five blocks that are chained using sum symbols when they describe the structure and contents of the query result or a dot preceding the output file extension. The first block specifies the source(s) of interest to query. In the ATMCdT case, only two different sources are considered: *ATM cards* and *TP single-ride tickets*. The second block contains the filters to apply. There are different kinds of filters, the most important being those used to filter the data by date, time, fare type, or some spatial filters (depending on the spatial layers included in the scenario). In the third block,

Table 1. List of *MobilityFNC* terms adapted from the ATMCdT case study.

Category	Terms
Aggregation	Operations used to calculate (e.g. count, diff, totals, subtotals, top.N or htotal)
Attributes	Attributes listed in the ER model (Fig. 3)
Boolean	Any boolean operator defined over the attribute (e.g. pop.over, pop.less, pop.between, pop.equal or applied to other associated attributes)
Ranges	The -*ly* termination referred to a known ranging (e.g. monthly, yearly, etc.), or predefined ones (e.g. summerly or nonsummerly)
Sources	ATM smart cards and TP (single tickets)
Spatial	*coastal, municipality, land use*, but it could be extended adding more spatial layers

the dimensions of the query result are defined (rows and columns) including attributes of the tables or derived aggregates. The fourth block includes the aggregation operations performed to achieve the resulting table. The final part of the syntax is the extension of the desired output data format. Until now, only two extensions have been used for storing the query results: **.csv* when the result is a regular table and **.geocsv* when the result contains a spatial column. However, any other extension compatible with this logic could be applied (such as: xlsx, json, geojson, shp, and gpkg).

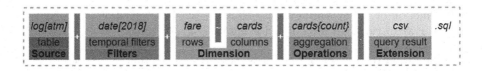

Fig. 4. Example of a query filename encoded with *MobilityFNC*.

A Workflow for Using *MobilityFNC*. As noted earlier, *MobilityFNC* can be applied in different mobility scenarios. In this research work, the DSL is a bridge that enables semi-automating the process for creating new queries. Figure 5 shows an activity diagram that complements the previous sequence diagram (see Fig. 2). This activity diagram shows the whole workflow and includes the management of the code (SQL queries), and the repository of results (spreadsheets and GIS files). The activity diagram shows three different roles. The roles of the two researchers (mobility and database manager) have very specific activities: coding filenames using *MobilityFNC* and writing SQL queries respectively; while the repository holds the updated results. This task is automated using a GNU Make program (Makefile). In this workflow, for each query executed on the

Grammar 1. *MobilityFNC* grammar described using the extended Backus-Naur notation [24].

$Filenane ::= Source\_list,"+",[(Filters,"+")], Dimension, [("+", Operations\_list)], Extension$

$Source\_list ::= "log[", Sources, "]"$
$Sources ::= source | (source, ",", source)$

$Filters ::= Filter | (Filter, "-", Filter)$
$Filter \qquad ::= \qquad ("date[", TempCardTypes, "]") | ("cards[", TempCardTypes, "]") |$
$("municipality[", DemSpatial, "]")$
$TempCardTypes ::= ranges | (ranges, ",", ranges)$
$DemSpatial ::= DemSpatialType | (DemSpatialType, ",", DemSpatialType)$
$DemSpatialType ::= (spatial) | (boolean)$

$Dimension ::= Rows, " ", Colums$
$Rows ::= (Row, "-", Row) | Row$
$Row ::= (ComponentType, "[", atributeFeature, "]") | ComponentType | Filter$
$Columns ::= (Column, "-", Column) | Column$
$Column ::= (ComponentType, "[", atributeFeature, "]") | ComponentType | Filter$
$ComponentType ::= attribute | aggregation$

$Operations\_list ::= attribute, "\{", Operations, "\}"$
$Operations ::= aggregation | (aggregation, ",", aggregation)$

$Extension ::= [(ExtensionStoreFile)]".sql"$
$ExtensionStoreFile ::= ".csv" | ".geocsv"$

database, the system automatically creates the corresponding results file, which simplifies the work of the researchers. The central line that corresponds to the outputs repository encompasses all the tasks that can be easily automated (for example, similarity searches and saving or exporting files). Other tasks such as writing the SQL from a textual query are more complex.

3 Writing, Naming, and Sharing SQL Queries

The *MobilityFNC* language has been widely used throughout the project defined in Sect. 1. Currently, more than 56 queries have been created to analyse various metrics across the bus transport system in the context of a previous research [10]. In this subsection, three different queries are shown and followed for the proposed workflow. These queries provide the answers to various research questions by aggregating data and providing spatial context when necessary.

3.1 Do Tourists Prefer a Type of Fare?

A first simple example of a *MobilityFNC* query asks about which fares are most used by tourists. More specifically, the query counts the ATMCdT smart cards that were only used in the summer of 2018 (grouped by fare). These cards were active in 2018, and their activity was concentrated in a three-month period. When considering the specifics of each fare type, only the T-10 card (multi-personal, 10 to 30 transactions, and no expiry date) seems to be the right choice

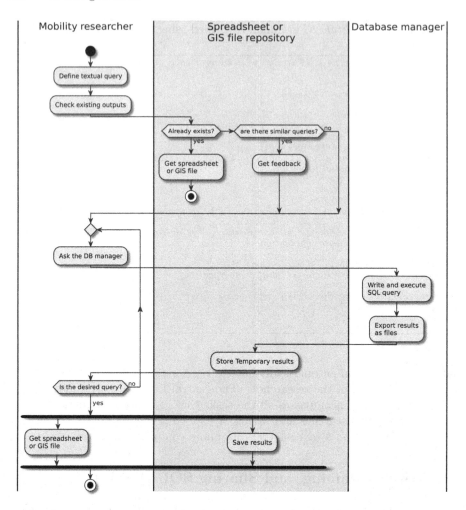

Fig. 5. Activity diagram showing a workflow. *MobilityFNC* is used when the user checks if the query exists and when the results are saved in the repository.

for short stay tourists. There are other fares that are used only in summer, but those fares are intended for longer activity periods and have a higher unitary price per trip. This simple statistic could be interesting for proposing optimisation measures and policies (i.e. better information campaigns). In addition, this query can be used to start a study about those journeys that are concentrated in the summer season. From top to bottom, Fig. 6 shows the different stages of the workflow: (1) the query requested by a mobility researcher; (2) the filename structured according to the *MobilityFNC*; (3) its SQL definition based on the proposed database schema; and (4) the associated query result as a table (*.csv).

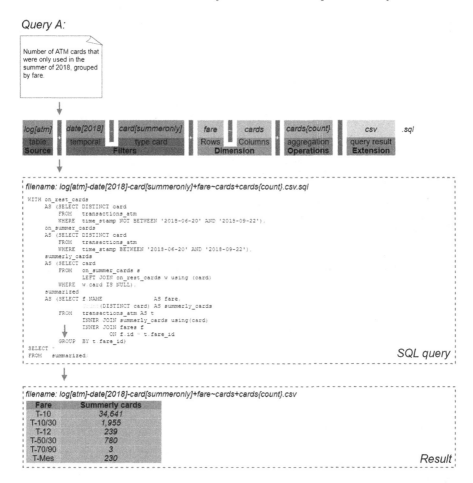

Fig. 6. Example of a query filename encoded with *MobilityFNC*.

3.2   Sale of Single-Trip Tickets in the Most Touristic Cities

A second more complex example is establishing in which period the single-ride tickets are most used in the most touristic cities during one year. The query counts the number of TP transactions (single-trip tickets) that were used in 2018, distinguishing if they took place in summer or during the rest of the year, and only in the most touristic municipalities of the study area (Cambrils, Tarragona, Salou, Reus, and Vila-Seca). The query result shows that the number of tickets sold is more stable in the larger cities (Tarragona and Reus) than in the other three touristic destinations (Cambrils, Salou, and Vila-seca). In these three municipalities, the number of tickets sold in the summer season exceeds those sold in the other nine months of the year. Furthermore, the number of single-trip tickets sold in medium-sized cities such as Cambrils or Salou is similar to or exceeds the number of tickets sold in Tarragona, which is almost four times

Query B:

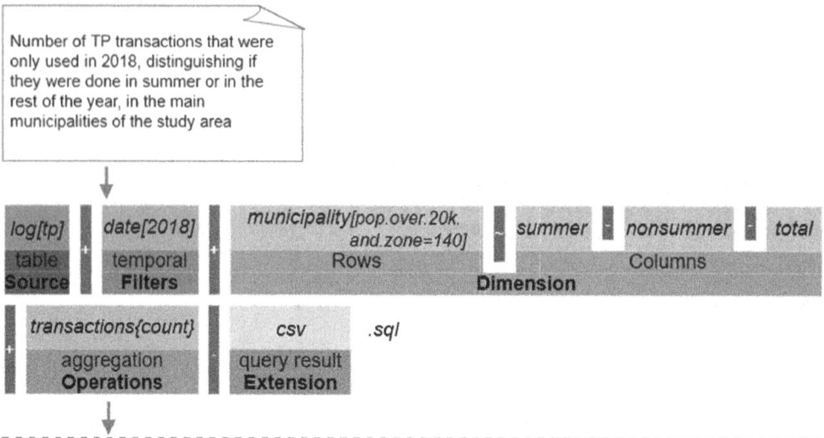

Number of TP transactions that were
only used in 2018, distinguishing if
they were done in summer or in the
rest of the year, in the main
municipalities of the study area

log[tp]	date[2018]	municipality[pop.over.20k. and.zone=140]	summer	nonsummer	total
table	temporal	Rows		Columns	
Source	**Filters**		**Dimension**		

transactions{count}	csv	.sql
aggregation	query result	
Operations	**Extension**	

filename: log[tp]-date[2018]+municipality[pop.over.20k.and.zone=140]~summer-nonsummer-total
+transactions{count}.csv.sql

```
WITH summarized
     AS (SELECT m.NAME      AS municipality,
                Count(CASE
                        WHEN ( time_stamp BETWEEN '2018-06-21' AND '2018-09-23' ) THEN 1
                      END) AS summer_total,
                Count(CASE
                        WHEN ( time_stamp NOT BETWEEN '2018-06-21' AND '2018-09-23' ) THEN 1
                      END) AS non_summer_total,
                Count(t.id) AS total_count
         FROM   transactions_tp t
         INNER JOIN fares f
                ON t.fare_id = f.id
         INNER JOIN stops s
                ON t.stop_id = s.id
         INNER JOIN municipalities m
                ON s.municipality_id = m.id
         WHERE  m.pop_2018 > 20000
         AND zone_id = 140
         GROUP  BY municipality_id
         ORDER  BY total_count DESC)
SELECT *
FROM   summarized;
```

SQL query

filename: log[tp]-date[2018]+municipality[pop.over.20k.and.zone=140]~summer-nonsummer-total
+transactions{count}.csv

Municipality	Summer	Nonsummer	Total
Cambrils	322,533	257,645	580,178
Tarragona	193,190	373,845	567,035
Salou	304,237	211,504	515,741
Reus	93,732	186,581	280,313
Vila-seca	118,042	74,013	192,055

Result

Fig. 7. Example of a query filename with a partial filter, encoded with *MobilityFNC*.

larger than these others. These figures help to explain the high level of pressure
that tourism exerts on public services in the area.

The structure of Fig. 7 is the same as in the previous example, showing how
the query is computed and the resulting table. In this case, Boolean filters are

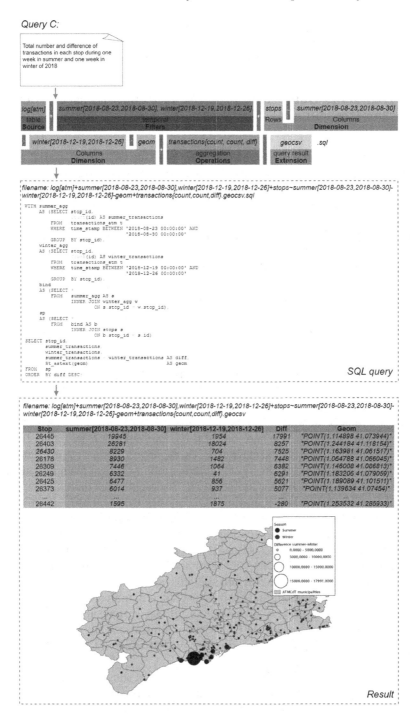

Fig. 8. Example of a query filename with a geospatial output, encoded with *MobilityFNC*.

used in the *dimension block* to avoid redundancy as municipality could also appear in the *filters block*. In this query, a list of totals is calculated to obtain the final count of single-ride transactions per city.

3.3   What is the Difference in the Use of Public Transport Between a Summer and a Winter Week?

This final query differs from the previous examples in that it takes advantage of the previously described feature of providing a result with a geospatial component as output (Fig. 8). A more specific temporal filter is also applied.

This query establishes a comparison to establish the spatial distribution of the greatest pressures on the public transport network, and for this task, only two representative weeks of each season are compared: a summer week and a winter week. In this way, it is possible to discern which stops are most stressed during the tourist period and which are also used throughout the year. As a result of this query, in addition to the columns with the number of transactions in each week and the difference between them, a column is included with the point geometry for each stop. This result is stored in a GeoCSV file, and can be easily uploaded for analysis or visualisation using geospatial data processing tools such as QGIS, gvSIG and R.

4   Concluding Remarks and Future Work

In this chapter, a solution to define and store SQL queries in a multidisciplinary research group is presented. The solution consists of a DSL acting as a file naming convention that strives to normalise the communication workflow between researchers in a project analysing public transportation smart card data. The *MobilityFNC* DSL supports the most common mobility concepts and it can apply temporal and geospatial filters. *MobitityFNC* is designed for mobility experts to be useful in the process of generating SQL queries by database administrators or developers. The SQL query is stored as content in the same file.

A remarkable aspect is the capability to support geospatial outputs in *MobitityFNC* by adding geometries such as point, line, or polygon. This feature can be useful to analyse and visualise the results using GIS software. Currently, this approach has been used in a real project [10], and more than 50 queries have been written, clearly named, and stored without any management issues.

This solution could serve as a bridge to start easily analysing data from other transport consortia and other AFCS, without limitations imposed by software or available resources. The proposed query repository could be publicly shared and the methods reused.

The proposed workflow still needs improvement on some important issues: (1) it is necessary to perform some validation in other projects, including projects studying different types of transport; (2) *MobitityFNC* needs to be used by different multidisciplinary research teams to obtain qualitative and quantitative results as feedback. This implies creating a public code repository for sharing the

SQL queries and checking for inconsistencies; (3) and finally, a future improvement would be the development of the capability to automatically generate SQL queries from the *MobilityFNC* format.

References

1. Alsger, A.A., Mesbah, M., Ferreira, L., Safi, H.: Use of smart card fare data to estimate public transport origin – Destination matrix. Transp. Res. Rec. J. Transp. Res. Board **2535**(1), 88–96 (2015). https://doi.org/10.3141/2535-10
2. Bagchi, M., White, P.R.: The potential of public transport smart card data. Transport Policy **12**, 464–474 (2005). https://doi.org/10.1016/j.tranpol.2005.06.008
3. Barth, R.S., Galante, R.: Passenger density and flow analysis and city zones and bus stops classification for public bus service management. In: SBBD, pp. 217–222 (2016)
4. Deursen, A.V., Klint, P.: Little languages: little maintenance? J. Softw. Maintenance Res. Practice **10**(2), 75–92 (1998)
5. Domènech, A., Gutiérrez, A.: A GIS-based evaluation of the effectiveness and spatial coverage of public transport networks in tourist destinations. ISPRS Int. J. Geo-Inf. **6**(3), 83 (2017). https://doi.org/10.3390/ijgi6030083, http://www.mdpi.com/2220-9964/6/3/83
6. Domènech, A., Miravet, D., Gutiérrez, A.: Mining bus travel card data for analysing mobilities in tourist regions. J. Maps **16**(1), 40–49 (2020). https://doi.org/10.1080/17445647.2019.1709578
7. Fabbiani, E., Vidal, P., Massobrio, R., Nesmachnow, S.: Distributed big data analysis for mobility estimation in intelligent transportation systems. In: Barrios Hernández, C.J., Gitler, I., Klapp, J. (eds.) CARLA 2016. CCIS, vol. 697, pp. 146–160. Springer, Cham (2017). https://doi.org/10.1007/978-3-319-57972-6_11
8. Gokasar, I., Simsek, K.: Using "big data" for analysis and improvement of public transportation systems in istanbul. In: Ase Bigdata/Socialcom/Cybersecurity Conference, Stanford University, 27–31 May 2014. Academy of Science and Engineering (ASE), ASE 2014 (2014)
9. Gokasar, I., Simsek, K., Ozbay, K.: Using big data of automated fare collection system for analysis and improvement of BRT-bus rapid transit line in Istanbul. In: 94th Annual Meeting of the Transportation Research Board, Washington, DC (2015)
10. Gutiérrez, A., Domènech, A., Zaragozí, B., Miravet, D.: Profiling tourists' use of public transport through smart travel card data. J. Transp. Geogr. **88**, 102820 (2020)
11. Gutiérrez, A., Miravet, D.: Estacionalidad turística y dinámicas metropolitanas: un análisis a partir de la movilidad en transporte público en el Camp de Tarragona. Revista de geografía Norte Grande **89**(65), 65–89 (2016). https://doi.org/10.4067/s0718-34022016000300004
12. Gutiérrez, A., Miravet, D.: The determinants of tourist use of public transport at the destination. Sustainability (Switzerland) **8**(9), 1–16 (2016). https://doi.org/10.3390/su8090908
13. Hudak, P.: Domain-specific languages. Handb. Program. Lang. **3**(39–60), 21 (1997)
14. Idescat: Institut d'estadística de catalunya. Web de l'estadística oficial de Catalunya (2019)

15. Kurauchi, F., Schmöcker, J.D. (eds.): Public Transport Planning with Smart Card Data. CRC Press, 1 edn. (2017). https://doi.org/10.1201/9781315370408, https://www.taylorfrancis.com/books/9781498726597

16. Li, T., Sun, D., Jing, P., Yang, K.: Smart card data mining of public transport destination: a literature review. Information 9(1), 18 (2018)

17. Lu, Y., Mateo-Babiano, I., Sorupia, E.: Who uses smart card? Understanding public transport payment preference in developing contexts, a case study of Manila's LRT-1. IATSS Res. 43(1), 60–68 (2019). https://doi.org/10.1016/j.iatssr.2018.09.001

18. Ma, X., Wu, Y.J., Wang, Y., Chen, F., Liu, J.: Mining smart card data for transit riders' travel patterns. Transp. Res. Part C 36, 1–12 (2013). https://doi.org/10.1016/j.trc.2013.07.010

19. Morency, C., Trépanier, M., Agard, B.: Measuring transit use variability with smart-card data. Transport Policy 14(3), 193–203 (2007). https://doi.org/10.1016/j.tranpol.2007.01.001

20. Pelletier, M.P., Trépanier, M., Morency, C.: Smart card data use in public transit: a literature review. Transp. Res. Part C Emerg. Technol. 19(4), 557–568 (2011). https://doi.org/10.1016/j.trc.2010.12.003

21. Prakasa, B., Putra, D.W., Kusumawardani, S.S., Widhiyanto, B.T.Y., Habibie, F., et al.: Big data analytic for estimation of origin-destination matrix in bus rapid transit system. In: 2017 3rd International Conference on Science and Technology-Computer (ICST), pp. 165–170. IEEE (2017)

22. Tao, S., Corcoran, J., Mateo-Babiano, I., Rohde, D.: Exploring BRT passenger travel behaviour using big data. Appl. Geogr. 53, 90–104 (2014)

23. Van Deursen, A., Klint, P., Visser, J.: Domain-specific languages: an annotated bibliography. ACM SIGPLAN Notices 35(6), 26–36 (2000)

24. Wirth, N.: Extended backus-naur form (EBNF). ISO/IEC 14977(2996), 2–21 (1996)

25. Wu, H., Tan, J.A., Ng, W.S., Xue, M., Chen, W.: Ftt: a system for finding and tracking tourists in public transport services. In: Proceedings of the 2015 ACM SIGMOD International Conference on Management of Data, pp. 1093–1098. ACM (2015)

26. Zaragozí, B., Gutiérrez, A., Trilles, S.: Towards an affordable GIS for analysing public transport mobility data: a preliminary file naming convention for avoiding duplication of efforts. In: Proceedings of the 6th International Conference on Geographical Information Systems Theory, Applications and Management, pp. 302–309. SCITEPRESS - Science and Technology Publications (2020). https://doi.org/10.5220/0009766303020309, http://www.scitepress.org/DigitalLibrary/Link.aspx?doi=10.5220/0009766303020309

27. Zaragozí, B.M., Trilles, S., Navarro-Carrión, J.T.: Leveraging container technologies in a giscience project: a perspective from open reproducible research. ISPRS Int. J. Geo-Inf. 9(3) (2020). https://doi.org/10.3390/ijgi9030138

Geolocation Inference Using Twitter Data: A Case Study of COVID-19 in the Contiguous United States

Bingnan Li$^{(\boxtimes)}$ ⓘ, Zi Chen ⓘ, and Samsung Lim ⓘ

University of New South Wales, Sydney, NSW 2052, Australia
{Bingnan.li,zi.chen1,s.lim}@unsw.edu.au

Abstract. Under the quarantine for the coronavirus disease 2019 (COVID-19) which has been spreading rapidly across the world since it was first identified in Wuhan City, China, in early December 2019, people are sharing their everyday life via social media more than ever before. Over the last decade, event-related information has been increasingly generated from Twitter by the growing popularity, and it is proved that the emergence and evolvement of events can be timely monitored and analyzed on the basis of this platform. Geographic information plays a crucial role in mining social media data, however, only about 2% of tweets hold accurate geographic information due to the operational complexity and privacy concerns. To overcome the geo-tagging restriction, finding effective geolocation inference methods is currently one of the main topics in this research field. Geographic information plays an important role in analyzing and monitoring the spread of an epidemic disease. In this study, we constructed a method of geolocation inference based on the whole potential location-related metadata of tweets. A crude form of geographic coordinate information can be obtained from every tweet's bounding box, while location-related information can be mined from the textual content, user location and place labels via Named Entity Recognition (NER) techniques. Three coordinate datasets of the United States counties are built and used as the coordinate references. Models with different data sources have been employed to predict the geolocations of the tweets related to COVID-19 in the contiguous United States. Results show that the models with four data sources, namely textual content, user location, place labels and bounding box of place, with Digital Boundary's Average (DBA), perform better than other models. When the area threshold of the bounding box is set to 10,000 km^2, the best model can successfully predict the geolocation of 90.8% of COVID-19 related tweets with the mean error distance of 4.824 km and the median error distance of 3.233 km. It is concluded that the proposed method enhances the granularity of geographic information of tweets and makes the surveillance of COVID-19 effective and efficient.

Keywords: COVID-19 · Social media · Geolocation inference · Twitter data · Data mining

1 Introduction

In December 2019, the initial cases of pneumonia associated with a novel coronavirus occurred in Wuhan City, China [1]. However, measures to control the spread of the virus

© Springer Nature Switzerland AG 2021
C. Grueau et al. (Eds.): GISTAM 2020, CCIS 1411, pp. 119–139, 2021.
https://doi.org/10.1007/978-3-030-76374-9_8

were not implemented effectively to keep its spread within China [2]. Since then, the coronavirus disease 2019 (COVID-19) has been rapidly spreading around the world, causing tens of millions of cases in more than 160 countries [1]. As of August 17th, 2020, almost 22 million (21,852,024) cases have been recorded, including 773,586 deaths where 25.48% (5,567,765) of those cases occurred within the United States, including 173,139 deaths according to the worldometer coronavirus pandemic tracker [3]. Therefore, an overarching objective of this study is to contribute to the identification of spatio-temporal patterns of the COVID-19 pandemic with a particular interest in the United States.

Over the past decade, the Internet has helped revolutionize every aspect of people's lives, and it is not only a source to get information, but also a platform to disseminate personal information [4, 5]. In addition, the development of mobile devices made it easier to send digital information (e.g., texts, location labels, and pictures). At the same time, social media platforms have experienced a tremendous and profound reform. Twitter and Facebook mainly provide basic services, but other types of social media are being used to connect online for different reasons, such as location-based services (e.g., Foursquare and Whrrl), media sharing services (e.g., Instagram, Snapchat, and Flickr), as well as other types of services (e.g., Quora, Medium, and LinkedIn). Users can establish online friendships based on mutual interests and share their everyday life with each other.

Supported by previous studies [4, 6–8], Twitter outshines other platforms in regard to social network analysis and event detection because of not only its excellent design, but also its vast user base of different age groups. According to the most up-to-date Twitter statistics for 2020, its monthly active users are around 330 million, which accounts for 23% of the Internet population, and about 500 million tweets are posted every single day [9]. Compared with Instagram and Snapchat regarding the demographics, Twitter is widely used by people of different ages and nearly 63% of them age between 35 and 65 [10]. The large quantity of user-generated contents is employed for data mining in various research areas [4]. Tweets with accurate geographic information can provide significant benefits to event response and monitoring, hence those without geographic information become useless unless geolocation inference is applicable. Accurate prediction of tweets' geolocation can effectively benefit the response and rescue in emergency events [11].

The development of Global Positioning System (GPS)-enabled mobile devices enables users to share and track their locations with accurate geographical coordinates. However, due to the operational complexity and privacy concerns, most users do not turn this function on [12]. As Laylavi et al. [13] illustrated, the percentage of tweets with geo-tags account for only 2%, which severely limits the development of associated applications. Therefore, accurate geolocation inference of tweets has become an urgent problem in this research field.

Nowadays, disease-related information is increasingly shared in real time through Twitter, while timely data with spatial and temporal information plays a significant role in surveillance of an epidemic disease [14, 15]. Every single tweet has its own metadata, which includes its creation time, but under most circumstances, does not contain its created geographical coordinates, hence geolocation inference of tweets is still a critical issue. Real-time data without any geographic information can be almost meaningless for emergency response and surveillance of an epidemic disease. Thus, this study aims to develop novel methods to predict geolocation of tweets based on their own metadata.

In this study, models based on multiple attributes of the tweet's metadata are built to predict the non-geotagged tweets' geolocation. Attributes of textual content, user location, place labels, and bounding box are fully used during the modelling process. The dataset used in this study was collected between the 10th and 30th of June 2020. During this time, the United States (US) was suffering a severe effect of the COVID-19 pandemic. The development of technologies, including Natural Language Processing (NLP) and Named Entity Recognition (NER) make it easier to extract location entities from textual data.

The main contributions of this paper are summed up as the following two points: (1) Exploring potential location-related attributes of the tweet's metadata and extracting location entities via NER techniques; (2) Three geographic coordinate datasets of counties are used to predict geolocation and the proposed models are built according to different priorities of location-related attributes.

The rest of this paper is structured as follows. Section 2 describes a literature review of relevant research. Section 3 presents a brief introduction of Twitter data's structure. Detailed explanation of the proposed models is described in Sect. 4. A case study of the COVID-19 in the contiguous US based on the models mentioned in Sect. 4 is illustrated in Sect. 5. The paper finally concludes in Sect. 6.

2 Related Works

Users sometimes add geo-information in their tweets, but in most cases, it is still not that complete or accurate. Therefore, various methods and algorithms from other fields are being used in the field of geolocation inference. With the development of technologies such as machine learning, deep learning, NLP as well as Geographical Information Systems (GIS), much more methods have made breakthroughs in this research field [16]. However, different from formal articles which are well written and grammatically correct, social media messages always contain informal elements, e.g., acronyms, emojis, hashtags and even typos, which is often attributed to the limit of character count and the use of mobile devices.

In the past few years, many studies of geolocation inference based on Twitter data have been published [16]. Ajao et al. [15] reviewed previous research related to geolocation inference of tweets, and summarized relevant methods and evaluation metrics. In the work of Cheng et al. [17], they discovered merely 20% of Twitter users in the US prefer to show cities where they live in their user profiles, and only 5% of them provide geographical coordinates information. The study of Hecht et al. [18] illustrated that even though self-described addresses are shown in their profiles, some of them are not accurate or valid, and geo-tagged tweets account for merely 0.77% of the whole. From the study of Ryoo et al. [19], the percentage of tweets with geographic information is only about 0.4%. Bartosz et al. [20] as well as Priedhorsky et al. [21] showed the similar percentages in their studies. More importantly, geolocation inference of social media data is the basis of other relevant studies. Consequently, further research in this area is needed.

When tweets are posted, some places information in the textual content enables us to understand them better. Textual content is used to predict the geolocation of tweets in the studies of Cheng et al. [22], Chandra et al. [23] as well as Chang et al. [24]. However, Ikawa et al. [25] described that some users always mention places that are not exactly where they are. In the study of Abrol et al. [26], they researched the social network relationships among their online friends. Backstrom et al. [27] and Bouillot et al. [28] described that geolocation inference of tweets can be achieved by the user profile in their studies.

NLP techniques enable various methods and algorithms of this field to be used in information extraction and geolocation inference. Techniques of NER and part-of-speech tagging (POS) have been introduced in the research of Lingad et al. [29]. Li et al. [30] introduced methods of machine learning and probabilistic to geolocation inference. Takhteyev et al. [31] used gazetteers and location databases in their research. In the study of Huang et al. [12], deep learning models are used to predict geolocation of Twitter data. Previous studies have obtained a great achievement in this field and have the potential to pursue more accurate results of geolocation prediction [32].

Most studies conducted on geolocation inference of tweets focus on either textual content or other location-related attributes. However, this research aims to implement all feasible combinations of potential attributes related to location to predict the geolocation of tweets.

3   Structure of Twitter Data

Twitter was released in March 2006 and now has about 330 million active users per month. Tweets can be posted by users via this platform. In its early days, every tweet can contain up to 140 characters, but the length of it was doubled in 2017 [33]. This increase provided users more space to express their ideas and saved more time of text compression than before. Every tweet's metadata contains a wealth of information about itself, while it is only visible to developers, not common users. Twitter data can be collected based on Twitter application programming interfaces (APIs) and stored with the format of JavaScript Object Notation (JSON). JSON format is lightweight and easy for both human beings and machines to understand and use. A JSON object contains a key/value pair and is normally enclosed in a pair of curly braces [34]. The structure of Twitter data consists of several objects, including tweet object, user object, coordinates object, place object, and bounding box object, which are all encoded in JSON format. For every tweet, the metadata can tell us its username, textual content, unique identification (ID), created time, and occasionally geographic details of where it was posted. In general, every tweet's metadata contains more than 150 attributes, while only spatio-temporal information related attributes (shown in Fig. 1) are taken into consideration in our research.

Figure 1 shows the spatio-temporal information related attributes in a tweet's metadata. The attribute of "location" is an element of the user object and is defined by user himself/herself, therefore, it can be a location that does not exist in the real world or cannot be recognized by computers. Another one is "geo_enabled", which means if the current user can attach geographic data or not. This attribute is very important for location-related studies, although it does not contain any essential geographic information.

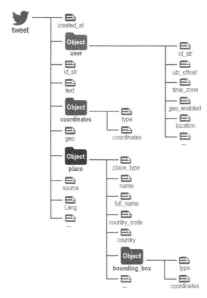

Fig. 1. Spatio-temporal attributes of a tweet's metadata.

Both attributes of "coordinates" and "geo" represent the specific longitude and latitude of the tweet's location, as a collection in the form [longitude, latitude]. However, "geo" has been deprecated according to the twitter official document, hence we used the attribute of "coordinates" to acquire accurate geo coordinates of tweets [35].

Place object contains various location-related attributes. The attribute "place_type" represents the type of location of this place and it has five values to choose from. Table 1 shows five values of attribute of "place_type" and statistics of our research dataset. For POI, it represents the specific location of a place, e.g., Washington Square Park, while the other four values stand for a certain area. Due to the large regional extent of city, admin, and country, we used data from only POI and neighborhood. Attributes of "name" and "full_name" are two ways to describe the place's names. While "country_code" and "country" provide the short code and exact name of the country of the place. The attribute of "bounding_box" is four lon/lat pairs of each corner of a box that contains the place [35].

4   Proposed Method

Figure 2 plots the workflow to illustrate the architecture of the proposed method of this research. This method is generally divided into three modules. In the first module, real time tweets within a bounding box are collected. Tweets data are initially stored into text files and then read based on JSON format. Then the data enters the preprocessing and geotagging stage, after which a dataset with geo-tagged tweets is created. In the second module, location entities are extracted from textual content, user location and place labels via NER techniques. Combining geometric properties of the place's bounding box, as well as coordinate datasets of gazetteers and digital boundaries of the US, all

Table 1. Typical values and statistics of "place_type" attribute.

Category	Amount	Percentage	Example
POI	119,655	0.96%	Washington Square Park
Neighborhood	25,183	0.20%	Downtown Jacksonville, FL
City	10,301,683	82.98%	Los Angeles, CA
Admin	1,942,596	15.65%	California, USA
Country	26,105	0.21%	Canada

these data are fed into 16 models to predict tweets' geolocation. Finally, predicted results are evaluated by mean error distance (MED) and median error distance (MDED).

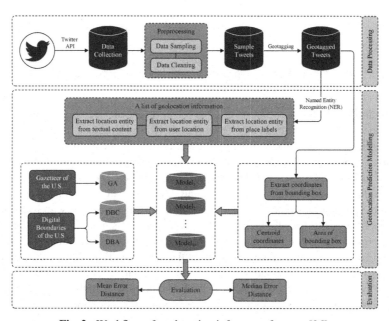

Fig. 2. Workflow of geolocation inference of tweets [36].

4.1   Data Collection

Twitter data can be gathered from both business companies and Twitter API which is available free of charge. As for commercial purchases, the companies can provide both historical and real time tweets from all over the world, but the price is very high. Twitter API can help collect tweets freely, but only real time tweets within the specific bounding box can be collected. Therefore, it normally takes several months to collect the whole research data using Twitter API. In this study, data collection was done via Twitter API, and it was implemented by the *tweepy* library of python [13, 37]. The data were collected from June 10th to June 30th, 2020 in the contiguous US during the COVID-19 pandemic. During this period, 12,408,538 unduplicated tweets were collected and stored into local text files. Only tweets located in the area of longitudes from 66°W to 125°W and latitudes from 24°N to 49°N are collected, as shown in Fig. 3. While within the bounding box, some tweets from Canada, Mexico, and the Bahamas were also included, but excluded in this research.

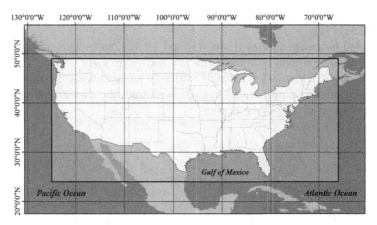

Fig. 3. Area of data collection.

4.2   Data Preprocessing

Data Cleaning. In the textual content of every tweet, it often contains noises, including hashtags, mentions, emojis and Uniform Resource Locator (URL) links, hence preprocessing operation is necessary. In this step, we used regular expressions to process textual data. A regular expression is a pattern that attempts to match with input text and can be implemented by python *re* library [38]. URL links started with "https://" and "http://" were removed from the textual content since they do not contain any location related information. We replaced unnecessary punctuation marks into a space, and consecutive spaces into one. Marks of user mentions, hashtags, non-English letters as well as stop words were all deleted [37]. As for the user location, it can be modified by users at will, thus the information was processed in the same manner.

Data Sampling. A workflow was plotted to illustrate how useless tweets are filtered out and generated a new dataset. The dataset was mainly processed via the python *pandas* library. Firstly, the method of "drop_duplicate" is employed to delete duplicated tweets from the dataset. The attribute of "lang" indicates the language used by every tweet, and only English tweets are kept in our study. As noted above, tweets posted outside the contiguous US are also removed from the dataset.

Another problem is that many tweets are meaningless to this study, such as those posted by advertisers or spambots. This kind of tweets is mainly posted by computers, therefore, only tweets posted by mobile devices (e.g., iPhone, Android, iPad, and Instagram) are kept, and the attribute of "source" was used to implement this function [13, 37]. Then tweets without geo-tags were filtered out and implemented by the "coordinates" attribute. Finally, the COVID-19 related tweets were extracted by using the keywords to match the "text" attribute of every tweet. We introduced Term Frequency-Inverse Document Frequency (TF-IDF) to get keywords from news articles about the COVID-19 pandemic in the US, and TF-IDF score helped us extract keywords from the related articles [39].

Supported by recent studies [1, 40, 41] and TF-IDF techniques, we used the following keywords: "corona", "coronavirus", "covid", "covid-19", "ncov", "sarscov2", "ncov2019" and "2019ncov" to extract COVID-19 related tweets. Through data sampling, 3,600 corresponding tweets were retrieved from the Twitter dataset. Figure 4 shows the whole data sampling process.

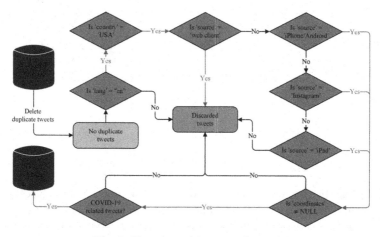

Fig. 4. Flowchart of data sampling [36].

4.3 Location Information Extraction

Named Entity Recognition. NER can be used to recognize and classify different types of entities (e.g., location names, person names, and organizations) from unstructured texts. It has been extensively studied in the last few years in machine learning and NLP. While it does not work well on informal texts like tweets since it is usually built on the basis of formal texts [29]. As for this technique, it can help to answer many real-world questions, such as: does a tweet contain the name of a person or does the tweet provide a person's current location? In this study, we use NER to identify locations from textual content, user location, and place labels of the tweet based on Stanford NER, spaCy, and Natural Language Toolkit (NLTK). After testing all tools in real tweet dataset, spaCy showed a much better performance than the other two tools, therefore, spaCy is used to identify location-related information from tweets in this research.

Bounding Box. The bounding box is a specified 4-sided geographic area and matching the tweet's location falling into the area. Unlike other location related geographical metadata, the bounding box contains the accurate lon-lat coordinates of the four points enclosing the place. Due to different types of places, bounding box has different areas. For instance, four points of a bounding box are $Point_1 = (\lambda_1, \varphi_1)$, $Point_2 = (\lambda_2, \varphi_1)$, $Point_3 = (\lambda_2, \varphi_2)$ and $Point_4 = (\lambda_1, \varphi_2)$, then Eq. 1 can be used to calculate the area of this bounding box.

$$S = R^2 \cdot |(\lambda_2 - \lambda_1) \cdot (sin\ \varphi_2 - sin\ \varphi_1)| \tag{1}$$

where R refers to the earth radius; λ_1 and λ_2 represent the longitudes of the bounding box, and φ_1 and φ_2 refer to the latitudes of the bounding box.

Equation 1 can be used to calculate the size of the bounding box. The bounding box's centroid can be reckoned as the predicted location of a tweet, therefore, if the bounding box's area is smaller, it can provide a relatively more accurate prediction. For city, admin and country, the bounding box is too large to be used to predict the geolocation.

4.4 Modelling

The location-related information is obtained from the four sources: textual content, location of user profile, place labels, and bounding box. Three coordinate datasets of counties are constructed based on gazetteers and digital boundaries of the US.

United States Gazetteers. The national gazetteers of the US were used as the data source and called GA in this study. It is a dataset including county's names and information related to geography in the US. This data is provided by the United States Census Bureau, and researchers can download it for free [42]. There are totally ten fields in the dataset, and some of them are displayed in Table 2. The field of "NAME" can provide duplicate names, but they locate in different states which means they have different values of "USPS". Fields of "INTPTLAT" and "INTPTLON", respectively, refer to latitude and longitude of the specific county.

Table 2. Data fields of US gazetteers.

Field	Description
USPS	United States Postal Service state abbreviation
GEOID	Unique geographic identifier for each feature
NAME	Name of the feature
INTPTLAT	Latitude of the feature in decimal degrees
INTPTLON	Longitude of the feature in decimal degrees

Digital Boundaries of the United States. Digital boundaries of the US are in the format of Environmental Systems Research Institute (ESRI) *lpk*. This group layer can be freely downloaded from the website of ESRI and presents counties of the US in the 50 states, the District of Columbia, and Puerto Rico. The detailed datasets are represented as polygons with over 40 fields [43].

In this paper, we only used digital boundaries of US counties due to the coarse granularity of location inference based on the city and state level. In order to obtain geographic coordinates of each county, we developed two ways to compute them and named them Digital Boundary's Centroid (DBC) and Digital Boundary's Average (DBA). DBC is calculated based on geometric properties of every county's polygon, and the value can be calculated by the centroid of the polygon. On the other hand, DBA is calculated by tweets falling into the county's polygon and the value can be calculated by their average latitude and longitude. For instance, suppose there are m counties in the contiguous US which are $County_1, \cdots, County_j, \cdots, County_m$ and $P\_tweet_1 = (\lambda_1, \varphi_1), \cdots, P\_tweet_i = (\lambda_i, \varphi_i), \cdots, P\_tweet_n = (\lambda_n, \varphi_n)$ are geographic coordinates of n tweets located in $County_j$, then the predicted coordinates of $County_j(P\_county_j)$ can be calculated by Eq. 2. This method can help compute the average longitude and latitude of geotagged tweets falling into the county's polygon.

$$P\_county_j = (\overline{\lambda}, \overline{\varphi}) = \left(\frac{\sum_{i=1}^{n} \lambda_i}{n}, \frac{\sum_{i=1}^{n} \varphi_i}{n} \right) \tag{2}$$

After calculating all polygons' coordinates based on DBA and DBC, Fig. 5 shows the distribution of distances between DBA and DBC of counties in the contiguous US. This figure illustrates that the distance difference is less than 20 km in most countries, especially for the smaller ones, while for some larger counties in the west and northeast corner, the difference is about 40 km or more. Smaller distance difference means two predicted methods are close to each other. When the distance difference is larger, the better method of coordinates prediction can achieve a better performance.

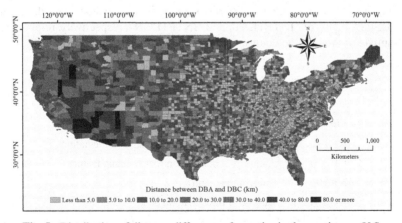

Fig. 5. Distribution of distance difference of counties in the contiguous U.S.

Modelling. As demonstrated in Fig. 2, the model is on the basis of four location-related attributes of the tweet's metadata: textual content (T), user location (U), place label (P) and bounding box (B). Location entities are extracted from T, U, and P by NER techniques, and then query them through coordinate datasets of GA, DBC, and DBA.

Equation 3 illustrates how the three predicted matrices are computed. The value will be stored as "null" if there is no county found based on NER. When we use NER to query the specific county's name, sometimes several results will be found since there are duplicate names of different counties. Therefore, the distance between the predicted point and centroid of the tweet's bounding box should be computed first, if it is within the specific threshold range, the predicted point can be reckoned as a valid result, otherwise will be discarded.

$$
\begin{bmatrix}
Text_1 & UserLoc_1 & Place_1 \\
\vdots & \vdots & \vdots \\
Text_i & UserLoc_i & Place_i \\
\vdots & \vdots & \vdots \\
Text_n & UserLoc_n & Place_n
\end{bmatrix}
NER
\begin{Bmatrix}
GA \\
DBC \\
DBA
\end{Bmatrix}
\implies
\begin{cases}
\begin{bmatrix}
T_{GA_1} & U_{GA_1} & P_{GA_1} \\
\vdots & \vdots & \vdots \\
T_{GA_i} & U_{GA_i} & P_{GA_i} \\
\vdots & \vdots & \vdots \\
T_{GA_n} & U_{GA_n} & P_{GA_n}
\end{bmatrix} \\
\begin{bmatrix}
T_{DBC_1} & U_{DBC_1} & P_{DBC_1} \\
\vdots & \vdots & \vdots \\
T_{DBC_i} & U_{DBC_i} & P_{DBC_i} \\
\vdots & \vdots & \vdots \\
T_{DBC_n} & U_{DBC_n} & P_{DBC_n}
\end{bmatrix} \\
\begin{bmatrix}
T_{DBA_1} & U_{DBA_1} & P_{DBA_1} \\
\vdots & \vdots & \vdots \\
T_{DBA_i} & U_{DBA_i} & P_{DBA_i} \\
\vdots & \vdots & \vdots \\
T_{DBA_n} & U_{DBA_n} & P_{DBA_n}
\end{bmatrix}
\end{cases}
\tag{3}
$$

where $Text_i$, $UserLoc_i$, and $Place_i$ are respectively textual content, user location, and place label of a tweet; T_{GA_i}, U_{GA_i}, and P_{GA_i} are predicted coordinates corresponding to $Text_i$, $UserLoc_i$, and $Place_i$, respectively, based on GA; T_{DBC_i}, U_{DBC_i}, and P_{DBC_i} are predicted coordinates corresponding to $Text_i$, $UserLoc_i$, and $Place_i$, respectively, based on DBC; T_{DBA_i}, U_{DBA_i}, and P_{DBA_i} are predicted coordinates corresponding to $Text_i$, $UserLoc_i$, and $Place_i$, respectively, based on DBA;

T_{GA_i}, U_{GA_i}, and P_{GA_i} can be "null" if corresponding counties are not found in GA; T_{DBC_i}, U_{DBC_i}, and U_{DBC_i} can be "null" if corresponding counties are not found in DBC; T_{DBA_i}, U_{DBA_i}, and U_{DBA_i} can be "null" if corresponding counties are not found in DBC.

Equation 4 shows how the area and centroid's coordinates are computed by the tweet's bounding box.

$$\begin{bmatrix} BBox_1 \\ \vdots \\ BBox_i \\ \vdots \\ BBox_n \end{bmatrix} \begin{cases} Area \\ Centroid \\ \Longrightarrow \end{cases} \begin{bmatrix} B_{AREA_1} & B_{CEN_1} \\ \vdots & \vdots \\ B_{AREA_i} & B_{CEN_i} \\ \vdots & \vdots \\ B_{AREA_n} & B_{CEN_n} \end{bmatrix} \qquad (4)$$

where $BBox_i$ is the tweet's bounding box; B_{AREA_i} and B_{CEN_i} are the area and centroid's lon-lat coordinates of $BBox_i$, respectively.

Because every tweet has the attribute of bounding box, every model in our study contains this attribute and is placed in the last position. UPTB is one model and designed according to the order of U, P, T, and B. Figure 6 illustrates a flow diagram of how UPTB works based on GA.

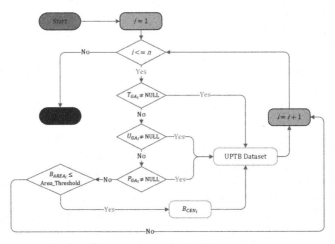

Fig. 6. Working principle of UPTB based on GA.

As shown in this flow chart, n elements are traversed in the outermost. Then, if T_{GA_i} is not "null", it is passed directly to the UPTB dataset, otherwise indicated by U_{GA_i}. If U_{GA_i} is not "null", it is passed directly to the UPTB dataset, otherwise indicated by P_{GA_i}. If P_{GA_i} is not "null", it is passed directly to the UPTB dataset, otherwise indicated by B_{AREA_i}. If the value of B_{AREA_i} is not more than the $Area\_Threshold$, B_{CEN_i} is passed to the UPTB dataset and then a new loop starts, otherwise a new loop starts directly and the final result will be set as "null". When the predicted result is "null", it means geo coordinates of this tweet cannot be predicted based on this model.

The other models are implemented with the same mechanism. That is, six models (i.e., TUPB, TPUB, UTPB, UPTB, PUTB, and PTUB) contain four parameters, six models (i.e., TUB, TPB, UTB, UPB, PTB, and PUB) contains three parameters, three models (i.e., TB, UB, and PB) contain two parameters and one model (B) contains merely one parameter. A total of 16 models are implemented in this study.

5 Experimental Results

We applied models mentioned in Sect. 4 to the sample dataset and evaluated their performance based on different metrics.

5.1 Research Data

Table 3 shows the Twitter dataset that we used in this study. We collected these tweets from 10th to 30th of June 2020 in the contiguous US during the COVID-19 pandemic spreading around the world. The total number of collected tweets are 12.4 million and tweets with geo-tags account for 6%. Only geo-tagged tweets related to COVID-19 are applied to the models described in Sect. 4, and the number is 3,600.

Table 3. Statistical information about Twitter dataset.

Item	Content
Database size	61.0 GB
Date of data gathering	2020.06.10–2020.06.30
Total number of tweets	12,415,222 tweets
Total number of unique tweets	12,408,538 tweets
Total number of tweets from mobile devices	11,475,982 tweets
Total number of tweets from Instagram	401,610 (3.24%)
Total number of English tweets	10,056,767 tweets
Number of geo-tagged tweets	758,946 tweets (6.11%)
Number of geo-tagged tweets related to COVID-19	3,600 tweets (0.029%)

As shown in Table 3, geo-tagged tweets account for 6.11% of the total Twitter dataset. These tweets were extracted, then plotted with digital boundaries of the contiguous US. Figure 7(a) [42] shows the population distribution of the contiguous US counties (i.e., people per square kilometer of 2018), and Fig. 7(b) shows the geo-tagged tweets distribution based on the contiguous US counties (i.e., geotagged tweets per 1,000 square kilometers between June 10th and June 30th, 2020).

In statistics, the Pearson's correlation coefficient (PCC) is a statistic that measures linear correlation between two variables. The value range of PCC is between -1 and 1, and the higher the value, the better the positive linear correction. Equation 5 shows how to calculate PCC based on two paired data $\{(x_1, y_1), \cdots (x_i, y_i) \cdots (x_n, y_n)\}$ consisting of n pairs.

$$r_{xy} = \frac{\sum_{i=1}^{n}(x_i - \bar{x})(y_i - \bar{y})}{\sqrt{\sum_{i=1}^{n}(x_i - \bar{x})^2}\sqrt{\sum_{i=1}^{n}(y_i - \bar{y})^2}} \tag{5}$$

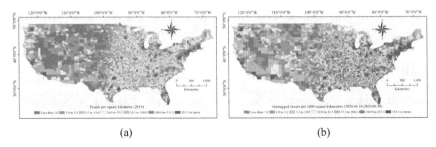

Fig. 7. Population and tweets distribution in the contiguous U.S.

In this study, x_i means people per square kilometer in every county, and y_i means tweets per 1,000 square kilometers in every county. PCC of the two variables in this study is 0.88, which indicates a strong positive correlation. Figure 7 also shows that population distribution and tweets distribution have a high correlation, hence we can detect real world events based on geo-tagged tweets or tweets with predicted geolocation.

5.2 Evaluation Metrics

Models' performance can be evaluated by the distance between the predicated geolocation and the real geolocation of a tweet. The actual distance between two points on the earth's surface can be calculated by the great circle distance. For instance, the great circle distance of two points, $p_1 = (\lambda_1, \varphi_1)$ and $p_2 = (\lambda_2, \varphi_2)$, can be calculated by Eq. 6.

$$Dist(p_1, p_2) = 2R \, arcsin\left(\sqrt{sin^2\left(\frac{\varphi_2 - \varphi_1}{2}\right) + cos(\varphi_1)cos(\varphi_2)sin^2\left(\frac{\lambda_2 - \lambda_1}{2}\right)}\right) \quad (6)$$

where R is the earth radius; λ_1 and λ_2 refer to the longitudes of points, and φ_1 and φ_2 refer to the latitudes of points.

Mean error distance (MED) and median error distance (MDED) are two metrics to evaluate models in our research, and are implemented by Eq. 7 and Eq. 8, respectively.

$$MED = \frac{1}{n_{tweets}} \sum_{i=1}^{n_{tweets}} Dist\left(\hat{p}_i, p_i\right) \quad (7)$$

$$MDED = median_{i=1}^{n_{tweets}} Dist\left(\hat{p}_i, p_i\right) \quad (8)$$

where $\hat{p}$ represents the predicted geolocation and p_i refers to the real geolocation of a tweet.

The tweet's metadata indicates that the value of bounding box is always not null, therefore, it can be used to predict the geo coordinates of the tweet. But its area varies a lot among different tweets and the error distance can be affected dramatically. Figure 8 shows the variation of MED and its percentage based on different area thresholds of the bounding box. For example, if the area threshold is set to 1,000,000 km^2, almost 100% of tweets can predict the geo coordinates, but the MED is almost 25 km. When the area threshold is set to 5,000 km^2, almost 90% of tweets can be valid to predict, and the MED improves to 5 km. As shown in Fig. 8, when the area threshold is set to 5,000 km^2 and 10,000 km^2, the MED and percentage can achieve a relatively better performance, thus the following experiments were conducted by these two values.

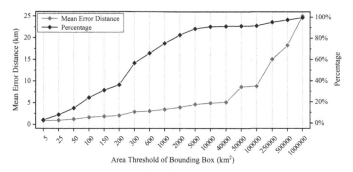

Fig. 8. MED and percentage of different area thresholds.

Sometimes users mention some other location names rather than the place where tweets are posted. But in most cases, users are more likely to be within or around the place. In addition to this, there often exist duplicate names of different counties in the datasets of GA, DBC, and DBA. Therefore, sometimes several counties were extracted by NER from a tweet. To resolve this issue, we only focus on the predicted location in the bounding box and the distance between it and the bounding box's centroid is within the specific range. In this study, we chose the distance threshold from 1 km to 10 km. For example, when the distance threshold is set to 6 km, only the first result with distance of predicted point and bounding box's centroid no more than 6 km has been kept. Figure 9 shows MED of TUPB in three datasets with different distance thresholds, when the area threshold is set to 5,000 km^2. As illustrated in this figure, the distance threshold has no obvious effect on datasets of DBC and GA, but it has a significant impact on DBA. When distance is set to 6 km, the MED is lowest, hence we chose 6 km as the distance threshold in this study.

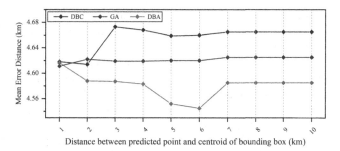

Fig. 9. MED based on different distance thresholds.

5.3 Results

Combining models mentioned in Sect. 4, three coordinate datasets of counties of the US and Eq. 6, MED ($B_{AREA_i} \leq 5,000$ km^2 and $B_{AREA_i} \leq 10,000$ km^2) can be computed and shown in Table 4 and Fig. 10. When the area threshold is set to 5,000 km^2, about 88.9% of sample tweets are successfully predicted, and the percentage has improved to 90.8% when the area threshold is set to 10,000 km^2.

Table 4. MED of models based on two area thresholds.

Models	MED ($B_{AREA_i} \leq 5,000$ km^2)			MED ($B_{AREA_i} \leq 10,000$ km^2)		
	DBC	DBA	GA	DBC	DBA	GA
TUPB	4.660	4.545	4.620	4.936	4.824	4.897
TPUB	4.660	4.545	4.620	4.936	4.824	4.897
UTPB	4.660	4.545	4.620	4.936	4.824	4.897
UPTB	4.660	4.545	4.620	4.936	4.824	4.897
PUTB	4.660	4.545	4.620	4.936	4.824	4.897
PTUB	4.660	4.545	4.620	4.936	4.824	4.897
TUB	4.654	4.572	4.627	4.930	4.850	4.904
TPB	4.660	4.545	4.620	4.936	4.824	4.897
UTB	4.654	4.572	4.627	4.930	4.850	4.904
UPB	4.631	4.583	4.612	4.908	4.860	4.890
PTB	4.660	4.545	4.620	4.936	4.824	4.897
PUB	4.631	4.583	4.612	4.908	4.860	4.890
TB	4.654	4.572	4.627	4.930	4.850	4.904
UB	4.619	4.619	4.619	4.896	4.896	4.896
PB	4.631	4.583	4.612	4.908	4.860	4.890
B	4.619	4.619	4.619	4.896	4.896	4.896

From Fig. 10(a), one can see that GA has a relatively steady performance for all models, and all values of MED are around 4.62 km. DBC has a similar performance to GA, but the models with four sources have relatively worse performances compared to other models. While DBA has a clear trend of variation based on different models, the models with three or four sources have better performances than other models. Figure 10(b) shows MED's variation with respect to DBC, GA, and DBA based on 16 models when the area threshold of the bounding box is set to 10,000 km^2. One can see that three lines from Fig. 10(b) have similar trend patterns as those from Fig. 10(a).

There often exist some abnormal values in the dataset, and these values can pose a significant impact on the mean value, hence the median value can reduce the impact of abnormal values. Table 5 and Fig. 11 show the median error distance with the bounding box's area of 5,000 km^2 and 10,000 km^2.

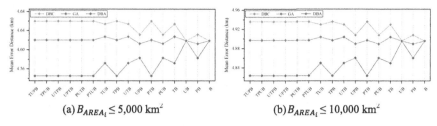

(a) $B_{AREA_i} \leq 5,000$ km^2 (b) $B_{AREA_i} \leq 10,000$ km^2

Fig. 10. MED of models based on two area thresholds.

Table 5. MDED of models based on two area thresholds.

Models	MDED ($B_{AREA_i} \leq 5,000$ km^2)			MDED ($B_{AREA_i} \leq 10,000$ km^2)		
	DBC	DBA	GA	DBC	DBA	GA
TUPB	3.239	3.095	3.245	3.327	3.233	3.373
TPUB	3.239	3.095	3.245	3.327	3.233	3.373
UTPB	3.239	3.095	3.245	3.327	3.233	3.373
UPTB	3.239	3.095	3.245	3.327	3.233	3.373
PUTB	3.239	3.095	3.245	3.327	3.233	3.373
PTUB	3.239	3.095	3.245	3.327	3.233	3.373
TUB	3.183	3.135	3.244	3.280	3.243	3.367
TPB	3.239	3.095	3.245	3.327	3.233	3.373
UTB	3.183	3.135	3.244	3.280	3.243	3.367
UPB	3.239	3.195	3.239	3.324	3.239	3.259
PTB	3.239	3.095	3.245	3.327	3.233	3.373
PUB	3.239	3.195	3.239	3.324	3.239	3.259
TB	3.183	3.135	3.244	3.280	3.243	3.367
UB	3.239	3.239	3.239	3.255	3.255	3.255
PB	3.239	3.195	3.239	3.324	3.239	3.259
B	3.239	3.239	3.239	3.255	3.255	3.255

From Fig. 11(a), one can see that the line of GA is almost straight, and all values are around 3.25 km. DBC shows a similar performance to GA, but three models of DBC performed relatively better. While DBA performs vary depending on different models, especially the models with four sources show better performances than other models. Figure 11(b) shows MDED's trend of DBC, GA, and DBA based on 16 models when the area threshold of the bounding box is set to 10,000 km^2. One can see that the models with four sources have the same performance regardless of DBC, GA, and DBA. But the values of MDED change a lot when less than four sources are used.

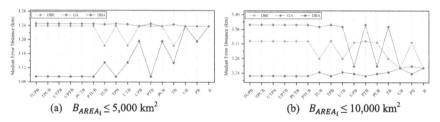

(a) $B_{AREA_i} \leq 5,000 \text{ km}^2$ (b) $B_{AREA_i} \leq 10,000 \text{ km}^2$

Fig. 11. MDED of models based on two area thresholds.

From Fig. 10 (MED of the models) and Fig. 11 (MDED of the models), it shows that DBA has the best performance in all cases, GA performs better in MED, and DBC performs better in MDED. Compared with MED, MDED have smaller error distances for all models.

6 Conclusion

Twitter has demonstrated its importance for gathering and publishing up-to-date information during a real-world event. Geographic information plays an important role in emergency response and event monitoring. However, only 2% of tweets are with geotags, hence geolocation inference of tweets is still a major challenge. In this study, we proposed various models to predict geolocation of tweets, as organized as follows: (1) Twitter data collection; (2) data cleaning and extract geo-tagged tweets related to COVID-19; (3) location entity extraction from location-related metadata of tweets based on NER; (4) construction of three coordinate datasets on the basis of gazetteers and digital boundaries of the US; (5) model implementation based on different area thresholds of bounding box; (6) model evaluation.

The proposed method has fully used all potential location-related attributes to predict tweets' geolocation. When the area threshold of the bounding box is set to 10,000 km², the best model can successfully predict the geolocation of 90.8% of COVID-19 related tweets with the mean error distance of 4.824 km and the median error distance of 3.233 km. This method has achieved the best performance compared with previous methods.

There still exist some deficiencies in this study. Firstly, the library of NER is limited and does not contain every county's name, which results in some useful information being filtered out. Secondly, even though the distance threshold is introduced to reduce the interference caused by duplicate county names, there still exist counties with the same name located in the same bounding box. Thirdly, in some cases, several location entities can be extracted based on NER, but in this study, only the first location entity that meets the criteria is chosen. However, the real location-related information does not always appear in the first position.

For further study, the proposed method can be applied to other emergency datasets (e.g., bushfires, typhoons, and earthquakes). When computing the average lon-lat coordinates of geo-tagged tweets located in a county, different weights can be added to each tweet. In addition, techniques such as natural language processing and deep learning models can strengthen text analysis and promote the development of this research field.

Acknowledgements. This research is sponsored by China Scholarship Council (CSC).

References

1. Singh, L., et al.: A first look at COVID-19 information and misinformation sharing on Twitter (2020)
2. Banda, J.M., et al.: A large-scale COVID-19 Twitter chatter dataset for open scientific research--an international collaboration (2020)
3. Worldometers. https://www.worldometers.info/coronavirus/
4. Prieto, V.M., Matos, S., Alvarez, M., Cacheda, F., Oliveira, J.L.: Twitter: a good place to detect health conditions. PloS One **9**, e86191 (2014)
5. Paul, M.J., Dredze, M.: You are what you tweet: analyzing Twitter for public health. In: Fifth International AAAI Conference on Weblogs and Social Media
6. Steiger, E., De Albuquerque, J.P., Zipf, A.: An advanced systematic literature review on spatiotemporal analyses of Twitter data. Trans. GIS **19**, 809–834 (2015)
7. Crooks, A., Croitoru, A., Stefanidis, A., Radzikowski, J.: #Earthquake: Twitter as a distributed sensor system. Trans. GIS **17**, 124–147 (2013)
8. Sinnenberg, L., Buttenheim, A.M., Padrez, K., Mancheno, C., Ungar, L., Merchant, R.M.: Twitter as a tool for health research: a systematic review. Am. J. Public Health **107**, e1–e8 (2017)
9. 50+ Twitter statistics & facts for 2020. https://www.websitehostingrating.com/twitter-statistics/
10. 10 Twitter Statistics Every Marketer Should Know in 2019. https://au.oberlo.com/blog/twitter-statistics
11. Ajao, O., Hong, J., Liu, W.: A survey of location inference techniques on Twitter. J. Inf. Sci. **41**, 855–864 (2015)
12. Huang, C., Tong, H., He, J., Maciejewski, R.: Location prediction for tweets. Front. Big Data **2**, 5 (2019). https://doi.org/10.3389/fdata
13. Laylavi, F., Rajabifard, A., Kalantari, M.: A multi-element approach to location inference of Twitter: a case for emergency response. ISPRS Int. J. Geo-Inf. **5**, 56 (2016)
14. Allen, C., Tsou, M.-H., Aslam, A., Nagel, A., Gawron, J.-M.: Applying GIS and machine learning methods to Twitter data for multiscale surveillance of influenza. PloS One **11**, e0157734 (2016)
15. Gao, Y., Wang, S., Padmanabhan, A., Yin, J., Cao, G.: Mapping spatiotemporal patterns of events using social media: a case study of influenza trends. Int. J. Geogr. Inf. Sci. **32**, 425–449 (2018)
16. Li, W., Serdyukov, P., de Vries, A.P., Eickhoff, C., Larson, M.: The where in the tweet. In: Proceedings of the 20th ACM International Conference on Information and Knowledge Management, pp. 2473–2476. ACM
17. Cheng, Z., Caverlee, J., Lee, K.: A content-driven framework for geolocating microblog users. ACM Trans. Intell. Syst. Technol. (TIST) **4**, 2 (2013)
18. Hecht, B., Hong, L., Suh, B., Chi, E.H.: Tweets from Justin Bieber's heart: the dynamics of the location field in user profiles. In: Proceedings of the SIGCHI Conference on Human Factors in Computing Systems, pp. 237–246. ACM

19. Ryoo, K., Moon, S.: Inferring Twitter user locations with 10 km accuracy. In: Proceedings of the 23rd International Conference on World Wide Web, pp. 643–648. ACM

20. Hawelka, B., Sitko, I., Beinat, E., Sobolevsky, S., Kazakopoulos, P., Ratti, C.: Geo-located Twitter as proxy for global mobility patterns. Cartogr. Geogr. Inf. Sci. **41**, 260–271 (2014)

21. Priedhorsky, R., Culotta, A., Del Valle, S.Y.: Inferring the origin locations of tweets with quantitative confidence. In: Proceedings of the 17th ACM Conference on Computer Supported Cooperative Work & Social Computing, pp. 1523–1536. ACM

22. Cheng, Z., Caverlee, J., Lee, K.: You are where you tweet: a content-based approach to geo-locating twitter users. In: Proceedings of the 19th ACM International Conference on Information and Knowledge Management, pp. 759–768. ACM

23. Chandra, S., Khan, L., Muhaya, F.B.: Estimating Twitter user location using social interactions--a content based approach. In: 2011 IEEE Third International Conference on Privacy, Security, Risk and Trust and 2011 IEEE Third International Conference on Social Computing, pp. 838–843. IEEE (2011)

24. Chang, H.-W., Lee, D., Eltaher, M., Lee, J.: @ Phillies tweeting from Philly? Predicting Twitter user locations with spatial word usage. In: Proceedings of the 2012 International Conference on Advances in Social Networks Analysis and Mining (ASONAM 2012), pp. 111–118. IEEE Computer Society (2012)

25. Ikawa, Y., Vukovic, M., Rogstadius, J., Murakami, A.: Location-based insights from the social web. In: Proceedings of the 22nd International Conference on World Wide Web, pp. 1013–1016. ACM

26. Abrol, S., Khan, L.: Tweethood: agglomerative clustering on fuzzy k-closest friends with variable depth for location mining. In: 2010 IEEE Second International Conference on Social Computing, pp. 153–160. IEEE (2010)

27. Backstrom, L., Sun, E., Marlow, C.: Find me if you can: improving geographical prediction with social and spatial proximity. In: Proceedings of the 19th International Conference on World Wide Web, pp. 61–70. ACM

28. Bouillot, F., Poncelet, P., Roche, M.: How and why exploit tweet's location information? In: AGILE 2012: 15th International Conference on Geographic Information Science (2012)

29. Lingad, J., Karimi, S., Yin, J.: Location extraction from disaster-related microblogs. In: Proceedings of the 22nd International Conference on World Wide Web, pp. 1017–1020. ACM

30. Li, R., Wang, S., Deng, H., Wang, R., Chang, K.C.-C.: Towards social user profiling: unified and discriminative influence model for inferring home locations. In: Proceedings of the 18th ACM SIGKDD International Conference on Knowledge Discovery and Data Mining, pp. 1023–1031. ACM

31. Takhteyev, Y., Gruzd, A., Wellman, B.: Geography of Twitter networks. Soc. Netw. **34**, 73–81 (2012)

32. Li, C., Sun, A.: Fine-grained location extraction from tweets with temporal awareness. In: Proceedings of the 37th International ACM SIGIR Conference on Research & Development in Information Retrieval, pp. 43–52. ACM

33. Tweeting Made Easier. https://blog.twitter.com/official/en_us/topics/product/2017/tweetingmadeeasier.html

34. An Introduction to JSON. https://www.digitalocean.com/community/tutorials/an-introduction-to-json

35. Tweet Location Metadata. https://developer.twitter.com/en/docs/twitter-api/v1/data-dictionary/overview/geo-objects

36. Li, B., Chen, Z., Lim, S.: Geolocation prediction from tweets: a case study of influenza-like illness in Australia. In: GISTAM, pp. 160–167

37. Singh, J., Dwivedi, Y., Rana, N., Kumar, A., Kapoor, K.: Event classification and location prediction from tweets during disasters. Ann. Oper. Res. **283**(1–2), 737–757 (2017). https://doi.org/10.1007/s10479-017-2522-3

38. Regular Expression Language - Quick Reference. https://docs.microsoft.com/en-us/dotnet/standard/base-types/regular-expression-language-quick-reference

39. Marujo, L., et al.: Automatic keyword extraction on Twitter. In: Proceedings of the 53rd Annual Meeting of the Association for Computational Linguistics and the 7th International Joint Conference on Natural Language Processing (Volume 2: Short Papers), pp. 637–643

40. Kouzy, R., et al.: Coronavirus goes viral: quantifying the COVID-19 misinformation epidemic on Twitter. Cureus **12**, e7255 (2020)

41. Chen, E., Lerman, K., Ferrara, E.: Tracking social media discourse about the COVID-19 pandemic: development of a public coronavirus Twitter data set. JMIR Public Health Surveill. **6**, e19273 (2020)

42. The National Counties Gazetteer File. https://www.census.gov/geographies/reference-files/time-series/geo/gazetteer-files.html

43. USA Counties. https://www.arcgis.com/home/item.html?id=a00d6b6149b34ed3b833e10fb72ef47b

Digital High-Scale Food Security Analysis: Challenges, Considerations and Opportunities

Timothy Mulrooney$^{(\boxtimes)}$ (ID) and Tysean Wooten (ID)

North Carolina Central University, Durham, NC, USA
tmulroon@nccu.edu

Abstract. Geospatial tools such as GIS (Geographic Information Systems) serve as a popular technology to assess and evaluate spatial dimensions of the food environment. While local-level policy decisions can be aided using GIS analysis and GIS data, little work has been invested in the holistic understanding of the data on which these decisions are made. In this paper, we address what entails high-quality geospatial data, challenges and opportunities that exist in the field of geospatial data development as applied to local-scale food environment research. We further explored factors of geospatial data quality assessment and quality control (QA/QC) for a commercially available business (CAB) database typically used in high-scale geospatial data analysis of the food environment. Factors related to the physical location of all food sources such as grocery stores and farmers markets and individualized vehicular transportation (roads) rated highest. They outweighed those related to land cover, utilities and zoning, which are more important in medium and low-scale (national level) analysis. When ranking various dimensions of data quality, subject matter experts found positional accuracy and attribute accuracy to be the most important in data development. However, errors related to temporal accuracy (age of data) exhibited the greatest number of errors within a CAB database. This schism serves as the impetus of this project and further addresses challenges between conceptual and practical geospatial data development policies and procedures.

Keywords: Geographic information system · Geodatabase data development · Geospatial standards · GIS data quality · Food environment

1 Introduction

Patterns of negative health-related outcomes such as obesity, hypertension, and diabetes are spatial in nature and when mapped highlight patterns of geostatistical clustering and spatial autocorrelation. While lifestyle choices and genetics contribute to individual and household vulnerability that lead to these differential health outcomes, it is possible to identify social and environmental factors, sometimes associated with geographic location, that have an effect on larger groups, and might be considered as critical indicators to address in any mitigation plan. While "All Americans, rich and poor, have more access to healthy—and unhealthy—food choices than ever" [1], individual-level choice to purchase a particular item is dependent upon a variety of factors. There is, however, a

© Springer Nature Switzerland AG 2021
C. Grueau et al. (Eds.): GISTAM 2020, CCIS 1411, pp. 140–166, 2021.
https://doi.org/10.1007/978-3-030-76374-9_9

strong relationship between health and diet and it seems clear the accessibility of sources for fresh meats, fruits, and vegetables is an important factor in the overall health of a community. Even in low-income neighborhoods, food stamp recipients who live close to supermarkets ate more fresh food and vegetables [2]. Spatial proximity is the principal determinant to patronize a particular grocery for about half (48%) of US residents [3] and more than half (53.9%) of residents in Detroit often shopped within 2 miles of their residence [4]. Those who bypass the closest store cite reasons such as lower prices, lower prices on wanted items, better selection and better quality of fresh foods as reasons for doing bypassing these closer stores [3]. Lower income residents may not have the means to be as selective and are subjected to the grocery store and their options, or lack thereof, that geography dictates. While it is safe to say that geography is not a prime determinant in explaining or even justifying health outcomes, it does have more of a role than one would think.

The United States Department of Agriculture (USDA) has utilized the term *food desert* to underscore regions within low-income communities that have limited accessibility to fresh food via supermarkets. Although some research has focused on rural areas [5–8] most of the knowledge base on the subject has been associated with urban areas which bring about other variables such as pedestrian access and public transportation which are typically not options in rural regions. In addition, the number of large retailers is decreasing or consolidating, but increasing in size to accommodate all shoppers, both grocery and non-grocery [9]. Combined with the fact retailers are migrating to the suburbs from downtowns [10], retailers tend to locate near high-volume roads that are less accessible to non-vehicular individualized transportation (i.e. walking, public transit or riding a bike) [11]. Research [12] has highlighted this disparity of distribution when it found unhealthy food options greatly outweighed healthy counterparts in Los Angeles while other research found poor and minority neighborhoods had less healthy food options than their richer and whiter counterparts [13]. As a result, typical sources of fresh and 'healthy' foods such as supermarkets and farmers' markets are being replaced by fast food restaurants and convenience stores which offer food options that are convenient (easily prepared and physically closer) and inexpensive, but typically less healthy. The long-term ramifications on community health far outweigh any of these tangible and intangible gains. In response to this increasing disproportion, research has explored the notion of *food swamps* which represent areas with tremendously high number or ratio of unhealthy food options compared to healthy options. Research at high scales [14, 15] has shown food swamps predict obesity and other negative health outcomes better than food deserts.

Geospatial tools such as Geographic Information Systems (GIS) serve as a popular technology to represent spatial dimensions of the food environment. A GIS serves as the means by which information about spatially-explicit phenomena can be created, stored, analyzed and rendered in the digital environment. GIS serves as the technological arm in the study of geography (i.e. the study of 'where'). Experts in many dissimilar fields have seen the utility of GIS as a means of quantifying and expanding their research. GIS is used in disciplines such as business, sociology, justice studies, surveying and the environmental sciences. As applied to food security, GIS can be used to measure the distance between residents and large supermarkets or supercenters, or the density of food outlets within an enumeration unit (census block group or zip code) as a commonly used proxy for availability and access [16, 17]. These regions of high and low access can be analyzed and mapped across both space and time [18] as shown in Fig. 1 [19], as well as the socio-economic factors that may help explain this access such as median family income (Fig. 2). These make powerful visual products disseminatable and understandable to the entire public that can have long-term practical and policy implications.

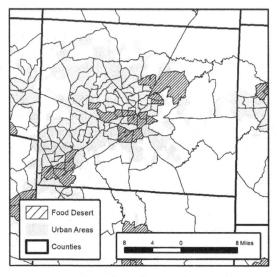

Fig. 1. Map of USDA food deserts in Guilford County, North Carolina [19].

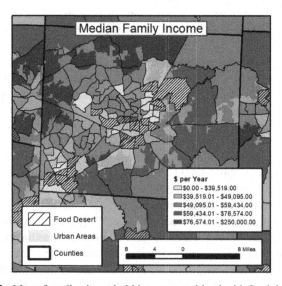

Fig. 2. Map of median household income combined with food deserts.

While many only see the output of GIS data and analysis in the form of maps, resources must be dedicated to creating high-quality data at a local scale. The manner in which these data are captured varies. Some methods include the use of a Global Positioning System (GPS) unit, extracting from or improving upon existing GIS data, downloading data from a web site, connecting to a web service, the use of an Unmanned Aerial Vehicle (UAV) or some other remote sensing platform, or creating data from an analog format via digitization or georectification. Regardless of the method, the resources (e.g., the computers, time and people dedicated to the process of collecting, creating, processing and cataloguing geospatial data) are the most time-consuming portion of a GIS-related project. This research holistically explores the types of geospatial data needed to perform high-quality analysis in support of analyzing and mapping spatial dimensions of the food environment at high scales. These database needs are quite different than data that may be required to remediate food insecurity at the individual/household level (such as Public Use Microdata) or coarser data at a national or sub-national scale. Little research has explored this field of database development, whether for the pure sake of science research and applied decision-making or policy that can be implemented in the field.

In the United States, food insecurity has been described as a "serious public health problem associated with poor cognitive and emotional development in children and with depression and poor health in adults" [20]. Given that women and children have much higher rates of food security than their male and more senior counterparts in the United States, some have called for a rights-based approach to addressing food security [20]. In support of understanding this multi-faceted problem, this research explores both technical and non-technical issues of the data required to represent the tangible and intangible food environment.

2   Literature Review

While the concepts 'food desert' and 'food swamp' have many theoretical definitions, they have applied applications. They exist in the real world and people have a practical understanding of them (Fig. 3).

Fig. 3. Sign outside of vacant grocery story building in Gibsonville, Guilford County, North Carolina.

Food security is considered to be the state "when all people, at all times, have physical and economic access to sufficient, safe and nutritious food to meet their dietary needs and food preferences for an active and healthy life" [21]. Contemporary literature has used terms such as *availability, accessibility, proximity, disparity, inequality, density, variety, affordability, walkability, connectivity* and *quality* as well as the aforementioned *food desert* and *food swamp* to describe quantitative measures of the food environment and ultimately food security. These can all be captured using a GIS in some way, shape and form at various scales.

The mapping and demarcation of food-insecure areas within the digital environment has been made exponentially easier using GIS technologies. While first used as an aesthetic tool to map study areas [22] or highlight underlying explanatory variables such as income [23], GIS has since been used to measure real-world distances and calculate densities, quantitatively express proximity and render this proximity with statistical significance using a variety of analytical, geostatistical and cartographic tools. Among the first to do this in the field of food desert research were Donkin et al. [24], Lovett et al. [25] and Pearce [26] while more recent research [27, 28] has quantitatively calculated and mapped the spatial extent of the aforementioned food swamps at high (sub county) scales.

Within a GIS, ways to express spatial dimensions of the food environment vary. Some research has expressed access and availability (or lack of access and availability) as linear units such as kilometers or miles [29], travel time in minutes [30, 31] and densities such as the number of food options per square mile by census tract [32], as well as more complex metrics based on the cost to operate a car [33]. More recently, unitless metrics expressed as ratios [15, 34] have been used as alternatives to absolute measures because these absolute measures are meaningless if not placed within some context. A ten-minute drive time to the nearest fresh food source in an urban area means something much different than a ten-minute drive to the nearest fresh food source in a rural area. The proper and prudent use of absolute measures requires more analysis and interpretation. Food swamp research using GIS utilizes existing metrics such as the Retail Food Environmental Index (RFEI) and the Expanded RFEI [14] while others [27, 28] have derived their own metrics and to define spatial extents of food deserts and swamps using variations of the RFEI, Expanded RFEI, Modified RFEI [35] and Food Balance Metric [36].

However, coarser scales of analysis also exist. In studies that model the supply and demand forces from farm to plate at a national scale, geospatial data regarding farm locations, their arrangement, land cover, flood plains, rivers, climate and population change which support burgeoning sustainable planning, management and development efforts, especially in developing countries are required [37–39]. At this scale, food security at a small scale can be considered a function of the socio-economic and political environment regarding factors such as macro-economy, natural resources, market conditions, education, political climate, food safety/quality and health care practices. These are not considerations in local-scale analysis where proximity to known food sources are correlated with explanatory variables to define food-needy regions. In addition, the geospatial data needs required for local (community) level food analysis are scale dependent and much different in nature than data required at a coarser national or sub-national scale.

These geospatial data required for local research vary in scope, ranging from roads and business locations to sidewalks and municipal boundaries. For example, research in Vermont looked at the quality of food in conjunction with point-to-point distances along a vector road network in which was then grouped into polygonal enumeration units (towns/townships) [5]. Other pioneers [16, 36, 40] also used vector GIS data at some level (individual point, census block group, tract, etc.) to express food security using distance and density calculations derived from GIS data. In national-scale analysis of this type, analyzing thousands to hundreds of thousand sources traveling to thousands of destinations is resource-intensive and requires large, ancillary data layers such as roads in support of this analysis as well as the abovementioned interpretation to be useful. For a large county in North Carolina (~500,000 people) and using Dijkstra's Shortest Path First (SPF) algorithm with a road network of more than 98,000 vertices [41] a best-case scenario for calculating just one drive-time calculation between two locations requires a minimum of 98,000 calculations and a worst-case scenario of more than 9 billion ($98,000^2$) calculations [42]. There are literally trillions of possible calculations between sources and potential destinations at the national scale along a much more robust road network, which essentially make desktop computing solutions impossible. While applications using Python, Stata [43] and R programming solutions make this process more efficient than Esri's Network Analyst calculations using a GUI (Graphical User Interface), they are less intuitive for the average GIS user and impossible for the average computer.

In the United States, guidance on the mapping of the food environment begins with the United States Department of Agriculture Food Access Atlas (https://www.ers.usda.gov/data-products/food-access-research-atlas/go-to-the-atlas/). Food access takes into account both the availability or proximity of food sources to residents as well as having readily-available transportation. Information collected and mapped at the census tract level includes the aforementioned food desert metric (low income and limited access) as shown in Fig. 4 as well as individual components that make up this metric and ancillary measures such as income, poverty, race/ethnicity, vehicle access and high-density housing. They are provided as tabular data that can be brought into a GIS and mapped accordingly. As shown in Fig. 4, census tracts can take on varying sizes and shapes. These larger census tracts, one of which is 322 sq. miles (834 sq. km) in size, in the middle of the diagram located in Columbus, Pender and Sampson Counties in North Carolina are especially problematic because they may be too large to highlight high-scale food security patterns necessary for community-based research. As a result, higher-scale food environment analysis using block groups [30, 44, 45] or even pixels using raster-based calculations [27] better elucidate local-level patterns, drives local policy and decision-making, and ultimately serves as a focus of this research.

While there is boundless value in performing local-scale food environment analysis using GIS, little research has been performed on the actual themes or topics that necessitate high-quality research at a high scale. In particular, little work has been performed to determine how important roads are in food security research at the local level. What about elevation? In addition to the actual features, there are various questions about the individual attributes required for high-quality food desert research. Is income (at the census block group level) a necessary attribute for sub-county food desert research? What

Fig. 4. USDA Food Access Atlas of Southeastern North Carolina showing low income and low access census tracts [19].

about road length? This research explores how can these themes and attributes can be prioritized when time and personnel constraints, which are a reality in the professional world, exist.

In a GIS sources and destinations used in the spatial assessment of the food environment are represented as points. Depending upon the focus and scale of analysis, the number of points utilized can range from the dozens [46, 47] to hundreds [40, 48] and even thousands. As a basis for this research on high-scale food security in North Carolina, GIS work highlighted metrics to measure food security at the block group level [27, 46, 49]. A variety of themes were used in these studies, ranging from roads, business locations and rivers to municipal boundaries, farmers' markets and fast food outlets. Each of these layers were developed or extracted from existing data at a scale appropriate for this type of detailed analysis. However, little insight is provided into what quality assessment was performed for the many consumers of these data. If a supermarket is not provided in the GIS database when one in reality exists (error of omission), one may be mapping food deserts and providing subsequent remediations where it is not needed. On the other hand, if a food source is attributed as a supermarket when it only serves a minimal sampling of fresh food (error of commission), researchers may not be properly identifying the food desert that exists in the area. The significance of data-driven considerations has caused researchers to think critically about the objective assessment, evaluation and reporting of data quality to data users.

In addition to determining what data layers best address the phenomena of food security, it is of paramount importance that these data are also correct. While most end-uses only want the end-products of GIS analysis typically in the form of maps, the largest cost of any GIS project is developing the data which go into high-quality research and the personnel resources attached to this data development. It goes without saying that in an era with limited resources such as personnel, space and time, database developers must be intentional in how, when and to what extent (temporal, spatial and topical) data must be developed. While attempts have been made to estimate the actual and tangible costs [50, 51] and value [52, 53] of geospatial data, it is impossible to place a monetary value on data although various entities have tried to estimate it [54, 55].

Spatial data quality is the end-product of processes designed to ensure newly created data are correct (Quality Assurance) while also identifying existing data that are incorrect (Quality Control). Applications of QA/QC extend well beyond the GIS world, such as banking, manufacturing, software, medicine and even taxonomy [56]. While some research [57] has distinguished between QA and QC, the two concepts are usually termed as a pair and felt that one cannot exist without the other. Although the QA/QC of spatial data within a GIS is required as per Federal Geographic Data Committeee (FGDC) standards and various organizations have processes in place to ensure the various accuracies are adhered to that best fit their needs, resources and limitations, it is not has been at the forefront of GIS research when compared to other facets of Geographic Information Science.

Nonetheless, the resources dedicated to data creation, especially high-quality data, are extraordinarily high. One opinion is that data quality has no inherent value or worth, but is ultimately realized when an action is taken on information pertaining to data quality [58]. Along those same lines, the end goal of information quality was to satisfy customer needs, in this case being the many users who utilize these data, many of whom assume that the data have undergone some validation [59]. Various components contribute to spatial data quality to include: horizontal accuracy, attribute accuracy, temporal accuracy and attribute completeness.

Horizontal accuracy represents the distance a GIS data layer deviates from geographic reality. It essentially measures the distance a GIS data feature is from where it 'should' be. It is impossible to tell the exact location of where a feature should be placed, as geo-rectified imagery and even high precision Global Position Systems (GPS) data have inherent error attached to them. Some data used food security research (grocery stores) were created via the process of geocoding in which a relative location such as an address is converted to a point with absolute location (latitude and longitude). Researchers found the positional accuracy (the actual location versus what the geocoding algorithm represents as the address) of geocoded rural addresses to be poorer than urban counterparts [60–62]. This can be problematic a large study area.

Attribute accuracy describes how well the assigned attribute values match the actual characteristics of the objects. Attributes are the non-spatial characteristics of an entity used to describe each individual segment. Food source attributes are uniform across an entity, and serve to distinguish one object from another. Attribute values can be text descriptions (e.g., CONAME = 'Food Lion' or NAICS = '44511003') or numerical values (SALESVOL = 1655). In other cases, InfoUSA, a supplier of geospatial business data, uses domain fields to describe particular attributes. For example, the square footage of the store, represented by the field name SQFTCODE, can only have one of four values: A: 1–2, 499 Square Feet, B: 2,500–9,999 Square Feet, C: 10,000–39,999 Square Feet, D: 40,000 + Square Feet.

Attribute completeness measures the degree to which all required attributes have been populated. This does not necessarily mean that they are correct. For example, the SQFTCODE must be populated and can be one of only the four possible aforementioned values matched through a domain table. In some cases, it is left blank in the data. For the

SALESVOL attribute, which represents sales volume in thousands of dollars, it must be an integer. In some cases where it is not provided or unknown, a value of '0' is provided. These missing or unknown values may skew analysis when agglomerated with known values.

Temporal accuracy refers to the age of the data compared to the usage or publication date. Issues of temporal accuracy arise when the GIS data indicates that a feature is open but has since closed. The assessment of temporal accuracy can be problematic because time is rarely treated as a separate entity within spatial databases and even in metadata, except for historically explicit databases such as the decennial census [63].

Early pioneers of GIS recognized the importance of data quality largely due to the legal ramifications in publishing incorrect spatial information which may lead to accidents from the misuse of data [64]. Even then, they understood the reconciliation between accuracy, the cost of creating the most accurate of data and the inevitability that some error will still exist. This concession is what is referred to as *uncertainty absorption* [65]. Given multitude of individual GIS data features required for this type of analysis, it is impossible to field verify every single feature used in analysis.

As applied explicitly to GIS applications related to the quality of spatial food environment data, work has proliferated as research in the spatial analysis and representation of the food environment has increased and a need has arisen to answer questions about the validity of data on which decisions are made. Research [66] has understood these challenges, which include the reliability and validity of data (proper addresses and classifications of stores) as well detail and completeness (enough information is stored that can be useful in food environment analysis). Other research [67] further expounded on these dimensions to include the quality of geocoding processes, the definition of food outlet constructs (what is the definition of healthy, use of proprietary codes, etc.) and ways to measure access and via a reportable standard called Geo-FERN (Food Environment Reporting).

Comprehensive studies [68, 69] explored the quality of large spatial databases purchased from independent sources, referred to as Commercially Available Business (CAB) data, among and between disparate datasets and providers which serve as the basis for retail businesses. Larger-scale studies [70–73] were performed for Durham, Chicago, Albany and Pittsburgh respectively. All cited some degree of difference between different CAB databases such as InfoUSA, Dunn and Bradstreet, TDLinx, as well as field-based and automated methods, noting that caution must be taken when using CAB databases. Further research [74] reinforced the idea of uncertainty absorption within this narrow focus (validity of GIS data in measuring the food environment), highlighting the reconciliation that must be made between the sheer number of data sources provided by CAB databases, the time needed for field verification and the need for high-quality data.

As part of a study on food access and spatial disparity in rural Texas, the addresses of food sources provided via public lists such as Internet telephone directories, telephone directories and the Texas Department of Agriculture were ground-truthed [48]. 18.9% of food sources provided via these public lists could not be verified for a variety of reasons. These reasons included 1) businesses were no longer open 2) business where food source was formerly located was now occupied by non-food source 3) address did not exist or able to geocode and 4) located denoted as a food source was a residence with no apparent food business. In addition, they found 35.7% of food sources within their study area were only identified through ground-truthing, as these food sources were not provided through public lists. In a similar study, field verification was performed on twenty-one different food source categories (Restaurant, Pub/Bar, Supermarket, Takeaway Food, etc.) across different combinations of socio-economic status (SES) and population densities (urban, rural, mixed) in England. For the rural low SES, more than 36% of food sources provided via a secondary source could not be found in the field [75].

Above and beyond these facets of data quality, the Federal Geographic Data Committee (FGDC) and spatial data transfer standards (SDTS) consider vertical accuracy (error in measured vs. represented elevation), data lineage (source materials of data) and logical consistency (compliance of qualitative relationships inherent in the data structure) components of data quality [76, 77]. Within the GIS community, temporal accuracy (age of the data compared to usage date) and semantic accuracy or "the quality with which geographical objects are described in accordance with the selected model" may also be considered elements of data quality [78] as well as metadata, the formal cataloguing of GIS data. Metadata has been used to describe data quality measures taken during the data development process and subsequent updates. Most generally thought of as "data about data", metadata serves as a formal framework to catalog the lifeline of a particular GIS data set. Feature-level metadata has been able to capture data quality information [79, 80], but is typically limited to quantitative measures of positional accuracy and qualitative information related to data lineage within eight of the more than 400 entries that comprise a complete FGDC-compliant metadata file. Even now, the population of these metadata elements is not fully automated and some entries must be done by the GIS data steward. Given the efficiency at which metadata population is done by each steward, data quality assessment done solely via the extraction of metadata entries is not advised.

3 Procedures

As a means to prioritize data layers, attributes and dimensions of spatial data quality, a Likert-type survey was developed and distributed to the GIS community that focuses on local-scale food security research. It is composed of twelve questions that not only ask about users' GIS experience, but also asks users questions about their preferences for particular GIS data layers used in analysis (Fig. 5) and the attributes attached to those layers (Fig. 6).

As shown in these figures, respondents were asked to give responses to these questions on a 5-point Likert-type scale, representing "Not Applicable at All" through "Essential to Research". The Likert scale uses ordered responses on a bipolar scale to assess the level of favorability with a particular statement. Some scales do have an even number of responses (4, for example), which force respondents to choose one side of the mean or the other. However, this one does not.

As applied to ranking dimensions of data quality, respondents were given a survey to rank six facets of data quality. An example of this survey and explanations of these facets are highlighted in Fig. 7.

You are developing a GIS database in order to conduct food security analysis. How important are the following GIS data layers to your research and analysis?

	Not Applicable at All	Slightly Important	Moderately Important	Very Important	Essential to Research
Building Footprints	O	O	O	O	O
Bus Routes	O	O	O	O	O
Businesses (All)	O	O	O	O	O
Census Units (block groups, tract, etc.)	O	O	O	O	O
Churches	O	O	O	O	O
Cities and Towns	O	O	O	O	O
Counties	O	O	O	O	O
Crime	O	O	O	O	O
Elevation	O	O	O	O	O
Farmers Markets	O	O	O	O	O

Fig. 5. Likert-type assessment used to rate importance of GIS data themes for use in food desert research. 23 layers were used in this assessment [19].

You are developing a GIS database in order to conduct food security research. How important are the following categorical or numerical attributes to your research?

	Not Applicable at All	Slightly Important	Moderately important	Very Important	Essential to Research
Average Household Size	O	O	O	O	O
Building Size	O	O	O	O	O
Distance to Nearest Resource	O	O	O	O	O
Education Attainment	O	O	O	O	O
Housing Status (Owner-Occupied / Rental / Vacant)	O	O	O	O	O
Income	O	O	O	O	O
Median Age	O	O	O	O	O
Median Rent Paid	O	O	O	O	O
North American Industry Classification Standard (NAICS) Code	O	O	O	O	O

Fig. 6. Likert-type assessment used to rate importance of attributes for use in local-level food desert research. 18 attributes were used in this assessment [19].

This survey was created and distributed to the food desert community via message boards, e-mails and online forums in the Fall of 2017 and Spring 2018. 32 respondents answered the survey.

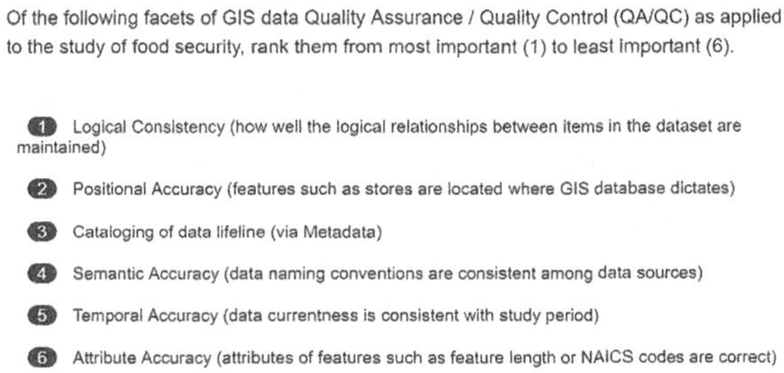

Of the following facets of GIS data Quality Assurance / Quality Control (QA/QC) as applied to the study of food security, rank them from most important (1) to least important (6).

1 Logical Consistency (how well the logical relationships between items in the dataset are maintained)

2 Positional Accuracy (features such as stores are located where GIS database dictates)

3 Cataloging of data lifeline (via Metadata)

4 Semantic Accuracy (data naming conventions are consistent among data sources)

5 Temporal Accuracy (data currentness is consistent with study period)

6 Attribute Accuracy (attributes of features such as feature length or NAICS codes are correct)

Fig. 7. Dimensions of spatial data quality that respondents were asked to rate using online assessment tool [19].

4 Results

4.1 Prioritization of Data Layers

Respondents were asked to rate data layers on 5-point Likert-type scale ranging from "Not Applicable at All" to "Essential to Research" where each response was assigned a point value as highlighted in Table 1.

Table 1. Respondents were asked the question *"You are developing a GIS database in order to conduct local-scale food security analysis. How important are the following GIS data layers to your research and analysis?"* regarding GIS data layers (street network, for example). The following scale assigned point values to their answers [19].

Response	Point value
Not applicable at all	1
Slightly important	2
Moderately important	3
Very important	4
Essential to research	5

For each layer, a weighted average based on responses was calculated from the values in Table 1 and ranked according to all 23 data layers in the survey. For example, for the Roads data layer, there were no responses for "Not Applicable at All", one for "Slightly Important", five for "Moderately Important", twelve for "Very Important" and the remaining fourteen responded with "Essential to Research". This would compute to a value of 4.22 and this value would be ranked among the other 22 data layers selected for this survey. In this case, the Roads layer ranked 2nd amongst the 23 data layers in the questionnaire. The "Grocery Stores" data layer ranked with the highest with a score of 4.25, followed closely by "Roads", "Farmers' Markets" and "Urban Areas" as highlighted in Table 2.

Table 2. Rank of Layers/Themes as Voted by GIS User Community [19].

Rank	Layer
1	Grocery stores
2	Roads
3	Farmers markets
4	Urban areas
5	Census units (block groups, tract, etc.)
6	Cities and towns
7	Fast-food restaurants
8	Counties
9	Bus routes
10	Businesses (All)
11	Non-census sub-county units (boroughs, townships, etc.)
12	Schools
13	Zoning
14	Sidewalks
15	Land cover
16	States
17	Churches
18	Walking/Jogging trails
19	Building footprints
20	Crime
21	Utilities (Electrical/Gas/Cable/Phone)
22	Elevation
23	Golf courses

In addition, users were asked to name themes not mentioned in the above list that would be useful in this type of analysis. Themes mentioned include: Parks, Greenhouses, Arable Land, Irrigation Pathways, Rivers, Access to Water, Food Banks, Food Assistance Organizations, Community Gardens, Non-Profit Businesses, Health Agencies, Corner Stores, Partial Markets (Walgreens, for example), Liquor Stores, Bus Stops and County Agencies.

4.2 Prioritization of Attributes

The same conventions were applied to attributes used to describe the data layers from Table 1. After averaging values marked by uses, the "Distance to Resource" attribute was ranked highest, followed by "Income" and "Race/Ethnicity (by enumeration unit)". These results are highlighted in Table 3.

Table 3. Rank of Attributes to Layers/Themes as Voted by GIS User Community [19].

Rank	Attribute
1	Distance to nearest resource
2	Income
3	Race/Ethnicity (by enumeration unit)
4	Population density
5	Average household size
6	Population
7	Education attainment
8	Housing status (Owner-Occupied/Rental/Vacant)
9	Transportation (# of vehicles by enumeration unit)
10	Median age
11	Median rent paid
12	Spending patterns (by enumeration unit)
13	Zoning type
14	North American industry classification standard (NAICS) Code
15	Road length
16	Building size
17	Number of employees by business
18	Speed limit

4.3 Dimensions of Data Quality

Using the facets of data quality addressed above, users were asked to rate six different dimensions of data quality from 1 (most important) to 6 (least important). These data dimensions speak to how the data are created, described and catalogued as part of the data development process. Scores for each facet were merely averaged and ranked. These rankings are highlighted in Table 4.

5 Opportunities for Development

5.1 Practical Applications of Data Quality Research

The importance and concepts of positional, temporal and attribute accuracies tie in with burgeoning opportunities in field of data quality assessment. These facets of data quality were rated highest of the six addressed in the survey as per Table 4. Research is beginning to realize the importance of testing data quality for store locations which entail a combination of field techniques and database analysis [69–73].

Table 4. Rank of Dimensions of Data Quality [19].

Rank	Facet of data quality
1	Positional accuracy (features such as stores are located where GIS database dictates)
2	Attribute accuracy (attributes of features such as feature length or NAICS codes are correct)
3	Temporal accuracy (data currentness is consistent with study period)
4	Logical consistency (how well the logical relationships between items in the dataset are maintained)
5	Semantic accuracy (data naming conventions are consistent among data sources)
6	Cataloging of data lifeline (via Metadata)

In support of this work, the research team developed a short field-based QA/QC project. 400 randomly selected food sources from an eleven-county region in southeastern North Carolina were divided between each of two major divisions of food ('healthy' vs. 'unhealthy') within urban and rural food sources. In order to maintain consistency in field verification for hypothesis testing, 100 urban healthy (UH) sources were randomly selected, as well as 100 rural healthy (RH), 100 urban unhealthy (UU) and then 100 rural unhealthy (RU). As a result, 200 urban features within the GIS database were field checked against 200 rural food sources in the same database. 200 healthy sources were to be checked against 200 unhealthy counterparts.

All 400 points were randomly selected and placed into a database for on-site field verification. The goal of field verification was to determine 1) if the business was actually located where the GIS database dictated 2) if the business was still in operation 3) if the business activity (fast food, for example) is attributed correctly. Also noted in the database were other issues that may contribute to questions of data integrity and subsequent food desert analysis, such as 1) geocoding errors where that point is located nearby, but not exactly where it should be and 2) points that could be attributed differently. This may occur where a small grocery store could have been attributed as a convenience store. Attributes were created specifically for field verification that contained placeholders for these notations that could be done in the field.

400 points were inspected to determine how well these GIS data and various permutations of these data aligned with geographic reality as well as cohorts against each other. Of the 400 total points inspected, 310 (77.5%) of them were accurate. Of the 90 that were deemed as incorrect, the following is a summary of the errors (Table 5):

Table 5. Summary of errors in QA/QC process.

Description of error	Number of occurrences	Type of error
Food source permanently closed	32	Temporal accuracy
Point is actually a residential location	24	Attribute accuracy
Nothing exists at the point	18	Horizontal accuracy
New business occupying Location	9	Temporal accuracy
Does not sell food directly to public (Distributor)	3	Attribute accuracy
Business name is the same, but is not a food source	2	Attribute accuracy
Located far distance from actual feature	2	Horizontal accuracy

All 90 errors were generalized into one of seven general descriptions as shown in Table 3. The most popular error, representing 35.6% of all errors, was that the food source represented in the GIS databases, was permanently closed. One example of these temporal inaccuracies is shown in Fig. 7 (Fig. 8).

Fig. 8. Rural Supermarket Now Permanently Closed. This Location Was Represented in the GIS Database as Being Open.

These 90 errors were broken down between various cohorts of the food environment as shown in Table 4. Most notable is the difference between urban and rural accuracy. 82.5% of all 200 urban features checked were correct compared to 72.5% of rural counterparts using the same sample size. These differences were also expressed between healthy food (82% urban vs. 70% rural) and unhealthy food (83% urban vs. 75% rural). Of the three different cohorts of food sources field verified, all of them had urban accuracy to be greater than rural accuracy.

An independent t-test of two proportions was run between the two sets of results to determine if there was a difference between the percentages computed. Using the derived accuracy percentages for each cohort ($\hat{p}_1$ and $\hat{p}_2$), the combined accuracy ($\hat{p}_0$) and the sample sizes for each cohort (n_1 and n_2), this test helps determine the criteria in order to reject the Null hypothesis (percentage from each cohort is equal to each other) and accept the alternate hypothesis (percent from each cohort are not equal to each other).

$$Z = \frac{\hat{p}_1 - \hat{p}_2}{\sqrt{\hat{p}_0\left(1 - \hat{p}_0\right)\left(\frac{1}{n_1} + \frac{1}{n_2}\right)}}$$

Permutations of the were run against each other using the test of two proportions as shown in Table 6. There are differences between urban and rural accuracy for the some of the six different cohorts of food stores inspected. Most significant was the distinct differences between the accuracy for all urban food sources and less accurate rural food sources at the $\alpha = .05$ level. These differences must be noted in working with unverified CAB data.

Table 6. Result for test of two proportions.

Null hypothesis	p-value
Urban Healthy (n = 100) = Rural Healthy (n = 100)	.0483[**]
Urban Unhealthy (n = 100) = Rural Unhealthy (n = 100)	.1664
All Urban (n = 200) = All Rural (n = 200)	.0170[**]

[*]$\rho < .1$ [**]$\rho < .05$ [***]$\rho < .01$

In addition to the actual quality of geospatial data being provided in a CAB database highlighting differences between urban and rural cohorts, other research has explored store-level metrics such as the linear shelf space of healthy food [81] and the amount of bruising of foods within stores [82]. These ideas further perpetuate the concepts of the relatively new idea of spatial justice/injustice which explores how access to both tangible and intangible assets [83, 84], such as food quality and even high-quality data in this case, vary across space. Further research opportunities into issues of data collection methods, field verification, data collection frequency and logical consistency can address the reasons for these distinct differences as applied to the narrow scope of spatial data accuracy within the confines of the food environment.

5.2 Standards-Based Approach to Database Development

Data standards such as the Spatial Data Standards for Facilities Infrastructure and Environment (SDSFIE) are used by the Department of Defense (DoD) to maximize interoperability and understandability across installations and branches by dictating naming conventions, attributes and domain values for spatial data layers. The name *spot_elevation_point* is denoted as "a point on the surface of the earth of known elevation" and is consistent across all DoD installations instead of using layer names such as *point, landmark* or *landmarks*. The *spot_elevation_point* feature class contains 23 attributes, which is relatively little compared to the *road_centerline* feature class which contains 55 attributes. The FGDC has defined data standards for landmarks, addressing, thoroughfares and parcels (FGDC, 2011) in order to standardize attributes so features can geocoded, described and represented fully entirely by the GIS user community. While the development of a database dedicated solely to food security is still being realized, point and polygonal features representing municipal and census-based units such as zip codes, towns, census tracts and census block groups have attributes that can be seamlessly integrated with attributes that rank highly in this study such as super-market density and access to transportation, as well as socio-economic indicators such as poverty, race/ethnicity, education attainment, population and population density. The development of these attributes may require further processing or the import of data using simple GIS operations from various spatial databases such as the 2010 Census, Esri Demographic Database, Esri Spending Patterns and American Community Survey.

In order to catalog both the data and the aforementioned processing, it is necessary to catalog administrative, structural and descriptive information about the geospatial data and the processes by which they were developed. Metadata serves as the formal means to describe a dataset, and provides the standardized framework for providing information about a dataset's lineage, attributes, age and creators using both qualitative and quanti-tative entries. In the GIS community, the FGDC-endorsed Content Standard for Digital Geospatial Metadata (CSDGM) is slowly being replaced by an International Standards Organization (ISO)-based metadata standard that accounts for evolving technologies such as remotely sensed imagery, online services and ontologies that did not exist when the original CSDGM (formally known as *FGDC-STD-001-1998*) was first published in 1998.

More than 400 individual elements comprise a complete metadata record and the state of North Carolina has developed a State and Local Government Profile, based on the ISO 19115, 19115-1 and 19119 standards. This standard streamlines these 400 elements into about 75 elements that best capture the information about a data layer which enable content consistency and improves the search and discoverability of data through online data repositories such as NCOneMap. This standard, as well as guidance for its use, is provided by the North Carolina Geographic Information Coordinating Council (NCGICC) through the NCOneMap online portal [85].

Using the State and Local Government Profile as a template, data layers developed in support of high-scale food security research should be cognizant of the following entries that already exist within this profile which speak explicitly to the aforementioned facets of data quality and help perpetuate data discoverability:

1) Topic Category: A theme keyword that adheres to at least one of the ISO Topic Categories.
2) Process Description: A repeatable element that provides a description of how the data were created and indicate the data source, where applicable. This process description should include any geoprocessing and/or field calculations used to derive spatial and attribute data derived for the sole purpose of food security research. This process description should also contain the source scale denominator and publication date

of source information, where available to clarify positional and temporal accuracy respectively.

3) Feature Catalogue: Entity and Attribute Descriptions and Citations referenced to ISO 19110, where possible.

In addition, the following Data Quality elements not explicitly addressed in this profile should be completed to catalog attempts to maintain the highest possible accuracies of data used in analysis. While not required, this cataloguing should strive to achieve popular positional (horizontal and vertical) accuracy standards such as the National Mapping Accuracy Standards (NMAS) for paper maps [86] and more recent National Standard for Spatial Data Accuracy (NSSDA) applied to purely digital data [87].

1) Attribute Accuracy Report: an explanation of the accuracy of the identification of the entities and assignments of values in the data set and a description of the tests used. This may be useful if food sources and/or destinations have been field checked for attribute errors.

2) Quantitative Attribute Accuracy Assessment: a value assigned to summarize the accuracy of the identification of the entities and assignments of values in the data set and the identification of the test that yielded the value.

3) Attribute Accuracy Value: an estimate of the accuracy of the identification of the entities and assignments of attribute values in the data set.

4) Logical Consistency Report: an explanation of the fidelity of relationships in the data set and tests used. This may be applicable if data used in the same analysis or derivation of attributes come from multiple data sources and/or at different scales.

5) Completeness Report: information about omissions, selection criteria, generalization, definitions used, and other rules used to derive the data set. Useful for both spatial data and attribute completion.

6) Horizontal Positional Accuracy Report: an explanation of the accuracy of the horizontal coordinate measurements and a description of the tests used. This may be useful when field checking the locations of food sources and/or destinations.

7) Horizontal Positional Accuracy Value: an estimate of accuracy of the horizontal positions of the spatial objects.

8) Horizontal Positional Accuracy Explanation: the identification of the test that yielded the Horizontal Positional Accuracy Value.

9) Vertical Positional Accuracy Report (where applicable): an explanation of the accuracy of the vertical coordinate measurements and a description of the tests used [76].

6   Conclusions

Spatial dimensions of the food environment can be measured using GIS. While GIS has increasingly become a powerful tool to map spatial dimensions of food security and the factors that help explain it, practitioners have little understanding of the challenges and opportunities in working with data at various scales. The comprehensive development of high-scale spatial data in support of the food environment elicits a number of both quantitative and qualitative considerations discussed in this paper. Among the considerations included in this paper include the data themes necessary for research, the attributes for said themes, the importance of various dimensions of data quality, efforts to assess and evaluate data quality in the field, data quality and the role of metadata in the cataloguing of these data.

Given data and the people that develop it are the most expensive component of any GIS project, this is especially important when resources such as time, personnel, storage space, processing speeds and bandwidth must be compromised. This data development can take on many forms, ranging from the downloading of existing data, processing of existing data, extraction from currently existing databases such as the aforementioned CAB databases, geocoding or the use of remotely sensed imagery, either purchased, procured or captured using a UAS (Unmanned Aircraft System). Regardless of the methods, resources must be utilized in order to create the spatial information and derive the attributes that facilitate food security research while cataloguing the people, processes and resources via metadata that can be discoverable across various, especially online, platforms.

As highlighted in this paper, the GIS database requirements for food security analysis at a local scale are much different than those needs at the national/sub-national scale. National scale and sub-national (state) studies in food security explore the economics of food production and links between this food and those who need it using data such as land cover, supply chains, zoning, soil type, low-scale transportation networks (both road and railroad), state and county outlines using coarse data. High-scale analysis at the block group and even pixel scale requires more specialized data, analysis, attribution and cataloguing than data grouped at census tracts, the standard for much research, including the United States Department of Agriculture Food Access Atlas. Types of data required include high-scale road networks (which include speed limits and derived travel times), business locations and spending patterns. From a data development standpoint, the realization of a database in support of local-scale food security research requires a reconciliation between developing the correct data layers, developing them at an appropriate scale that allows for local-level (sub county) scale analysis, rendering within appropriate budgets (time, people, money, etc.) that can be practically applied through policy and/or decision-making.

Utilizing a survey of 32 GIS professionals who integrate GIS data in support of food environment research, they provided their opinions on the importance of various themes attached to food desert analysis the relative importance of dimensions of data quality. Themes directly contributing to the physical procurement of healthy food such as grocery stores, roads and farmers' markets were ranked highest by these professionals. Furthermore, analysis utilizing census tracts and block groups were ranked higher than counties, further articulating the opinion that county level analysis is too just coarse to guide meaningful decision making.

GIS-based exploratory data analysis is a useful tool for model development as it allows analysts to interrogate diverse geographically linked datasets to identify inherent patterns and develop testable hypotheses regarding factors contributing to those observed patterns. This data-driven approach minimizes bias from imposition of untested assumptions derived from studies for other purposes at other scales in other settings. Information related to proximity (physical distance from resources) and socio-demographics such as income, race/ethnicity and household size were deemed as most important. These factors are essential to food desert research and specifically the USDA definition of a food desert, which contain both distance and poverty components. Lastly, dimensions of data quality were identified and users were asked to rank them in their order of importance. Positional accuracy and attribute accuracy ranked highest while the cataloguing of data in the form of metadata was ranked lowest. Research in the field of geospatial data quality assessment is evolving using field-based (virtual and otherwise) and programmatic techniques.

This focus on positional and attribute accuracy within this research was especially interesting because errors related to temporal accuracy (age of data) exhibited the most number of errors within a CAB database (food business locations) used for high-quality food environment research. In a field assessment and evaluation of 400 randomly selected data features in southeast North Carolina, 90 of these data points were found to be incorrect. 46% of the errors were related to temporal accuracy of the data, whether the business in question no longer existed at that location or a new type of business was occupying the food business location when checked in the field. 32% of errors were related to attribute errors where 1) the location was in fact a residential location) 2) the business name was correct, but it did not sell food and 3) the business did not sell directly to the public. The remaining 22% of errors were related to horizontal accuracy where the business location in the GIS was located far from the actual business, most likely due to geocoding error.

In exploring differences between various preselected cohorts of these data sources, distinct differences were found between accuracies for rural and urban cohorts. For n = 200, the geospatial data representing rural food sources (72.5%) was less accurate than urban cohorts (82.5%) at $\alpha = .05$. In addition, rural healthy food sources were statistically less accurate than urban healthy cohorts at that same significance level. While rural communities are disproportionately affected by unhealthy food environments [16] and some research has shown that disparities in food access are also greatest in rural communities [88, 89], this disproportionality also extends to the accuracy data sources within these regions. These schisms, which also include the difference between our concerns and perceptions with respect to geospatial data error and the true empirical error in geospatial data, serves as an impetus for future work and further addresses challenges between conceptual and practical geospatial data development policies and procedures.

High-quality data serves as the fundamental basis for decision-making. GIS data, whether provided through the United States Census or through other vendors can be easily converted to geospatial format if they are not already provided in that format. Another of the challenges in working with these data at various scales is its reliability, or lack thereof. Explanatory demographic data are typically collected within enumeration units such as the census block group, tract, county and state level through the American Community Survey (ACS), a program through the United States Census that samples data in non-decennial census years. Inherent in all ACS data is a sampling error, which represents "errors that occur from making inferences about the whole population from only a sample of the population" [90]. Within quantitative calculations of error is an enumeration unit's determination of reliability which are a result of scale, sampling methods and sampling size. Three classes of reliability exist for ACS data: High, Medium and Low. These classes can give users and decision makers insight into the data used for analysis at a particular scale. These factors must also be considered when developing data or overlaying them with other geospatial data given the propagation of error inherent in multiple inaccurate or unreliable data sources.

The specific focus of this work has been on the collection, integration, analysis, assessment and systematic description of geospatial data via formal metadata that is of a type and level of detail to be of practical value in the development, implementation and evaluation of interventions and policies addressing local-level food security. This holistic approach necessitates an understanding of the technical skills needed to develop high-quality geospatial data as well as the qualitative understanding to While the results of this work can be used as pure research in and of itself, it is anticipated that results can be used in helping to facilitate decision-making and dictate policy at directly addressing and remediating the phenomenon of food deserts as well a proliferating research in disparate fields such as meta-metadata (information about metadata), data mining, field assessment and data quality. Furthermore, this work addresses the technical components of geospatial database development such as attribution, naming conventions and metadata according to existing standards such as the ISO-based North Carolina State and Local Government Metadata Profile. While some minor questions still remain unanswered such as the potential for cross-validation or the integration of qualitative data given food desert research has been trending towards a mixed-methods approach (combining qualitative and quantitative data), it is our hope to further explore cost-effective methods for needs assessment that take into account both causal complexity, perhaps via longitudinal studies, and programmatic challenges imposed by the combination of the increase of chronic disease, the contribution of unhealthy eating to chronic disease, limited resources and increased demand. If done correctly, integrating GIS technologies with intervention planning has the potential to be a cost-effective means for organizations to conduct effective planning aimed at improving food and nutritional security at multiple spatial and temporal scales. Practical database development and the efficient use of resources serves as the cornerstone of this planning and implementation.

Nonetheless, the framework approach described in this research is flexible and broadly applicable, and can be useful for comparing and exploring spatial relationships among scales, accuracies and standards between different study areas if resources exist. We suggest that the approach, methods and results described in this paper be used to inform analysts and end-users of geospatial data research of any implicit or explicit error that may explain, elucidate, undermine and reinforce results using these data.

Acknowledgements. The project was supported by the Agricultural and Food Research Initiative Competitive Program of the USDA National Institute of Food and Agriculture (NIFA), grant number 2016-67023-24904.

This material is also based upon work supported by the National Science Foundation under Grant No. 1824949. Any opinions, findings, and conclusions or recommendations expressed in this material are those of the author(s) and do not necessarily reflect the views of the National Science Foundation.

References

1. Brat, I.: Do 'food deserts' cause unhealthy eating? Wall Street J. (2015). https://www.wsj. com/articles/do-food-deserts-cause-unhealthy-eating-1436757037. Accessed 21 Mar 2020
2. Rose, D., Richards, R.: Food store access and household fruit and vegetable use among participants in the US food stamp program. Public Health Nutri. **7**(8), 1081–1088 (2004)
3. Food Marketing Institute: U.S. Grocery Shopping Trends, 2016. Food Marketing Institute, Arlington, VA (2016)
4. Zenk, S., et al.: Food shopping behaviors and exposure to discrimination. Public Health Nutri. **17**(5), 1167–1176 (2013)
5. Van Hoesen, J., Bunkley, B., Currier, C.: A GIS-based methodology toward refining the concept of rural food deserts: a case study from Rutland County, Vermont. J. Agric. Food Syst. Comm. Develop. **3**(2), 61–76 (2013)
6. Gross, J., Rosenberger, N.: Food Insecurity in Rural Benton County: An Ethnographic Study. Working Paper No. 05-02, Rural Studies Program, Oregon State University, Corvallis, OR (2005)
7. Blanchard, T., Lyson, T.: Access to low cost groceries in nonmetropolitan counties: Large retailers and the creation of food deserts. Paper presented at the Measuring Rural Diversity Conference, Washington, DC, pp. 1– 24 (2006)
8. Morton, L., Bitto, E., Oakland, M.: Solving the problems of Iowa food deserts: food insecurity and civic structure. Rural Sociol. **70**(1), 94–112 (2005)
9. Clarke, G., Heather, E., Guy, C.: Deriving indicators of access to food retail provision in british cities: studies of Cardiff. Leeds Bradford. Urban Stud. **39**(11), 2041–2060 (2002)
10. Furey, S., Strugnell, C., McIlveen, H.: An investigation of the potential existence of "food deserts" in rural and urban areas of Northern Ireland. Agric. Hum. Values **18**, 447–457 (2001)
11. Mamen, K.: Facing Goliath: challenging the impacts of supermarket consolidation on our local economies, communities, and food security - policy brief. Oakland Inst. **1**(3), 1–8 (2007)
12. Lewis, L.B., et al.: African Americans' access to healthy food options in South Los Angeles restaurants. Am. J. Public Health **95**(4), 668–673 (2005)
13. Powell, L.M., Slater, S., Mirtcheva, D., Bao, Y., Chaloupka, F.: Food store availability and neighborhood characteristics in the United States. Prev. Med. **44**, 189–195 (2007)
14. Cooksey-Stowers, K., Schwartz, M., Brownell, K.: Food swamps predict obesity rates better than food deserts in the United States. Int. J. Environ. Res. Public Health **14**, 1366 (2017)
15. Zenk, S.N., Powell, L.M., Rimkus, L., Isgor, Z., Barker, D.C.: Relative and absolute availability of healthier food and beverage alternatives across communities in the United States. Am. J. Public Health **104**, 2170–2179 (2014)
16. Morton, L., Blanchard, T.C.: Starved for access: life in rural America's food deserts. Rural Realities **1**(4), 1–10 (2007)
17. Sharkey, J.R., Horel, S.: Neighborhood socioeconomic deprivation and minority composition are associated with better potential spatial access to the ground-truthed food environment in a large rural area. J. Nutr. **30**(5), 620–627 (2008)
18. Chen, X., Clark, J.: Interactive three-dimensional geovisualization of space–time access to food. Appl. Geogr. **43**, 81–86 (2013)
19. Mulrooney T., Wooten, T.: A public participatory approach toward the development of a comprehensive geospatial database in support of high-scale food security analysis. In: Proceeding of the 6th International Conference in Geographical Information Systems Theory Application and Management (GISTAM 2020), pp. 21–32 (2020)
20. Chilton, M., Rose, D.: A rights-based approach to food insecurity in the United States. Am. J. Public Health **99**, 1203–1211 (2009)

21. Food and Agriculture Organization of the United Nations: Declaration of the World Summit on Food Security 2009. ftp://ftp.fao.org/docrep/fao/Meeting/018/k6050e.pdf. Accessed 29 Feb 2020

22. Wrigley, N.: 'Food deserts' in British cities: policy context and research priorities. Urban Stud. **39**(11), 2029–2040 (2002)

23. Guy, C.M., Clarke, G., Eyre, H.: Food retail change and the growth of food deserts: a case study of Cardiff. Int. J. Retail Distrib. Manage. **32**, 72–88 (2004)

24. Donkin, A.J., Dowler, E.A., Stevenson, S.J., Turner, S.A.M.: Mapping access to food at a local level. British Food J. **101**(7), 554 (1999)

25. Lovett, A., Haynes, R., Sunnenberg, G., Gale, S.: Car travel time and accessibility by bus to general practitioner services: a study using patient registers and GIS. Soc. Sci. Med. **55**(1), 97–111 (2002)

26. Pearce, J., Witten, K., Bartie, P.: Neighbourhoods and health: a GIS approach to measuring community resource accessibility. J. Epidemiol. Community Health **60**(5), 389–395 (2006)

27. Mulrooney, T., McGinn, C., Branch, B., Madumere, C., Ifediora, B.: A new raster-based metric to measure relative food availability in rural areas: a case study in Southeastern North Carolina. Southeast. Geogr. **57**(2), 151–178 (2017)

28. Rose D., Bodor J.N., Swalm C.M., Rice J.C., Farley T.A., Hutchinson P.L.: Deserts in New Orleans? Illustrations of urban food access and implications for policy. Paper presented at: University of Michigan National Poverty Center/USDA Research Conference on Understanding the Economic Concepts and Characteristics of Food Access. USDA, Washington, DC (2004)

29. Jago, R., Baranowski, T., Baranowski, J.C.: Distance to food stores and adolescent male fruit and vegetable consumption: mediation effects. Int. J. Behav. Nutri. Phys. Activity **4**, 35 (2007)

30. Jiao, J., Moudon, A., Ulmer, J., Hurvitz, P., Drewnowski, J.: How to identify food deserts: measuring physical and economic access to supermarkets in King CountyWashington. Am. J. Public Health **102**(10), 32–39 (2012)

31. Ver Ploeg, M., Breneman, V., Farrigan, T., Hamrick, K., Hopkins, D., et al.: Access to affordable and nutritious food–measuring and understanding food deserts and their consequences: United States Department of Agriculture (Economic Research), Service Washington, D.C. (2009)

32. Block, J.P., Scribner, R.A., DeSalvo, K.B.: Fast food, race/ethnicity, and income: a geographic analysis. Am. J. Prevent. Med. **27**, 211–217 (2004)

33. Hallett, L., McDermott, D.: Quantifying the extent and cost of food deserts in Lawrence, Kansas, USA. Appl. Geogr. **31**, 1210–1215 (2011)

34. Clary, C.M., Ramos, Y., Shareck, M., Kestens, Y.: Should we use absolute or relative measures when assessing foodscape exposure in relation to fruit and vegetable intake? Evidence from a wide-scale Canadian study. Prevent. Med. (Baltimore) **71**, 83–87 (2015)

35. Centers for Disease Control and Prevention: Children's Food Environment State Indicator Report (2011). http://www.cdc.gov/obesity/downloads/ChildrensFoodEnvironment.pdf. Accessed 3 Mar 2020

36. Gallagher, M: Examining the impact of food deserts on public health in Chicago. Mari Gallagher Research and Consulting Group. http://www.marigallagher.com/site_media/dynamic/project_files/1_ChicagoFoodDesertReport-Full_.pdf. Accessed 22 Apr 2029

37. Babatunde, R.O., Omotesho, O.A., Sholatan, O.S.: Factors influencing food security status of rural farmers in North Central Nigeria. Agric. J. **2**(3), 351–357 (2010)

38. Obioha, E.E.: Climate variability, environment change and food security nexus in Nigeria. J. Hum. Ecol. **26**(2), 107–121 (2009)

39. Soneye, A.: Farm holdings in Northern Nigeria and implication for food security: a remote sensing and GIS assessment. Afr. J. Food Agric. Nutri. Develop. **14**(2), 1–15 (2014)

40. McEntee, J., Agyeman, J.: Towards the development of a GIS method for identifying rural food deserts: geographic access in Vermont, USA. Appl. Geogr. **30**(1), 165–176 (2010)

41. Dijkstra, E.W.: A note on two problems in connexion with graphs. Numer. Math. **1**, 269–271 (1959)

42. Melhorn, K.: Shortest Paths: Algorithm and Data Structures - The Basic Toolbox. Springer, New York (2008). https://doi.org/10.1007/978-3-540-77978-0

43. Huber, S., Rust, C.: Calculate travel time and distance with OpenStreetMap data using the open source routing machine (OSRM). Stata J. **16**(2), 416–423 (2016)

44. D'Acosta, J.: Finding food deserts: a study of food access measures in the phoenix-mesa urban area (Master's thesis) University of Southern California. Los Angeles, CA (2015)

45. Wang, Z.: Socio-demographic and economic determinants of food deserts (Master's thesis) University of Arkansas, Fayetteville, AR (2012)

46. Love, G., Mulrooney, T., Brown, L.: Using GIS to address food availability in Durham, North Carolina. North Carolina Geogr. **19**, 34–52 (2012)

47. Opfer, P.: Using GIS technology to identify and analyze 'food deserts' on the southern Oregon coast. Oregon State University Archives, pp. 1–52 (2010)

48. Sharkey, J.R., Horel, S., Han, D., Huber, D.: Association between neighborhood need and spatial access to food stores and fast food restaurants in neighborhoods of colonias. Int. J. Health Geogr. **8**(9), 1–17 (2009)

49. Major, E., Delmelle, E., Delmelle, E.: 2018 SNAPScapes: using geodemographic segmentation to classify the food access landscape. Urban Sci. **2**, 71 (2018)

50. Janssen, M., Charalabidis, Y., Zuiderwijk, A.: Benefits, adoption barriers and myths of open data and open government. Inf. Syst. Manage. **29**(4), 258–268 (2012)

51. Johnson, P.A., Sieber, R., Scassa, T., Stephens, M., Robinson, P.: The Cost(s) of geospatial open data. Trans. GIS **21**, 434–445 (2017)

52. Bernknopf, R., Shapiro, C.: Economic assessment of the use value of geospatial information. ISPRS Int. J. Geo-Inf. **4**, 1142–1165 (2015)

53. Both, A., Wauer, M., Garcia-Rojas, A, Hladky, D., Lehmann, J.: GeoKnow generator workbench – an integrated tool supporting the linked data lifecycle for enterprise usage. In: Proceedings of the 11th International Conference on Semantic Systems Posters and Demos, of SEM 2015, p. 92 (2015)

54. Koutnik, M.: The Benefits of GIS in Local Government: Examples from ESRI's User Community. Environmental Systems Research Institute, Inc. Redlands (1996)

55. Ledbetter, M., Hunt, C. Anderson, D.: Blueprints for a Citywide GIS: Scottsdale's Award-Winning System Provides a Profitable Example. GIS World, pp. 62–64, November 1997

56. Chapman, A.D.: Principles of Data Quality, version 1.0. Report for the Global Biodiversity Information Facility, Copenhagen (2005)

57. Taulbee, S.M.: Implementing data quality systems in biomedical records. In: Gad, S.C., Taulbee, S.M. (eds.) Handbook of Data Recording, Maintenance, and Management for the Biomedical Sciences, pp. 47–75. CRC Press, Boca Raton (1996)

58. Dalcin, E.C.: Data quality concepts and techniques applied to taxonomic databases. Thesis for the degree of Doctor of Philosophy, School of Biological Sciences, Faculty of Medicine, Health and Life Sciences, University of Southampton (2004)

59. English, L.P.: Improving data warehouse and business information quality: methods for reducing costs and increasing profits. Wiley, New York (1999)

60. Bonner, M.R., Han, D., Nie, J., Rogerson, P., Vena, J.E., Freudenheim, J.L.: Positional accuracy of geocoded addresses in epidemiologic research. Epidemiology **14**(4), 408–412 (2003)

61. Cayo, M.R., Talbot, T.O.: Positional error in automated geocoding of residential addresses. Int. J. Health Geogr. **2**(1), 10 (2003)

62. Ward, M.H., et al.: Positional accuracy of two methods of geocoding. Epidemiology **16**(4), 542–547 (2005)
63. Longley, P., Goodchild, M., Maguire, D., Rhind, D.: Geographical Information Systems: Principles, Techniques, Management and Application, 2nd edn. Wiley, Chicester (2005)
64. Epstein, E.F: Litigation over information: The use and misuse of maps. In: Proceedings, IGIS: The Research Agenda 1, pp. 177–184. NASA, Washington, D.C. (1988)
65. Bedard, Y. Uncertainties in land information systems databases. In: Proceedings of the 8th International Symposium on Computer Assisted Cartography (Auto Carto 8), Baltimore, MD, pp. 175–184 (1987)
66. Forysth, A., Lytle, L., Van Riper, D.: Finding food: issues and challenges in using geographic information systems to measure food access. J. Transp. Land Use **3**(1), 43–65 (2010)
67. Wilkins, E., Morris, A., Radley, D., Griffith, C.: Using Geographic Information Systems to measure retail food environments: Discussion of methodological considerations and a proposed reporting checklist (Geo-FERN). Health Place **44**, 100–117 (2017)
68. Auchincloss, A., Moore, K., Moore, L., Diez-Roux, A.: Improving retrospective characterization of the food environment for a larger region in the United State during a historic time period. Health Place **18**(6), 1341–1347 (2012)
69. Liese, A., et al.: Validation of 3 food outlet databases: completeness and geospatial accuracy in rural and urban food environments. Am. J. Epidemiol. **172**(11), 1324–1333 (2010)
70. Han, E., Powell, L., Zenk, S., Rimkus, L, Ohri-Vachaspati, P., Chaloupka, F.: Classification bias in commercial business lists for retail food stores in the U.S. Int. J. Behav. Nutri. Phys. Activity **9**, 46 (2012)
71. Hosler, A., Dharssi, A.: Identifying retail food stores to evaluate the food environment. Am. J. Prev. Med. **39**(1), 41–44 (2010)
72. Mendez, D., Kim, K., Hardaway, C., Fabio, A.: Neighborhood racial and socioeconomic disparities in the food and alcohol environment: are there difference by commercial data sources? J. Racial Ethnic Health Disparities **3**, 108–116 (2016)
73. Rummo, P., Albrecht, S., Gordon-Larsen, P.: Field validation of food outlet databases: the Latino food environment in North Carolina, USA. Public Health Nutri. **18**(6), 977–982 (2015)
74. Powell, L.M., Han, E., Zenk, S.N., et al.: Field validation of secondary commercial data sources on the retail food outlet environment in the United States. Health Place **5**, 1122–1131 (2011)
75. Lake, A.A., Burgoine, T., Stamp, E., Grieve, R.: The foodscape: classification and field validation of secondary data sources across urban/rural and socio-economic classifications in England. Int. J. Behav. Nutri. Phys. Activity **9**(1), 37 (2012)
76. Federal Geographic Data Committee (FGDC): Content Standard for Digital Geospatial Metadata Workbook. Federal Geographic Data Committee, Washington D.C. (2000)
77. United States Geological Survey (USGS): Spatial Data Transfer Standard (SDTS): Logical specifications. United States Geologic Survey, Reston, Virginia (1997)
78. Salgé, F.: Semantic accuracy. In: Guptill, S.C., Morrison, J.L. (eds.) Elements of Spatial Data Quality, pp. 139–152. Elsevier Science Ltd., New York (1995)
79. Devillers, R., Bédard, Y., Jeansoulin, R.: Multidimensional management of geospatial data quality information for its dynamic use within geographical information systems. Photogram. Eng. Rem. Sens. **71**(2), 205–215 (2005)
80. Qiu, L., Lingling, G., Feng, H., Yong, T.: A unified metadata information management framework for the digital city. In: Proceedings of IEEE's Geoscience and Remote Sensing Symposium, Anchorage, Alaska, pp. 4422–4424 (2004)
81. Farley, T., Rice, J., Bodor, J., Cohen, D., Blumenthal, R., Rose, D.: Measure the food environment: shelf space of fruits, vegetables and snack foods in store. J. Urban Health **86**(5), 672–682 (2009)

82. Cummins, S., et al.: Variations in fresh fruit and vegetable quality by store type, urban–rural setting and neighbourhood deprivation in Scotland. Public Health Nutri. **12**(11), 2044–2050 (2009)
83. Bailey, K., Grossardt, T.: Toward structured public involvement: Justice, geography and collaborative geospatial/geovisual decision support systems. Ann. Assoc. Am. Geogr. **100**(1), 57–86 (2010)
84. Soja, E.: Seeking Spatial Justice. University of Minnesota Press, Minneapolis (2010)
85. North Carolina Geographic Information Coordinating Council (NCGICC): North Carolina State and Local Government Metadata Profile for Geospatial Data and Services. North Carolina Geographic Information Coordinating Council, Raleigh (2018)
86. United States Bureau of the Budget: United States National Map Accuracy Standards. U.S. Bureau of the Budget, Washington, D.C. (1947)
87. Federal Geographic Data Committee (FGDC): Geospatial Positioning Accuracy Standards Part 3: National Standard for Spatial Data Accuracy (FGDC-STD-007.3-1998) Federal Geographic Data Committee, Washington, D.C. (1998)
88. Morland, K., Wing, S., Diez Roux, A.: Neighborhood characteristics associated with the location of food stores and food service places. Am. J. Prevent. Med. **22**(1), 23–29 (2002)
89. Smith, C., Wright-Morton, L.: Rural food deserts: Low-income perspectives on food access in Minnesota and Iowa. J. Nutri. Educ. Behav. **41**(3), 176–187 (2009)
90. ESRI (Environmental Systems Research Institute): The American Community Survey (2014). https://www.esri.com/library/whitepapers/pdfs/the-american-community-survey.pdf. Accessed 29 Mar 2020

Author Index

Printed in the United States
by Baker & Taylor Publisher Services